Heritage
Studies
for Christian Schools

Marilyn Elmer

Heritage Studies for Christian Schools®: Book 4

Produced in cooperation with the Bob Jones University Department of History of the College of Arts and Science, the School of Education, and Bob Jones Elementary School.

ISBN 0-89084-100-4

©1985 Bob Jones University Press
Greenville, South Carolina 29614

20   19   18   17   16   15   14   13   12   11   10   9

Contents

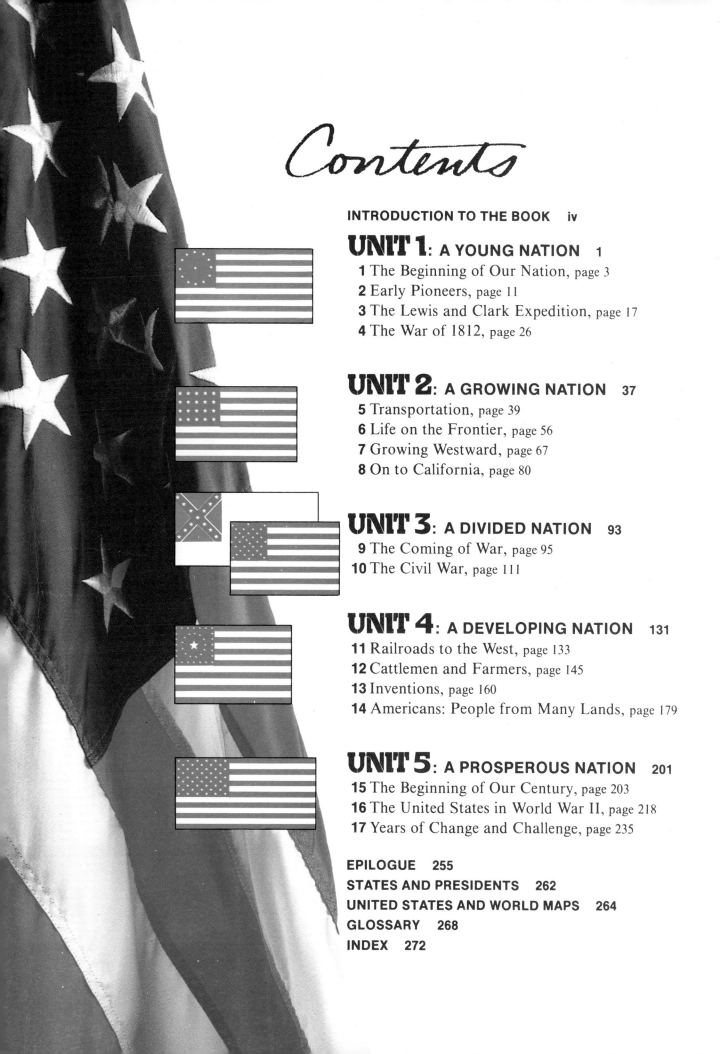

INTRODUCTION

This book is called a Heritage Studies book. What do you think the word *heritage* means? Why do you think we should study our heritage?

These children were not born in the United States. They do not speak English. Their food and clothing are different from yours. These children look, act, and speak as they do because they each have a different heritage.

A person's heritage is everything that has a part in making him who he is, what he is like, and what he does. No one chooses his own heritage. God chooses each person's family and country of birth. These two things are perhaps the most important part of a person's heritage.

People who are born in the United States have special blessings that people in many other countries do not have. One of these blessings is the opportunity to hear about God and to read His Word whenever they please. The United States was settled by people who believed in God and respected the Bible. These people made laws to guarantee the freedom of religion to all the citizens of this great land.

The Bible is the most important part of our heritage. We learn about God and His Son, Jesus Christ, from the

Bible. We learn that we are sinners. We learn how we can be saved from our sin by asking Jesus to forgive our sins and be our Saviour.

In the Bible God tells Christians how to live while they are on the earth. He commands fathers to be the head of the family. "For the husband is the head of the wife, even as Christ is the head of the church" (Ephesians 5:23). Both the father and the mother are to love and care for their children. Parents are to teach their children what is right. "Train up a child in the way he should go" (Proverbs 22:6). Children are to honor and to obey their parents. "Children, obey your parents in the Lord: for this is right. Honour thy father and mother" (Ephesians 6:1-2).

The Bible tells Christians how to be good citizens. God's people are to obey the laws of their country. "Submit yourselves to every ordinance of man for the Lord's sake" (I Peter 2:13). Of course, they are not to obey laws that would make them disobey God's Word. "Then Peter and the other apostles answered and said, We ought to obey God rather than men" (Acts 5:29). Christians are to be honest and to do their work well. "To do your own business, and to work with your own hands, as we commanded you; That ye may walk honestly toward them that are without, and that ye may have lack of nothing" (I Thessalonians 4:11-12). Christians are to pray for the rulers of their state and country. "I exhort therefore, that, first of all, supplications, prayers, intercessions, and giving of thanks, be made for all men;

For kings, and for all that are in authority; that we may lead a quiet and peaceable life in all godliness and honesty" (I Timothy 2:1-2).

Christians also learn from the Bible that God controls the affairs of this world. No country can become strong unless God permits it. And no country can be destroyed unless He allows it. This truth should comfort God's children. Hebrews 13:5-6 says, "For He hath said, I will never leave thee, nor forsake thee. So that we may boldly say, The Lord is my helper, and I will not fear what man shall do unto me."

In this book you will learn about the United States. This is the country God has chosen for us to live in. He has blessed each of us by making this nation part of our heritage. As you learn about America, you will also be learning about your own heritage.

The men and women who helped make our country showed in their lives "keys to character."

Obedience	Determination
Honesty	Joyfulness
Dependability	Gratitude
Industriousness	

Watch for examples of these important keys to character as you study this book. Some of them are marked with this symbol. Look for others as you read. Ask the Lord to help you make them a part of your life.

A Young Nation

ONE

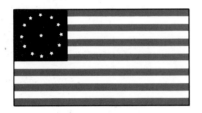

A New Flag On June 14, 1777, Congress decided that "the Flag of the United States be thirteen stripes alternate red and white and the Union be thirteen stars in a blue field." It did not decide on a particular design for the stars. The flag shown here was flown in some of the battles during the War for Independence. To honor our flag, we celebrate Flag Day every June 14.

UNIT GOALS

- I will be able to explain why the Constitution is important to our nation.
- I will be able to tell how the capital city of the United States was begun.
- I will be able to explain how the purchase of the Louisiana Territory helped the United States.
- I will be able to describe the trip made by Captain Lewis, Captain Clark, and their men.
- I will be able to quote some sayings and a song that came from the War of 1812.
- I will be able to locate Washington, D.C., the first thirteen states, the Mississippi River, and the Louisiana Territory on a map.

TIME LINE

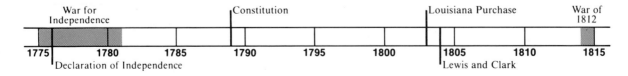

CHAPTER 1

THE BEGINNING OF OUR NATION

The Declaration of Independence was adopted on July 4, 1776. This document told the world that the thirteen British colonies in America were free and independent states. The king of England had refused to allow the colonists the rights that other Englishmen had and had refused to protect the colonies. Therefore, the colonies declared that they were free and that they no longer belonged to England.

Before England let the colonies go, she fought a long, hard war with the Americans. The War for Independence lasted until 1781. It proved that the colonists were serious about being an independent nation. The colonists' determination to be free helped them to win the war.

A New Government

People need some form of government to help them live and work

together. They need a leader as well as laws and rules. This is true at home, at school, at church, in a city, and in a nation.

The thirteen independent states in America needed a government. Men from each of the states met in Philadelphia to decide what would be the best kind of government for their new nation. They worked together for several months. At last they agreed on a plan and wrote it down on paper.

Their written plan of government is called the **Constitution of the United States**.

The Constitution starts with the words, "We, the People of the United States." These words remind everyone that the government of the United States belongs to the people. The United States is not governed by a king. It is governed by men and women who are elected by its citizens.

The Constitution could not be adopted until nine of the thirteen states voted for it. Some states would not vote for the Constitution until the Bill of Rights was added. The Bill of Rights says that every person has the right to worship God in his own way and to say what he believes is true. It also says that no officer of the law can enter a person's house without a permit. A person cannot be punished for a crime unless he is found guilty by a court of law. These and the other rights in this bill are important to the people of the United States.

The Constitution is the most important document in our government. It was written for the people, and only the people have the right to change it.

The Constitution

The Constitution states that the government of the United States should

The Bill of Rights
protects our rights to—

Worship freely   Speak freely

Be free from
unlawful searches

Have a fair trial

Three Branches of Government

Legislative branch
(Congress—makes laws)

Judicial branch
(Courts—settles disputes
about laws)

Executive branch
(President—enforces laws)

have three parts. First, there is to be a group of citizens called the **Congress** to make laws. Then there is to be a **president** who, with his aides, sees that everyone obeys the laws. Last, there are to be **judges** and **courts** to settle any disputes about the laws.

The Constitution gave many duties to the Congress. The men in the Congress were to decide what kind of money should be used in the new nation. The Congress was to collect taxes, oversee the building of roads and post offices, and arrange to have an army and navy. The first Congress was also to decide what to do with the western lands.

Starting the Government

The Constitution was only a plan written on paper, but the people of the United States at once started to put that plan to work. Each state elected men to be in the Congress. Judges were chosen and courts were set up. The people elected George Washington to be the first president.

In April, 1789, George Washington left his home in Mount Vernon, Virginia, to take charge of the new government in New York. (At this time New York City was our nation's capital.) People cheered him as he rode from town to town. Friends met him at the Hudson River, and thirteen men rowed him across in a barge. Thirteen cannons boomed as the boat reached the city. Bells rang and people cheered.

A few days later, George Washington placed his right hand on the Bible and vowed to obey the Constitution. He promised to carry out his duties as the new president.

Presidential Oath

"I do solemnly swear that I will faithfully execute the office of President of the United States, and will, to the best of my ability, preserve, protect, and defend the Constitution of the United States."

Some people thought that Mr. Washington should be called "His Excellency" or "His Highness, the President." These terms reminded Mr. Washington of England's king. He knew that the Americans had fought hard to be free from the king, and he was content to be called "Mr. President."

Building a New Capital City

At first the Congressmen and others who worked for the government met in New York City, but this location did not suit everyone. The men from the southern states were especially displeased. They wanted a meeting place closer to their homes.

In 1791 President Washington chose the location for the new **capital** of the United States. It was on the eastern bank of the Potomac River between

Our New Capital
Washington, D.C.

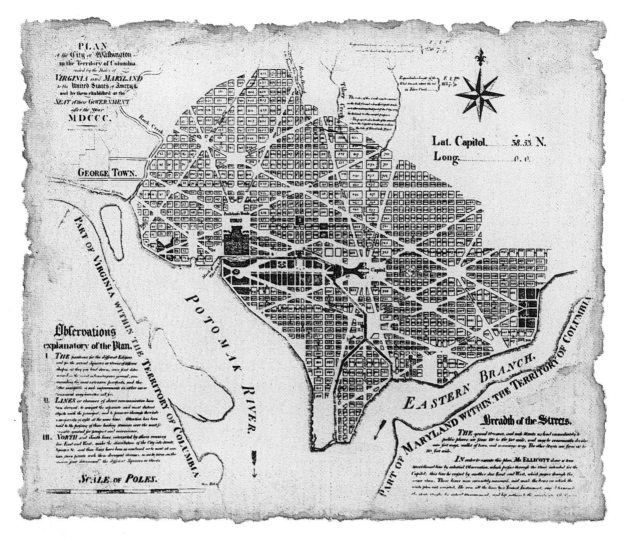

Virginia and Maryland. The city was to be named Washington, and the land around it would be called the District of Columbia.

President Washington hired a French engineer, Major Pierre Charles L'Enfant, to draw the plans for the new city. His plans called for streets to divide the city into squares. Major L'Enfant gave the streets running north and south numbers for names, and the streets running east and west letters. He also suggested that there be broad avenues to connect the most important buildings. These avenues were named after the states.

Construction on the new city began on February 1, 1791. Horses pulled carts and wagons loaded with building materials to the workers. Barges loaded with supplies floated down the

Benjamin Banneker

Benjamin Banneker helped survey the land and lay out the streets of Washington. Mr. Banneker was a free black man. He had not been able to go to school very much, but he had read many books. He was interested in astronomy and math, so he learned all he could about these subjects. He was also an inventor. He built the first clock made entirely of materials found in America.

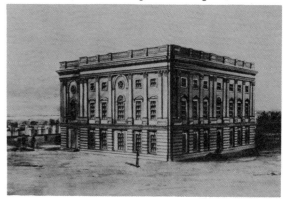

Potomac River. Slowly the laborers completed streets and buildings. Years passed, and still the men continued to work.

For the ten years that the city of Washington was being built, Philadelphia was the "substitute" capital. At last, in November, 1800, the Congress held its first meeting in the Capitol Building. At that time Washington, D.C., could hardly have been called a city since there were few buildings. Often the streets were ankle-deep with mud. By this time John Adams was the president. His wife

Abigail believed that Washington would be a great city. She wrote, "It is a beautiful spot, capable of every improvement, and the more I view it, the more I am delighted with it."

Things to know

1. The written plan for the government of our country is called the _____.

2. The three parts of the government are the _____, the _____, and the _____.

3. The first president of the United States was _____.

4. The part of the government that makes the laws is called the _____.

5. Any disagreements about laws are settled by the _____.

6. The _____ was added to the Constitution to protect the rights of the people.

7. The capital of the United States is now _____.

Things to talk about

1. What are some freedoms that are given in the Bill of Rights? What can you do that you could not do if you lived in a country that did not have these rights?

2. What are some rights each person in your class has?

3. Why do we choose leaders and make rules in our churches, clubs, and other groups?

4. How do the rules in your school, classroom, and home help you?

5. How do the rules that God gives in His Word help you?

6. What do you think it would be like if each state had its own kind of money and its own mail service?

7. How and why do you celebrate the Fourth of July? Flag Day?

8. Why do you think George Washington was rowed across the Hudson River by thirteen men and honored by the shooting of thirteen cannons?

Things to do

1. Make a list of the first thirteen states. Find each one on a map.

2. Elect a president and other officers for your class. Make laws for your class and plan penalties for those who break the laws.

3. Draw pictures to illustrate the rights given in the Bill of Rights.

4. Imagine that you are a newspaper reporter. Write a story about one of these events: the Constitution is adopted; Washington becomes the first president; the land for Washington, D.C., is chosen; the Adams family moves to Washington.

5. Find out where the Constitution is kept. Try to find a copy of it and read it as it was first written.

6. Memorize the Preamble to the Constitution.

7. Start a booklet of the flags of our country.

CHAPTER 2

EARLY PIONEERS

One duty facing the new Congress was deciding what to do with western lands. As the new nation settled down, the people began to wonder more about the West. Most Americans lived along the settled east coast. To the west rose the Appalachian Mountains. Beyond that stretched vast areas of unsettled land. For the next hundred years, Americans kept busy exploring and settling this land.

The men, women, and children who went to these new lands were called **pioneers**. A pioneer is someone who goes to an unsettled land and makes his home there. This unsettled land is called the **frontier**. When the first colonists came to America, the frontier was along the east coast. As more and more settlers came, the frontier moved farther inland. First the frontier lay east of the Appalachians. Then it moved over the Appalachians to the Mississippi River Valley. Later pioneers traveled farther west to the Plains and over the Rockies until they settled the

The First
Thirteen States
—1781

During the war Americans won this territory from the British. After the war the Northwest Territory came under the control of Congress.

Congress needed to raise money, so it decided to sell land in the Northwest Territory. The land did not cost much, so many families bought some and began the trip to the frontier. However, the government did not sell all the land. It gave some of the land to men who had been soldiers in the war. The government had not had money to pay these soldiers, but desired to thank them in some way. In all, thousands of men loaded their families and goods

Far West, and then the American frontier was gone. Before 1900, thousands of families had left their homes and become pioneers. They endured the hardships of frontier life to settle our great land.

The Northwest Territory

Even before the War for Independence, some pioneers had moved west. Daniel Boone and his men were some of the first people to cross the Appalachian Mountains and settle. They lived in what is now Kentucky. Other settlers went farther north into the area called the **Northwest Territory**.

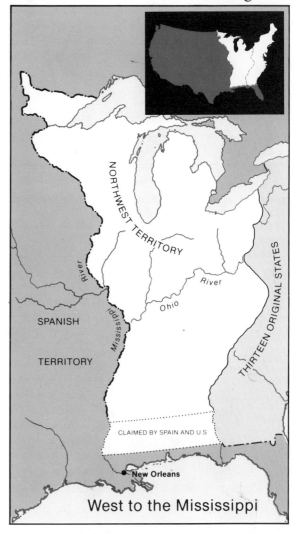

West to the Mississippi

on wagons or boats and made their way to their new homes. They left their old homes in the settled East to go into the wilderness. Later, families from Germany, France, and other European countries joined the groups of people going into the Northwest Territory.

Most of these settlers were farmers. They found that the land in the Northwest Territory was good for growing crops and raising animals. The farmers produced large amounts of flour, cornmeal, wool, and pork. Many settlers also did some trapping, and had furs to sell as well. If these men were to make any money from their goods, they had to have markets. The people in the East and in foreign countries would buy the products if the farmers could get them there.

Steps to Becoming a State

1. The people of an area ask Congress for permission to become a state.
2. Congress directs the people to write a constitution and submit it for approval.
3. Congress votes to admit the state.

New Orleans: A Valuable Port City

Transportation was the major problem in getting goods to market. Goods could be moved two ways: by land or by water. The trip over the mountains with pack horses was long and hard and often cost more than the goods were worth. Water travel was also long and hard, but it was cheaper. The choice was not hard to make.

Soon builders were busy with hammers and saws. Along the rivers of this area they built boats to carry goods to markets. These were flatboats. They were made of just a few logs fastened

Pioneers transporting goods on a flatboat

together. Farmers loaded their goods on them. Then they floated them to the Mississippi River and on to the large city of New Orleans.

There on the docks, men waited to buy the goods. These buyers loaded the goods onto sailing ships, which took the goods to New York, Philadelphia, and other cities in the East. Other ships went to foreign countries. New Orleans became an important city to the western farmers, because they could sell their goods there.

Find New Orleans on the map on page 15. Was it in territory that belonged to the United States? What countries owned the land around New Orleans?

New Orleans was located about one hundred miles upstream from the mouth of the Mississippi River. Frenchmen had first settled the city in 1718. This was long before very many English settlers moved west. The area of French settlement was called the **Louisiana Territory**.

In those days France dreamed of building a French nation in the New World. French explorers built forts along the Great Lakes and down the Mississippi River. But the dream never came true. France was busy fighting wars in Europe. In America, the Spanish were also France's enemies.

In 1803 President Thomas Jefferson was worried because neither France nor Spain was very friendly toward the United States. Both the French and the Spanish gave American farmers trouble when they came to New Orleans. Finally President Jefferson sent a message to both countries. He told them that the United States was willing to fight for the freedom to use the port of New Orleans.

The United States Gets a Bargain

Before the nation went to war, President Jefferson decided to try to buy the city of New Orleans. He sent Robert Livingstone and James Monroe

Thomas Jefferson

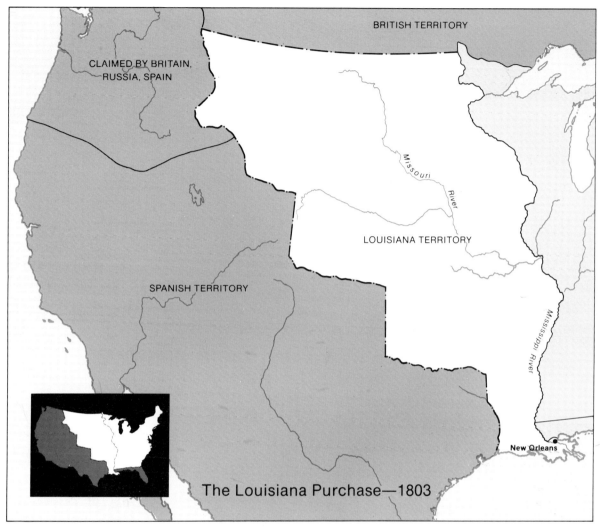

CLAIMED BY BRITAIN, RUSSIA, SPAIN

BRITISH TERRITORY

Missouri River

LOUISIANA TERRITORY

SPANISH TERRITORY

Mississippi River

New Orleans

The Louisiana Purchase—1803

to meet with Napoleon, the ruler of France at that time. Napoleon chose a man to talk with the Americans.

The two Americans made their request to buy the city. The Frenchman

thought for a while. France did not want to fight the United States. She was in danger of going to war with England, and her soldiers were needed at home. Besides, France needed the money. The Frenchman answered with a surprising offer. He offered to sell not only the city of New Orleans, but all of Louisiana!

All of Louisiana? The Americans could hardly believe their ears. They tried to hide their surprise, for they did not want to seem too eager. Soon the men agreed that the United States would pay 15 million dollars for all the

Louisiana Territory, including the city of New Orleans. This cost equaled about four cents an acre.

President Jefferson was greatly pleased with the purchase. The territory stretched from the Mississippi River in the east to the Rocky Mountains in the west. It more than doubled the size of the United States. The young nation had started to grow.

Things to know

1. New Orleans is located near the mouth of the _____ River.

2. New Orleans belonged to the country of _____ before 1803.

3. The land from the Mississippi River to the Rocky Mountains was called _____.

4. _____ was the president when the United States bought New Orleans and Louisiana from France.

5. The United States paid France _____ dollars for the land.

Things to talk about

1. Why are many large cities located near water?

2. Why was the French city of New Orleans so important to the American farmers of the West?

3. Why was water transportation often better than land transportation in the early years of our nation? What were some disadvantages of water transportation?

Things to do

1. List the states that were formed from the Louisiana Territory.

2. List rivers that flow into the Mississippi River.

3. Locate the main mountain ranges in the United States.

4. Imagine that you are shopping and that you spend $100 an hour, twelve hours a day, six days a week. How long would it take you to spend $15,000,000?

5. Find the cost of an acre of land where you live.

6. Add to your flag booklet.

CHAPTER 3

THE LEWIS AND CLARK EXPEDITION

President Thomas Jefferson had wanted to send explorers to the Louisiana Territory even before the United States bought it from France. First, he wanted to know more about Louisiana and the other lands west of the Mississippi River. Second, he hoped to find the source of the Missouri River. Third, he was interested in finding a route to the Pacific Ocean.

Jefferson persuaded Congress to give $2,500 to carry out his plan.

The Explorers

President Jefferson chose his private secretary, Meriwether Lewis, to lead an **expedition** to explore the new land. Captain Lewis was a quiet man and a man of great character. Determination was his most important trait.

When he set a goal, he did his best to reach it. Red-haired William Clark was the assistant captain. His cheerful spirit encouraged Lewis and the other men during the long, dreary months of the trip.

The explorers formed an interesting group. Among them were John Colter, who was just sixteen years old, and plump John Potts, a forty-one-year-old Dutchman. York was William Clark's slave. Patrick Gass was Irish; Hugh McNeal was Scottish; and George Drouillard was French. John Ordway was a soldier from New Hampshire; John Shields was a Kentucky blacksmith; and George Shannon was a farmer's son from Ohio.

Preparation for the Trip

The explorers met in St. Louis to prepare for their trip. Captain Lewis secured two large, open rowboats and a fifty-five-foot keelboat to carry their supplies. They took only a small amount of food: mostly flour, corn-meal, tea, dried soup, salt, and pepper. They would rely on their skill as hunters to provide fresh meat.

The route Lewis and Clark planned for the trip led through the lands of many Indian tribes. President Jefferson ordered the explorers to treat the Indians with respect and to make friends with them. They packed the keelboat with gifts for the Indians. Some of these gifts were beads, brooches, rings, bells, mirrors, brass kettles, and cans of paint. They also packed 4,600 needles and seventy yards of red cloth. As a special gift for the Indian chiefs, they took shiny medals with Jefferson's picture on them.

The group left St. Louis in May, 1804. All summer long the men pushed and pulled their boats up the muddy Missouri River. Before winter came they built Fort Mandan in what is now North Dakota.

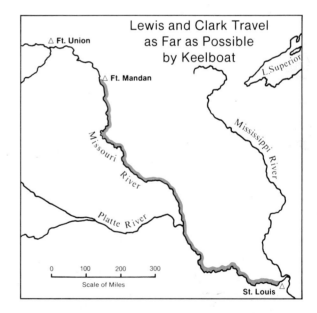

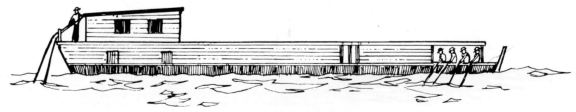

A keelboat

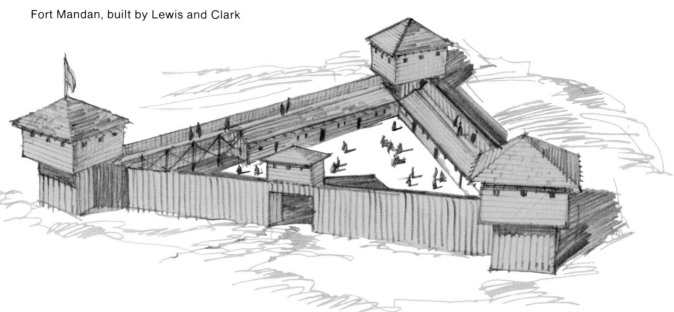

Fort Mandan, built by Lewis and Clark

In November, 1804, a French-Canadian fur trapper named Toussaint Charbonneau and his Indian wife, Sacajawea, joined the explorers. Sacajawea had been stolen from the Shoshone Indians many years before.

Statue of Sacajawea, put up in honor of her help to Lewis and Clark

She was eager to return to her homeland to see her people. The two offered to guide the men and to interpret their words to the Indians. During the winter, Sacajawea gave birth to a son whom the father named Baptiste.

Over the Mountains

When spring came in April of 1805, the explorers started again. The trip beyond Fort Mandan was long and difficult. The land became more and more mountainous. The explorers were entering the lower ranges of the mountains known today as the Rocky Mountains. The rivers became narrow, rushing streams. The keelboat was unable to travel these streams and had to be left behind. "We must have horses," Captain Lewis declared. "Without horses we shall leave our bones in these mountains." The men knew that they were near the land of the Shoshone Indians. That tribe had

THE LEWIS AND CLARK EXPEDITION   **19**

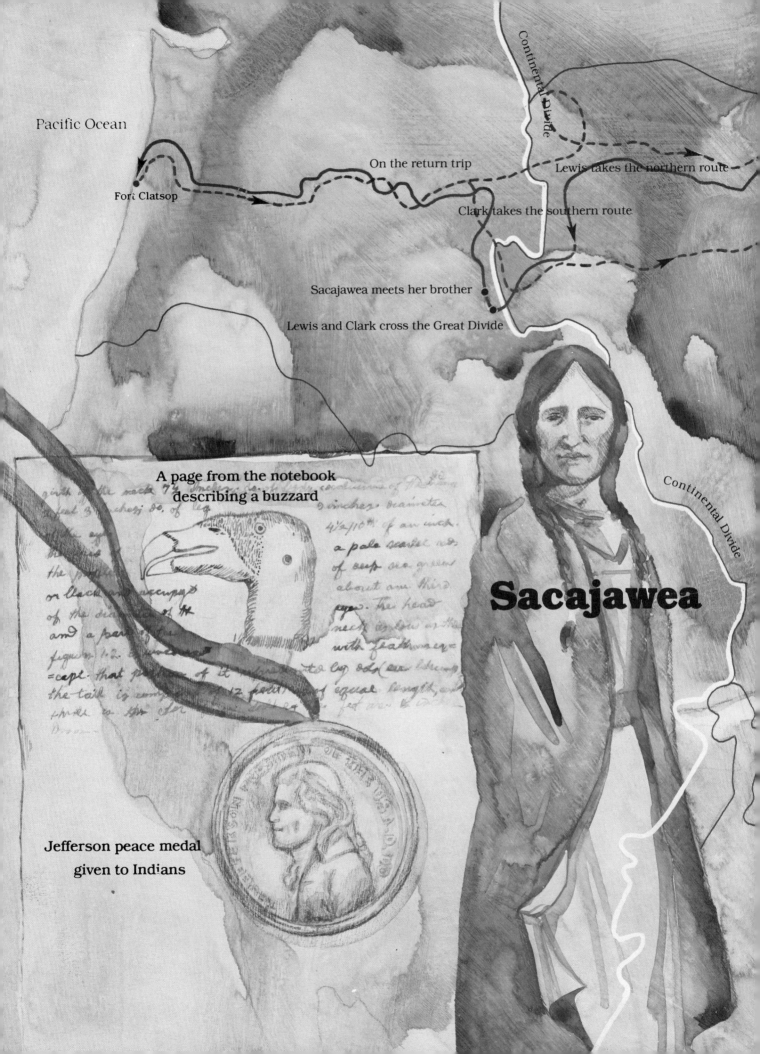

Pacific Ocean

Continental Divide

On the return trip

Lewis takes the northern route

Fort Clatsop

Clark takes the southern route

Sacajawea meets her brother

Lewis and Clark cross the Great Divide

Continental Divide

A page from the notebook
describing a buzzard

Sacajawea

Jefferson peace medal
given to Indians

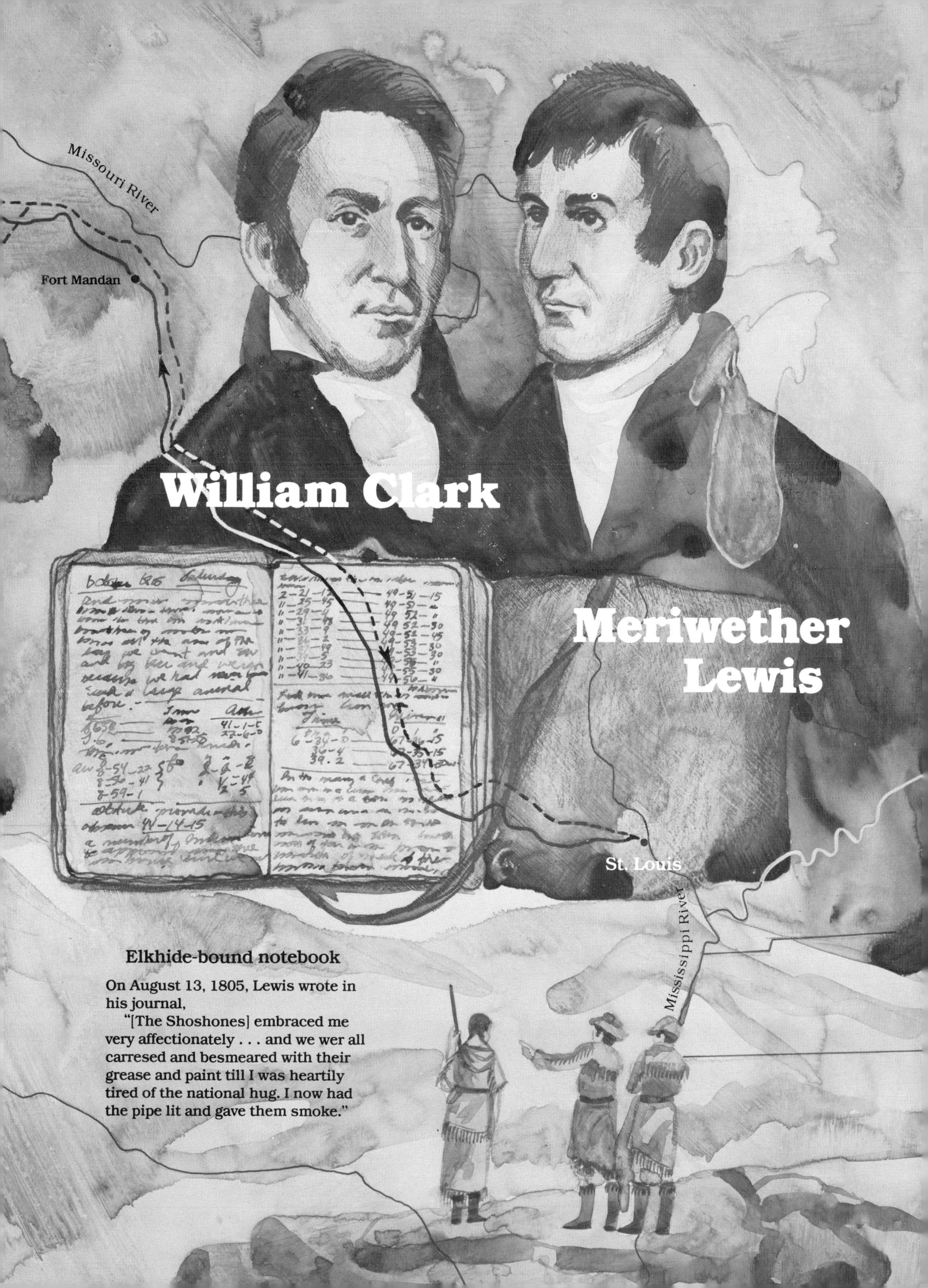

Missouri River

Fort Mandan

William Clark

Meriwether Lewis

St. Louis

Mississippi River

Elkhide-bound notebook

On August 13, 1805, Lewis wrote in his journal,

"[The Shoshones] embraced me very affectionately . . . and we wer all carresed and besmeared with their grease and paint till I was heartily tired of the national hug. I now had the pipe lit and gave them smoke."

many horses. The explorers hoped that Sacajawea's people would help them and sell them the horses they needed.

All summer they traveled through the mountains. When August came, the nights grew very cold. Everyone knew that they must get through the mountains before winter arrived. They knew that winter would come early to the mountains. One day Captain Lewis made a decision: he and three others would go ahead of the other explorers to look for the Shoshone.

Early one morning the four men started up the mountain near their camp. They followed a trickling stream, which below them had been the mighty Missouri River. Higher and higher they went, until finally the stream ended in a little spring. The men were excited, for they had found the source of the mighty Missouri River. They had reached one of their goals!

Quickly the men moved on. They noticed that now the mountain streams flowed westward. Instead of flowing eastward toward the Mississippi River, the water flowed toward the Pacific Ocean. The men had crossed the **Continental Divide**.

The four men continued westward. Suddenly they saw an Indian on a fine horse. Captain Lewis grabbed a blanket from his knapsack. He took it by the corners, waved it three times in the air, and spread it on the ground. This was the sign for "welcome" used by the Plains Indians. The Indian stopped and looked at him. Captain Lewis walked slowly toward the warrior. He rolled

up his sleeve and showed the pale skin of his upper arm. He called out, "Tabba bone! Tabba bone!" which means, "White man! White man!" Slowly the captain went closer, but the Indian whipped his horse and quickly rode away.

The next day the men saw sixty Indians mounted on prancing horses and frisky ponies riding toward them. Captain Lewis made signs of peace and offered them presents. He waved an American flag. "Ah hi e, ah hi e!" ("I am much pleased!") said the young Shoshone chief. Later the four white men and several Indians traveled back to where Captain Clark and the others waited. Imagine everyone's surprise when Sacajawea threw her arms around the Indian chief. He was her brother Cameah, whom she had not seen since she was a child.

Lewis and Clark bought forty good horses and three colts from the Indians. An old Shoshone offered to guide them through the rugged mountains. Captain Clark called him "Old Toby." Sacajawea said good-by to her people, and the explorers continued on their westward journey.

Then came the hardest part of the whole trip. Between the explorers and the Pacific was a range of the Rockies that was so high and so steep that it seemed impossible to cross. Old Toby pointed to a distant ridge split by deep cracks. One of the men said, "Captain, no man can travel that ridge."

"Sergeant," answered Lewis, "thirty-four men, a woman, and a baby start traveling that ridge on the day after tomorrow."

Following their brave captain, the group moved out. The days that followed were days of freezing cold, snow, and gnawing hunger. The food was almost gone, and no game could be found. The men ate the colts one after another. One night they killed a timberwolf. Its meat was tough and stringy, but it provided dinner for the hungry explorers. On the worst day of all, their only meal was a little dried soup mixed with snow and bear oil.

Finishing the journey seemed almost hopeless. One man was sick and coughed constantly. Captain Clark was in pain from a twisted hip. The only trail was along a narrow ledge that circled a cliff at least a thousand feet high. But the men were determined to keep on.

Finally the ledge widened and sloped downward. In the distance the men glimpsed a meadow of green grass. Some of them began to run toward it. Off to the west they saw low green hills. Everyone rejoiced, for they had crossed the Rockies.

Finishing the Journey

The rest of the journey was easier. Friendly Indians provided food until the men could hunt and fish again. They built boats and traveled downstream on rivers. When they reached the Columbia River, they knew their journey was almost over. On November 7, 1805, Captain Clark wrote in his journal: "Ocean in view! Oh! the joy." The explorers had reached their final goal, the Pacific Ocean. Later he carved this message on a tree.

WILLIAM CLARK DECEMBER 3, 1805 BY LAND FROM THE UNITED STATES IN 1804 & 1805

The men built Fort Clatsop near the mouth of the Columbia River and spent the winter months there. When spring came, they started their long trip back home.

The group of weary explorers arrived in St. Louis on September 23, 1806. They had traveled almost eight thousand miles in two years, four months, and twelve days.

Captain Lewis and Captain Clark had kept careful records in a journal of everything that had happened on their long trip. They had collected samples of plants and animals. They had made drawings and maps of the land they had seen. These records helped the American people learn about the great wealth and beauty of the new land that doubled the size of the United States.

Things to know

1. List three purposes of the Lewis and Clark expedition.

2. Arrange the following events in the order in which they occurred: (a) met Sacajawea's brother; (b) left St. Louis; (c) found the source of the Missouri River; (d) built Fort Mandan; (e) bought horses; (f) reached the Pacific Ocean; (g) arrived back in St. Louis; (h) crossed the Rocky Mountains from west to east.

3. How far did Lewis and Clark travel? How long did it take them?

Things to talk about

1. How did the personality and character of Captain Lewis help the men on the trip? How did the personality of Captain Clark help them?

2. If you had been on the trip, would your personality and character have been a help to the others?

3. Why was it important to be friendly with the Indians?

4. Why do you think the explorers did not take horses and large amounts of food?

5. Why do you think Lewis and Clark kept a journal? How was it valuable to them? to President Jefferson? to us?

6. Do you think you could eat a colt or a wolf? Why or why not?

7. What is meant by the term *Continental Divide?* Is that a good name?

Things to do

1. Draw the route of the Lewis and Clark expedition on a map. Draw pictures of the kinds of transportation the explorers used along the route.

2. List the states through which Lewis and Clark traveled.

3. Find out all you can about Sacajawea. What has been done to help people remember her?

4. Write a story describing Sacajawea's meeting with her brother.

5. Where do you think the Eastern Continental Divide is?

6. On a map, trace the path of the Missouri River. Tell where it joins the Mississippi River. List some rivers that flow into it.

CHAPTER 4

THE WAR OF 1812

The United States had purchased Louisiana while France was at war. Napoleon was still fighting in Europe, and by 1812 most of Europe was at war against him. Great Britain used her mighty navy to try to defeat the French. But Britain's actions during this war angered the Americans. The United States and Britain had not been very friendly since the War for Independence ended. This new trouble caused the Americans and British to fight again, this time in the War of 1812.

Into the War

To make her navy strong enough to win against France, Britain needed every man she could get. But many sailors deserted British ships. They knew they could get better treatment on American ships. Soon the British navy began to stop ships to search them for deserters. They took any man who could not prove that he was *not* a British sailor.

Few sailors could prove that they were American sailors. Many of them were "pressed," or forced to leave their ships and work on British ships. This practice was called **impressment**. This action angered the Americans. If the British could take American sailors, then the seas were not free. Because of these and other problems, Congress voted to go to war.

Sea Battles of the War

Most of the battles during the War for Independence were fought on land; however, many of the battles of the War of 1812 were fought on water. Great ships with white sails and powerful cannons were the pride of both navies.

One of America's greatest ships was the U.S.S. *Constitution*. This ship was made of the strongest oak the shipbuilders could find. Its bottom was covered with copper given by Paul Revere. The copper protected the ship from barnacles and helped it to move faster.

This mighty ship won many battles. The U.S.S. *Constitution's* first victory was off the coast of Canada near Nova Scotia. Later this same ship defeated the British H.M.S. *Java*. The U.S.S. *Constitution* was hit with heavy gunfire from the British fleet during these battles. But the cannonballs and gunshot seemed to bounce off its sides, and the American warship never lost. Americans nicknamed the ship "Old Ironsides." They were proud of its great victories.

The *Constitution* defeating a British ship

Two famous American sea captains fought for the United States during the War of 1812. They were Captain James Lawrence and Captain Oliver Hazard Perry. James Lawrence was the captain of the American ship called the U.S.S. *Chesapeake*. Captain Lawrence was a brave, devoted leader. He was wounded during a terrible battle, but he cried

The U.S.S. *Constitution*

out, "Don't give up the ship!" His brave words later became the motto of the United States Navy.

Later that same year, Captain Oliver Hazard Perry attacked British warships on Lake Erie. The powerful British guns destroyed several of Perry's ships. Finally they damaged the flagship, the ship Perry commanded. Rather than give up, Captain Perry rowed to a smaller vessel. He bravely sailed his small ship directly toward the British warships. His cannons and other guns sprayed the British ships with fire and shot. The British had not expected

The War of 1812

✴ Important Battles

Uncle Sam

If you have ever gone to a Fourth of July parade, you may have seen a man or a boy dressed in a red, white, and blue costume. His striped trousers and tall top hat with stars and stripes make him look very tall. His white beard makes him look old. When you see him, you might say, "Oh, look! There's Uncle Sam."

But you may not know that there was once a real person named Uncle Sam. He was Samuel Wilson. Sam was born in Arlington, Massachusetts, in 1766. His father and two older brothers fought in the War for Independence. Sam joined the army when he was just fourteen years old.

When the war was over, Sam settled in Troy, New York. He started a meat-packing plant there. He was known in Troy for his hard work, honesty, and common sense. During the War of 1812, Sam's packing plant supplied meat for the U.S. forces in northern New York.

The governor of New York and some officials came to visit Sam's plant. They saw meat packed in wooden barrels. On each barrel of beef the initials U.S. had been stamped. One of the visitors asked a workman what the "U.S." stood for.

"Uncle Sam," the workman replied.

A reporter who was along asked, "Uncle Sam who?"

Perry to fight. In their surprise they soon surrendered. Captain Perry reported his victory by saying, "We have met the enemy and they are ours."

An Attack on Washington

Not all Americans were fighting for freedom of the seas. Many settlers chose this time to try to take part of

The worker answered, "Why, Uncle Sam Wilson, of course—the man who is supplying the army with its meat." The term "Uncle Sam" spread, and soon people were saying that army supplies from beef to cannon balls to soldiers came from "Uncle Sam."

Uncle Sam soon became a national symbol, but at first he did not look like he does today. In the beginning he was usually shown as a young man. In the 1840s a clown named Dan Rice dressed as Uncle Sam. He was the first to use the clothes we see Uncle Sam wearing today. He also used stilts so that he would be taller and would be easier to see in the circus crowds. In 1869 a cartoonist named Thomas Nast drew Uncle Sam with his white beard.

Probably the most famous picture of Uncle Sam is the one on a World War I poster. The poster was used to get men to join the service. It has Uncle Sam pointing his finger and saying, "I want you!"

Unfortunately, some people have misused the idea of Uncle Sam in more recent years. They have made fun of him and have drawn him more as a bully than as a friend.

But Uncle Sam is still remembered and honored. In New York State, Samuel Wilson's birthday, September 13, is officially called "Uncle Sam's Day." In 1961 Congress passed a special resolution in honor of Uncle Sam Wilson. Today when you hear people talk about the government, especially in business dealings, they may speak of Uncle Sam. If you listen closely, you may hear grown-ups use the term. They may say something like "I work for Uncle Sam" if they work for the federal government. Or they may say "I pay taxes to Uncle Sam." You may surprise them by telling them who the real Uncle Sam was.

Canada from Britain. A small United States army attacked the city of York and burned some government buildings. (York is now called Toronto.) The British did not soon forget this attack on their city.

In 1814 British soldiers marched against Washington, D.C. President James Madison sent an urgent message from the Capitol to his wife, Dolley: "The British are marching on Washington. Leave at once!" Dolley did not panic but quickly went to work. She filled trunks with important government papers. She packed silver, valuable china, velvet curtains, and books and put them in a carriage. Then she noticed a painting of George

fire to the White House, the Capitol, the Treasury Building, and the War Office Building. Although important items were lost, Dolley Madison's quick action had saved many valuables.

Our National Anthem

After the attack on Washington, the British returned to their ships. With them they had a prisoner, an American doctor. Soon they set sail for Baltimore, the place of their next attack. The American victory there inspired the words to our national anthem.

Before the battle began, a lawyer from Washington named Francis Scott Key and a friend of his had gone aboard a British ship in the Baltimore harbor. They wanted to arrange for the release of their friend, the doctor taken prisoner during the attack on Washington. While they were on the

Washington that was bolted to the wall. Quickly she took a knife, cut the picture from its frame, and wrapped it so that she could carry it. Now she was ready to leave.

A short time after the Madisons and other government officials left Washington, the British arrived. They now took their revenge for York. They set ship, Key and his friend learned of the planned British attack. The British kept them on board so that they could not warn the Americans.

As the ship moved out into the water, Key could see the outline of Fort McHenry in the distance. This fort protected the city of Baltimore. Above the fort, on top of the tallest building, waved the American flag with its red and white stripes and fifteen stars. Seeing the flag made Key proud to be an American. He knew that the American flag, "Old Glory," would never be lowered unless the American soldiers surrendered.

A huge British warship with powerful cannons came into view. Key watched the mighty vessel turn slowly toward the fort. The heavy gray and black cannons of both the fort and the ship stood silent. Key could no longer

Francis Scott Key

see the American flag against the last bright red of the setting sun. The battle was about to begin. To keep the three Americans safe, the British moved them to a smaller ship behind the British fleet.

Suddenly the British cannons fired. They boomed and roared as great clouds of smoke filled the air. The shouts of men, the glaring fires, and the smell of burning wood came across the water. The battle raged all night long. Key and his friends watched from the safety of the British ship, but they did not know what was happening. Were the Americans defeated?

Then the battle ended as quickly as it had started. A strange silence fell over the water. There were no more cannon blasts. The fires were put out. Key's ship rocked slowly in the bay.

Key looked out over the water. He watched the large British warship moving off into the distance. The clouds in the sky caught the morning's first rays from the sun. The dark outline of Fort McHenry appeared with the first light.

"I see it! I see it!" exclaimed Key. "The flag is still there!" The Americans had not surrendered.

Pulling a crumpled letter from his pocket, Key began to write on the blank side. In just a few minutes, he scribbled the first stanza of a poem. When he returned to shore, he finished three other stanzas. The next day his poem was printed on handbills and handed out in the streets of Baltimore. Later the words were set to a familiar tune.

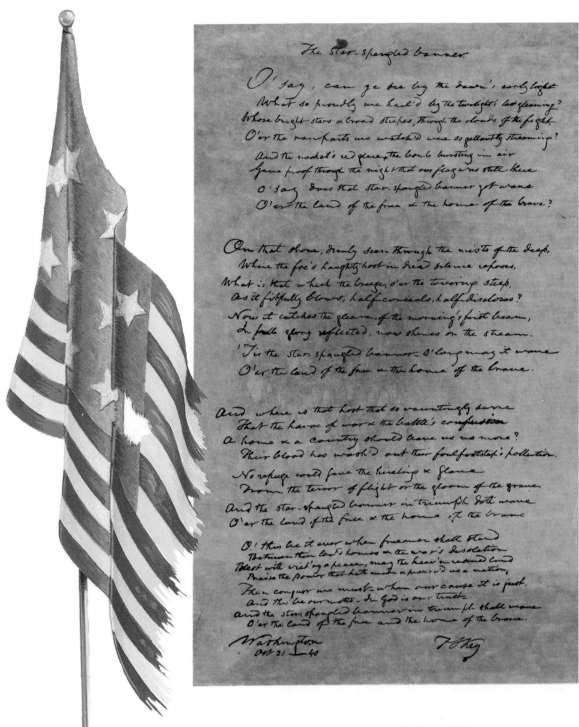

The new song became popular throughout the United States. Congress later voted it our national anthem. Today the words of "The Star-Spangled Banner" remind us of America's greatness even when under attack.

The End of the War

The last battle of the War of 1812 was fought on January 8, 1815. General Andrew Jackson was ordered to defend New Orleans. About eight thousand British soldiers arrived by sea to take the city. They attacked again and again,

Old Hickory

Andrew Jackson's father died just before his son's birth. Andrew lived with his mother in South Carolina and later moved to Tennessee. He did not go to school very long, but he taught himself. He became a lawyer, a senator, a judge, and an army general. General Jackson was stern and tough. "He's as tough as hickory," someone said. After this, Andrew Jackson was often called "Old Hickory."

but Jackson's expert riflemen from Tennessee and Kentucky drove them back each time. The British at last gave up. Over 300 British men were killed,

The Battle of New Orleans

1,250 were wounded, and 500 captured. Only 14 Americans were killed, 39 wounded, and 18 captured. "Old Hickory," as Andrew Jackson was called, had led his army to victory.

This battle made Andrew Jackson famous in the United States. It did not affect the war, however. Neither of the armies knew it, but a peace treaty had been signed fifteen days before that battle began.

After the War

The War of 1812 did not really settle the differences between the United States and Britain. The peace treaty did not even mention the impressment of sailors. Also, Canada stayed a British colony. These results hardly seemed to solve the problems that started the war.

Even so, the war did change life in America. Americans became more patriotic. Our land had been challenged by a foreign nation, and the citizens had joined together to fight the enemy. Because of the war, Americans now had a national anthem. Even today Americans' hearts are stirred when they hear the national anthem. It is a symbol of our country's greatness.

The war also helped the United States to become more **self-sufficient.** Before the war Americans had bought most of their manufactured goods from other countries. During the war this trade was stopped by British ships that formed a **blockade** outside U.S. harbors. The British blockaded the United States by anchoring ships off the coast and keeping merchant ships from entering. By keeping foreign goods out of U.S. stores, the British hoped to weaken the United States. The lack of goods hurt Americans for a while, but soon they began to manufacture their own goods. In the next unit, you will learn some of the ways in which the United States became more self-sufficient.

Things to know

1. Match the following names with the items below.

     ____ Dolley Madison

     ____ Francis Scott Key

     ____ Oliver Hazard Perry

     ____ Andrew Jackson

     ____ James Madison

     a. Wrote "The Star-Spangled Banner"

     b. Wrote, "We have met the enemy and they are ours."

     c. Was president during the War of 1812

     d. Saved a picture of George Washington

     e. American general at New Orleans

2. What ship was called "Old Ironsides"? Explain how it got that name.

3. Why do we remember the battles at Washington, D.C., at Baltimore, and at New Orleans?

Things to talk about

1. What are some ways in which wars in the 1800s differ from wars today?

2. Why do we sing "The Star-Spangled Banner" at the beginning of certain programs and ball games? Why do we stand up when we hear it?

3. What do these words in "The Star-Spangled Banner" mean: "hailed," "twilight's last gleaming," "perilous," "ramparts," "gallantly streaming"?

4. How did the rockets and bombs prove that "the flag was still there"?

5. Why is it important for a nation to manufacture most of its own goods?

6. What is an anthem?

Things to do

1. Draw a picture of a ship like those used in the War of 1812.

2. Find Washington, D.C., Baltimore, and New Orleans on a map.

3. Memorize the first verse of "The Star-Spangled Banner" if you do not know it already.

4. Figure out how many years have passed since "The Star-Spangled Banner" was written.

5. Plan a special program to honor our flag and our national anthem.

6. Add to your flag booklet.

A Growing Nation

36

TWO

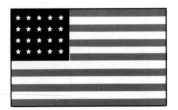

A Changing Flag   By 1791 the United States flag was out of date. Vermont had become the fourteenth state, and soon other states were added as the country grew. On April 14, 1818, Congress voted that the United States flag should always have thirteen stripes but that one star would be added for each state that joined the union. This flag became the official flag on July 4, 1818.

UNIT GOALS

- I will be able to describe ways in which the transportation needs of the new nation were met by roads, canals, steamboats, railroads, and clipper ships.
- I will be able to explain how Stephen Paxson helped spread the gospel among pioneer families.
- I will be able to tell about the disagreements between the white men and the Indians.
- I will be able to explain why and how Americans settled in Oregon and in Texas.
- I will be able to describe the gold rush days.
- I will be able to tell how the United States obtained the land west of the Mississippi River.
- I will be able to locate Texas, Oregon, and California on the map.

TIME LINE

National Road Construction Begins | First Railroad | Gold in California | Pony Express

1800 — 1810 — 1820 — 1830 — 1840 — 1850 — 1860

Clermont | Erie Canal Completed | Trail of Tears | Texas Becomes a State

CHAPTER 5

TRANSPORTATION

When George Washington became the first president of the United States in 1789, the nation was small. All the states of the Union stretched along the coast of the Atlantic Ocean. But the nation did not stay small. The country grew by leaps and bounds across the Appalachian Mountains and then over the Mississippi River. It stretched north and west and south as new territories were added. By 1860 the United States reached from the Atlantic to the vast Pacific. Indeed, these years were growing years.

Find the first thirteen states on the map at the end of the book. Which mountains are just west of these states? Which rivers can you see? Can you tell which way they flow?

The growing nation needed transportation. Settlers eager to claim new land wanted safe, easy transportation. Once settled, they needed to take their goods to market. You recall that many western settlers shipped their goods down the Mississippi River to sell them at New Orleans. The government needed transportation for mail and military orders. Friends needed transportation to visit each other, and businessmen often had duties far from home. Without better transportation, the nation could not have grown.

Sheffey, Unusual Films

Moving West Before Independence

The first English colonists settled close to the Atlantic Ocean. They wanted to be near the coast where the ships from England could reach them. Over the years, the East became more settled, and new settlers moved farther inland, away from the ocean. Often they traveled inland by water because that was easier than land travel. Then they chose places near the rivers or streams to clear land and build their homes. Soon villages grew up along the inland rivers. Rather than building roads to reach the villages, people simply traveled on the rivers.

The Appalachian Mountains stood in the way of settlers who wanted to go farther west. Few trails or rivers

provided travel routes through them. Trees covered these rugged mountains, and deep valleys lay between them. Winter storms brought heavy snows, and spring rains turned streams into roaring rivers. Only the bravest of the early pioneers dared to cross these mountains.

First among these brave pioneers was a group of frontiersmen led by Daniel Boone. They led the way across the Appalachian Mountains to the Kentucky country. Thousands of settlers who came after them used the road they made over the mountains.

These men worked hard building the road. Daniel went first. He cut notches or **blazes** in trees to mark the way. The other men followed behind and cleared the trail. They cut down small trees and brush. Scouts on both sides of the new trail watched for Indians. After days of hard work, the men reached the low place in the mountains that is now called the Cumberland Gap.

For the next fifty miles, Boone and his men widened an Indian trail called "Warriors' Path." Then "The Bison Street" stretched out before them. This

Boonesborough, Kentucky, under attack by Indians

was a path made by thousands of bison, or buffalo. Finally the men reached the Kentucky River. There they built Fort Boonesborough (see map on page 42).

The trail that Boone and his men cut was called the Wilderness Road. By 1800 about 200,000 pioneers had traveled over it to make new homes beyond the Appalachian Mountains. Farmers drove their livestock back to eastern markets over the road. Herds of animals walked along the way and ate what they could find as they went. Sometimes people called this road the "Kaintuck Hog Road" because so many hogs were driven over it.

The National Road

As the nation grew, the government decided to build a road between the western frontier and the East. The Great National Road was the first road paid for by the United States government. The road began at the city of Cumberland, Maryland. At first it ended on the Ohio River at what is now Wheeling, West Virginia. Later builders continued the road to Illinois. When it was completed in 1840, Congress had spent over 7 million dollars for the highway.

The National Road

As many as twenty-four horse coaches have been counted in line at one time on the road, and large, broad-wheeled wagons, covered with white canvas stretched over bows laden with merchandise and drawn by six horses, were visible all the day long at every point, and many times until late in the evening, besides numberless caravans of horses, mules, cattle, hogs, and sheep. It looked more like a leading avenue of a great city than a road through rural districts.

—*A man who lived near the National Road*

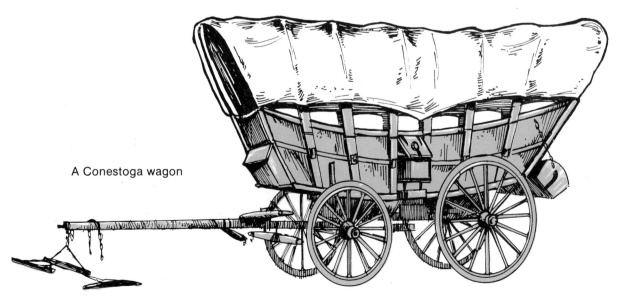

A Conestoga wagon

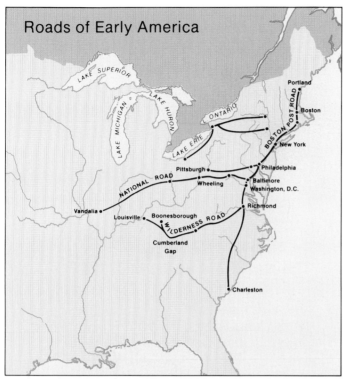

Roads of Early America

The National Road, also called the Cumberland Road, was always busy. Travelers filled it from dawn until dark. Wagons and coaches pulled by oxen or horses used the highway every day. Freight wagons carried produce to markets in the East and manufactured goods back to the West. Fancy stagecoaches traveled their routes both east and west. Mighty **Conestoga wagons** carried families and their belongings across the mountains.

More Roads to the West

Besides the government, American businessmen also paid to have roads built. Many people thought that each state government should build roads like the National Road. Since most of the states did not have enough money to do this, businessmen formed companies to build the roads instead.

Many roads built by these companies were **toll roads.** Toll roads had gates at special places along the way. Travelers stopped at each gate and paid some money before they could go on. The money paid was called a **toll.** At first the tollgate was a pole or pike set across the road. The pike was turned to the side of the road when the traveler

A stagecoach on the Cumberland Road

paid the toll. The people called these roads **turnpikes.** The money collected at these tollgates paid for the building of the roads. Extra money collected was a profit for the companies.

Travel over these early roads was sometimes difficult. The roads were bumpy, dusty, and after a rain, muddy. In the 1830s Fanny Kemble, an Englishwoman visiting the United States, described her travels on one of America's new roads:

Away galloped the four horses, trotting with their front and galloping with their hind legs: and away we went after them, bumping, thrumping, jumping, jolting, shaking, tossing and tumbling over the wickedest road, I do think the cruellest, hard-heartedest road, that ever wheel rumbled upon.

The National Road and these other roads brought much trade from the West to Baltimore, Philadelphia, and other eastern cities. The western farmers were grateful for the new roads. They no longer had to depend on water routes down the Mississippi River to New Orleans. The settlers living in the

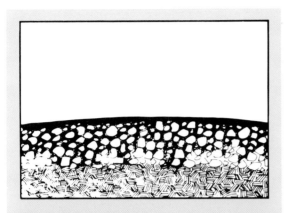

McAdam's Road

After 1825, parts of the National Road were rebuilt according to a plan made by John McAdam, an engineer in Scotland. First, the workmen dug a shallow trench where the road was to be built. Next, they filled the trench with broken stones and packed them down as much as possible. Finally, they dug a ditch on each side of the road to carry off the water when it rained.

Roads built in this way were smoother than the old dirt roads. They did not get ruts and holes so quickly. Wagons rolled along more easily on "McAdam's roads," and traffic speeded up.

Today some roads are called **macadam** *roads. Find out what they are like.*

northern area west of the Appalachians also needed an easier way to transport their goods to markets in New York City. Transportation on natural and manmade waterways solved their problems.

DeWitt Clinton and His Big Ditch

For years men had talked of building a **canal** to link the Great Lakes with the Atlantic Ocean. But the task seemed impossible. However, one man, DeWitt Clinton, the governor of New York, believed it could be done. He talked about the canal, wrote about the canal, and finally drew plans for the canal. He asked the United States Congress to build his canal, but it refused. Mr. Clinton never gave up. In 1815, the state of New York agreed to pay for his "Big Ditch," the Erie Canal.

Work on the canal began in 1817. First, the surveyors marked the route with red stakes. Next came the workers who chopped the trees, dug out the stumps, and scooped out the canal. Then came the carpenters and masons, who built bridges and **locks.** They used a new kind of cement that would harden underwater.

The job took eight years. The finished canal was 363 miles long and four feet deep. The canal was forty-two feet wide at the top but narrowed to only twenty-eight feet at the bottom. It connected Buffalo on Lake Erie with Albany on the Hudson River.

To complete the canal, workmen built a towpath next to the waterway.

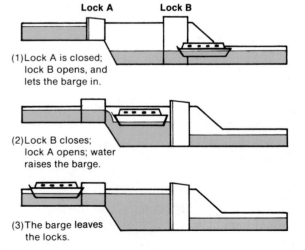

(1) Lock A is closed; lock B opens, and lets the barge in.

(2) Lock B closes; lock A opens; water raises the barge.

(3) The barge leaves the locks.

Mules walking on the towpath pulled boats as large as eighty feet long and fifteen feet wide through the canal. Many of these boats went only two miles an hour. The fastest passenger boats traveled between six and seven miles an hour. People no longer called the canal the "Big Ditch." Now they named it the "Grand Canal." Governor Clinton made the first trip between Buffalo and New York City, which took him ten days.

Towns along the canal built bridges over it. Many of these were very low. When a boat came near a town, the steersman called out, "Low bridge! Everybody down!" The passengers crouched in the bottom of the boat until they passed under the dangerous bridge. The steersman's cry was a common sound on the canal. It became part of a famous song about the Erie Canal.

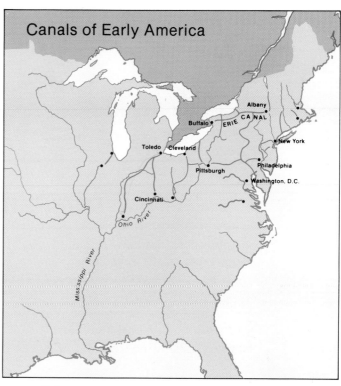

Canals of Early America

Many people used the Erie Canal to transport their goods to the Hudson River and then to markets in New York City. In addition to the cost of shipping,

Traveling by Canal

"I like traveling by canal boats very much. Ours was not crowded, and the country through which we passed was delightful. The only difficulties are the bridges over the canal, which are so very low that one is obliged to place oneself flat on the deck of the boat to avoid being scraped off it; and this experience occurs, upon the average, once every quarter of an hour."

—Fanny Kemble
Englishwoman

they paid a toll to use the canal. The tolls soon paid for the building of the canal, and the canal became a great success. Other canals were also built throughout the eastern United States.

De Witt Clinton

THE ERIE CANAL

I've got a mule, her name is Sal,
Fifteen years on the Erie Canal.
She's a good old worker and a good old pal,
Fifteen years on the Erie Canal.
We've hauled some barges in our day,
Filled with lumber, coal and hay
And every inch of the way I know
From Albany to Buffalo.

We better get along on our way, old gal,
Fifteen miles on the Erie Canal,
Cause you bet your life I'd never part with Sal.
Fifteen miles on the Erie Canal.
Git up there, mule, here comes a lock,
We'll make Rome 'bout six o'clock.
One more trip and back we'll go
Right back home to Buffalo.

Chorus

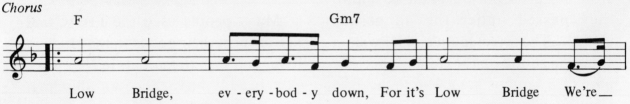

Low Bridge, ev-ery-bod-y down, For it's Low Bridge We're

com-ing to a town! You can al-ways tell your neigh-bor, You can

al-ways tell your pal, If you've ev-er nav-i-gat-ed on the

E - rie Ca - nal.___   E - rie Ca - nal.___

America's waterways were busy highways linking cities in the East with the towns in the North and the West.

A New Method of Transportation

The canals improved water transportation by connecting rivers. However, river travel was still slow. The flatboats and keelboats could not travel upstream well. But inventors went to work on that problem. Their answer was the **steamboat.**

The steamboat, like many other inventions, was the result of the ideas of several men. In 1769 James Watt invented a useful steam engine. About 1790 John Fitch tried adding the steam engine to a boat. However, his steamboat did not work well. In the early 1800s Robert Fulton took their ideas, improved them, and made them work. We remember him as the builder of the first successful steamboat in the United States.

Robert Fulton was born in Pennsylvania. As a young man, he traveled to England to study painting and art.

While there, he grew interested in canals and in underwater warfare. Always looking for good ideas, he thought up several ways to improve the building of canals. He even built a two-man submarine.

After a few years, Robert Fulton returned to the United States. He soon formed a partnership with another man who was interested in building steamboats. Fulton worked hard and built a steamboat, which he named the *North River Steamboat Clermont*. The boat was 140 feet long and 14 feet wide. The engine, made in England, pushed the side paddle wheels. These wheels turned in the water and moved the boat along. People laughed at the strange-looking boat. They called it "Fulton's Folly."

Robert Fulton and the *Clermont*

Ignoring their jeering, Fulton put his invention to the test. On August 17, 1807, a small group of passengers boarded the *Clermont* in New York City for a trip up the Hudson to Albany. Most people did not believe that the awkward craft would run. However, the steamboat slowly moved away from shore and pushed its way upstream.

The journey from New York City to Albany took two days. During the trip the passengers were splashed with water from the paddle wheels and sprinkled with soot from the smokestacks. At last, the steamboat arrived safely in Albany. Fulton's invention was a success. But when it was time for the return voyage, only two men were willing to repeat the trip.

Glad for his success, Fulton worked to improve the *Clermont*. Soon he opened regular steamboat service between New York City and Albany. No longer did people laugh at his invention. Instead they paid to ride it and ship goods on it.

After this, businessmen started steamboat lines in many parts of the United States. Steamboats carried large amounts of freight and many passengers. Faster than flatboats or canal boats, the steamships also traveled easily upstream or down. As more steamboats were built, freight charges and ticket prices came down.

The most famous of the steamboat lines were on the Mississippi River. The Mississippi riverboats were designed to

The riverboat *Golden Eagle* on the Cumberland River

The riverboat *Delta Queen*

travel in the river's shallow water. Builders put the engines on the main deck instead of below the water line. People even joked that one steamboat, called the *Washington,* "could float on a heavy dew."

Steamboats moved over the Missouri, the Ohio, and other rivers on into the great Mississippi. The cities along their routes grew into rich trading centers. The steamboat lines provided a better way for the people living on the frontier to get their produce to market and to bring back goods they bought. They made it easier to travel from place to place. Because of this, the western lands became more valuable.

The Railroad

About the same time that Robert Fulton was building his steamboat, other men were trying steam-powered cars that ran on rails. Before them, other inventors had built roads with wooden rails. Horse-drawn wagons and carts moved faster on rails than on regular roads. Putting the steam engine and rails together resulted in the railroad.

In 1825 in New Jersey, John Stevens built a small steam-powered **loco-motive** that ran on iron rails. Like Robert Fulton, he believed that steam-powered engines could solve America's transportation problems.

Although some agreed with these two men, not everyone believed in steam-powered transportation. To convince the doubters, a race was set up near Baltimore in 1830. Peter Cooper had built a little locomotive that he named *Tom Thumb.* A stagecoach owner challenged Cooper's locomotive to a race against one of his stagecoach line's fastest horses.

At the start of the race the horse quickly dashed ahead of the train. Then the train gained speed and inched past the galloping horse. Cooper shoved more wood and coal into his steam engine. The rider of the horse yelled and urged his horse to run even faster. The crowd shouted in excitement. Some cheered for the rider of the horse; others cheered for *Tom Thumb.* The steam engine strained and puffed. The

The *Tom Thumb* and its famous race

horse's hooves pounded against the earth.

Suddenly a belt slipped off the engine. Clouds of steam and smoke filled the air. The locomotive's wheels started to slide and grind against the iron rails. Before Cooper could replace the belt, the horse dashed across the finish line. *Tom Thumb* lost the race but proved that a steam-powered locomotive on an iron track was a good idea.

Word of *Tom Thumb*'s race against the horse spread across the country. People finally believed that the steam-powered engine could run as fast as the fastest horse. Businessmen formed companies to build railroads and locomotives. The first regular service

in the nation began in Charleston, South Carolina. On Christmas Day, 1830, a locomotive called the *Best Friend* made this company's first run.

The *Best Friend*

The new railroad companies began to grow rapidly. By 1835 workmen had laid a thousand miles of railroad track,

A railroad bridge built in 1869

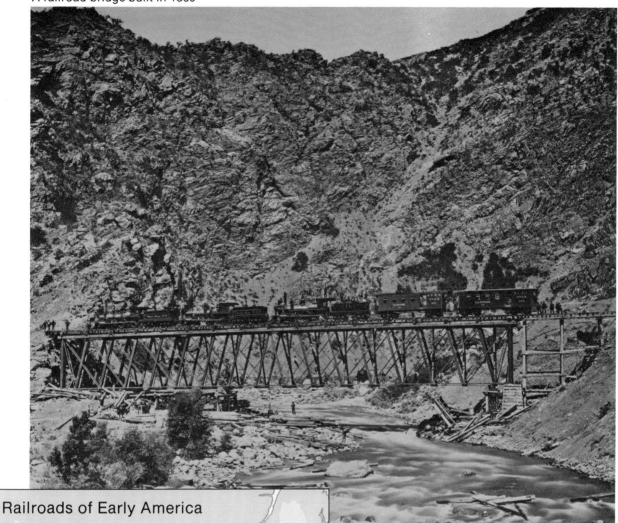

Railroads of Early America

Boston
Chicago
Cleveland
Philadelphia
Baltimore
Washington, D.C.
St. Louis
Charleston
New Orleans

and about two hundred trains operated over it.

By the middle of the 1800s, transportation in our nation had changed greatly. The iron horse on its iron rails tied together our nation's largest cities. Brightly painted riverboats carried freight and passengers back and forth on the rivers from New Orleans to locations in Ohio and Pennsylvania. Transportation between America and other nations changed as well. The desire for faster travel encouraged the growth of a new type

A steam locomotive

of transportation. The graceful clipper ships sailed the ocean, carrying cargo to and from Europe, Asia, and America.

The Clipper Ships

The **clipper** ships were famous for their beauty and speed. They had sharp, narrow hulls designed to cut smoothly through the waves. Their great, billowing sails were carefully arranged to catch the slightest puff of wind. The *Sea Witch,* one of the fastest clipper ships, once traveled from China to New York City in 74 days and 14 hours. This was over 100 days faster than ordinary ships. The average trip from New York City around South America to San Francisco lasted 160 days. However, the *Flying Cloud* set a record by completing the trip in only 89 days and 21 hours.

These great clipper ships attracted great men to sail them. Perhaps one of the best sea captains was Nathaniel Brown Palmer. Palmer first went to sea during the War of 1812 when he was only fourteen years old. At twenty-one

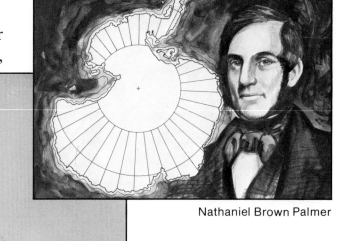

Nathaniel Brown Palmer

A clipper ship

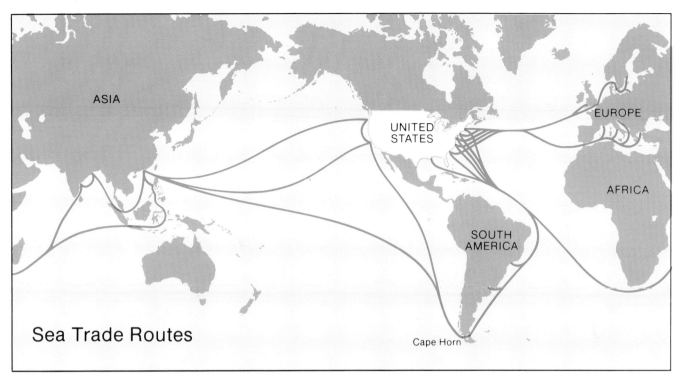

Sea Trade Routes

ASIA

UNITED STATES

EUROPE

AFRICA

SOUTH AMERICA

Cape Horn

he commanded a small ship on an expedition for seals at the tip of South America. While on this voyage, he discovered the continent of Antarctica.

Captain Palmer was a wise and cautious man. He understood his ships, the weather, and his men. It was said that during his career Palmer never lost a **spar** or a man. After retiring from the sea, Palmer designed clipper ships for other captains to sail. His life as a sea captain helped make him one of the greatest designers of American clipper ships.

During the 1800s the United States of America changed greatly. As people moved to new areas and produced more goods, they built roads and dug canals. They also built steamboats and trains and designed better ships. These improvements in transportation helped our country to become larger and greater.

America

Samuel Smith was a young man studying to be a minister. He had no classes to attend one cold February day in 1831. He liked being able to stay home and read. While leafing through a German hymnbook, he noticed a patriotic song. It had a nice melody that seemed easy to sing. Samuel immediately decided to write a patriotic song of his own that would fit the tune. He found a scrap of paper and began to write. In half an hour, he had completed all four verses. Samuel made a copy of the song and gave it to his friend, Lowell Mason.

Mr. Mason thought that the new song should be sung in public. Without telling Samuel, he arranged for a choir of five hundred boys and girls to sing it at a Fourth of July celebration in Boston. How surprised Mr. Smith was to hear his song sung on such a great occasion! Soon afterward, "America" was published in several hymnbooks and became popular throughout the country.

Things to know

1. Match the following men with the proper means of transportation.

   ____ De Witt Clinton   a. Clipper ships

   ____ Daniel Boone   b. Steamboats

   ____ Robert Fulton   c. Erie Canal

   ____ Peter Cooper   d. Wilderness Road

   ____ Nathaniel Palmer   e. Railroads

2. Choose the correct words to complete each sentence.

   a. The clipper ships were built mainly for (size, speed, safety).

   b. The Erie Canal connected the Hudson River and (the Mississippi River, the Atlantic Ocean, Lake Erie).

   c. The *Clermont* was first used in (Virginia, New York, Pennsylvania).

   d. The National Road was paid for by (the United States government, the state of Maryland, the men who built it).

   e. The first railroad service in the United States was in (Ohio, Massachusetts, South Carolina).

Things to talk about

1. Do we have any "national roads" today? If so, what are they called?

2. How are today's turnpikes like those of early days? How are they different?

3. How did the Erie Canal help the following people: (a) those who lived along the Great Lakes; (b) those who wished to "go west"; (c) those who lived along the canal; and (d) those who lived in Buffalo and New York City?

4. How did the steamboat make the lands west of the Appalachian Mountains more valuable?

5. If you lived near a place where a stagecoach changed horses, how could you make some money?

6. Why was speed important to the clipper ship builders and captains?

7. In what ways were trains better than stagecoaches? How were stagecoaches better than trains?

8. How can the character traits of DeWitt Clinton and Robert Fulton be examples to help us to be better Christians?

Things to do

1. Write a story about a day on the National Road.

2. Find out if there is a highway today where the National Road was first built.

3. Draw a picture of the *Clermont, Tom Thumb,* or a Mississippi River steamboat.

4. Find out how roads are built today. About how much does it cost to build one mile of a four-lane highway?

5. List the five Great Lakes. Find them on your map.

6. Make a list of the kinds of transportation you have used.

7. Learn the song "The Erie Canal."

8. Find out how locks on a canal work.

9. Add to your flag booklet.

10. Make a graph of the following information about the number of miles of railroad track there were in each of the following years.

Miles of Railroad Track	Year
23	1830
1,098	1835
2,818	1840
4,633	1845
9,021	1850
18,374	1855
30,626	1860

CHAPTER 6

LIFE ON THE FRONTIER

Which states were added to our country between 1790 and 1860? How many of these were west of the Appalachian Mountains?

The land west of the Appalachians promised Americans a new life. Many Americans dreamed of claiming this land for their farms and orchards. They dreamed of building busy towns and cities near the many rivers and streams. These settlers worked to make their dreams come true by pushing their way into the frontier. They answered the call, "Go west!" They led the way for a growing nation to follow. As more and more settlers traveled to the frontier, new states were made. In 1787

Congress had said that at least 60,000 free persons had to live in a territory before it could be made a state. From the map of new states, you can see that many Americans went to live on the frontier.

The Early Frontier

Most of the pioneers who traveled west were farmers. They tried to arrive at their new land in early spring. This gave them time to clear some land and raise a crop, build a log cabin, and get ready for the cold winter months. Every member of the family worked hard to provide the food, shelter, and clothing they needed. Over the years many pioneers built big farms.

Some of the people on the frontier lived much like many people in the East. They started stores, opened blacksmith shops and small factories, and published newspapers. They lived in growing towns and cities.

The log schoolhouse was an important building in the pioneer communities. Most schools had only one room, few books, and no chalkboards, charts, or maps. Without these supplies, the schools depended upon good teachers, good lessons, and good students.

New States—1790-1860

The students in nearly every school used the **McGuffey Readers**. First published in 1837, they were used for about seventy-five years to teach reading and spelling. They contained stories and lessons that taught children honesty, kindness, and love of God and His Word.

Most of the pioneers believed in God. Even those who did not trust the Lord Jesus as their Saviour believed that a person should go to church and try to do right. They respected the Bible and those who obeyed it.

Most pioneer towns held their church services in the schoolhouse until the settlers could build a church building. Many towns did not have a full-time pastor. Instead, a traveling preacher visited several towns regularly. He held services, baptized people, and held weddings and funerals. The people called him a "circuit-riding" preacher because he rode a horse from one settlement to another on a route known as a **circuit.**

Sometimes during the summer months, groups of preachers held camp

A circuit-riding preacher

Sheffey, Unusual Films

meetings. These services attracted families from many settlements. They gathered under a large shelter to sing songs and listen to the preaching. There were usually two or three services during the day and another one each evening. Camp meetings were a time of fellowship as well as spiritual blessing for the settlers. Between the services the families played games, visited old friends, made new friends, ate, and sang familiar songs. The song on the next page was sung at many of these camp meetings.

A camp meeting   *Sheffey*, Unusual Films

A New Way to Spread the Gospel

Robert Raikes started the first Sunday school in England in 1780, and the idea soon spread to America. The Sunday school was especially important on the frontier, where many churches did not have a regular pastor or weekly services. Missionaries went into the western lands to start Sunday schools. The greatest of these Sunday school missionaries was Stephen Paxson.

Stephen Paxson and his family lived in Illinois. Although Mr. Paxson was crippled and could not speak clearly, he was a good husband and a good father. One day his daughter asked him to go to Sunday school with her. She had promised to bring a visitor and did not know who else to ask. Even though Mr. Paxson thought that Sunday school was only for children, he went to please his little girl. Because he knew so little about the Bible, he returned week after week to learn what God's Word said. After four years he accepted the Lord as his own Saviour.

In 1848 God called Paxson to become a Sunday school missionary. During his forty years as a missionary, he traveled from the Great Lakes to the Gulf of Mexico and from the Allegheny Mountains to the Rockies. Everywhere he went he started Sunday schools.

Mr. Paxson traveled almost entirely by walking or on horseback. A church in Illinois took an offering for him to buy a "missionary horse." He used the money to buy a horse he named "Robert Raikes." This good horse carried Paxson for twenty-five years. Together they traveled more than 100,000 miles.

BRETHREN, WE HAVE MET TO WORSHIP

1. Breth - ren, __ we have met to __ wor - ship __
2. Let us __ love our God su - preme - ly, __

And a - dore the Lord our God; Will you __ pray with
Let us __ love each oth - er too; Let us __ love and

all your __ pow - er, __ While we __ try to
pray for __ sin - ners, __ Till our __ God makes

preach the Word? All is vain un - less the __ Spir - it
all things new. Then He'll call us home to __ heav - en,

Of the Ho - ly One comes __ down; Breth - ren, __ pray, and
At His ta - ble we'll sit __ down; Christ will __ gird Him -

ho - ly __ man - na __ Will be __ show - ered all a - round.
self, and __ serve us __ With sweet __ man - na all a - round.

"Robert Raikes" learned Paxson's habits so well that he stopped every time they met a child. He automatically turned in at every church and school. Children called the horse "Dear Old Bob."

In those days, a missionary did three things to start a Sunday school. First, he found a place to meet. Then, he found one or more persons to be teachers. Finally, he worked to get a donation of five dollars so that he could buy a collection of one hundred Christian books for the children and teachers to read.

With practice, Mr. Paxson taught himself to speak clearly and to walk without showing pain. He was not afraid of hard work. He once began forty Sunday schools in forty days. Afterwards, he wrote in a report, "I had to work day and night like a horse."

Sometimes during the winter, Paxson went to several large eastern cities to raise money for his work. People enjoyed hearing about his experiences. His "peach-basket" story was very popular. He told it something like this:

I visited a man named Mr. Allen to see if he would support a Sunday school in his neighborhood. He was peeling peaches on his back porch. He invited me to sit down and help myself to the peaches.

While we were eating, I asked if there were a Sunday school nearby.

"No," he answered, "and as for me, I am against education."

I tried to show him that children needed to be taught their duty to God and their responsibilities to others. Then I asked what his children did on Sundays.

"Climb trees and wear out their clothes," was his reply.

"Wouldn't it be better for them to be in Sunday school instead of wearing out their clothes?"

"Well, perhaps it would," he admitted.

I asked, "How many children do you have that are old enough to go to school?"

He started counting on his fingers. Then he called, "Wife, come here and name the children while I count." They counted thirteen.

I looked over the meadow and saw his hogs feeding on the clover. "How many hogs have you over there?" I asked.

"Eighty-three fine fat fellows," he said with pride.

"Now, see here, my friend. You have to count to see how many children you have, but you know how many hogs you have. Where is your mind—on your hogs or on your children?"

Mr. Allen looked up. "Old hoss, you've got me. It's too much on the hogs."

Two years later I visited the family again. The farmer had been saved and had joined the church.

Altogether, Stephen Paxson started 1,300 Sunday schools and helped the teachers in over 1,700 others. His greatest joy was serving the Lord. Later, his oldest son joined him in the work and started over 700 Sunday schools himself. Perhaps no one else did more than the Paxson family to spread the gospel in the West during those days.

Trouble with the Indians

When white men came to the New World, they found tribes of Indians. Some tribes lived in houses and raised crops of corn, squash, and beans. Some tribes lived in bark huts called wigwams. They traveled from place to place, hunting and gathering wild rice and berries. Other tribes lived in tepees made of animal skins or in other kinds of homes.

Each Indian tribe had its own laws, religion, and customs. These were passed from parents to children by stories and songs. No Indian tribe in North America had a written language.

Some colonists went as missionaries to the Indians. They wanted to tell the Indians of Christ's love. Often the missionaries to the Indians faced many hardships and troubles. Sometimes the Indians did not like the white missionaries and tried to hurt them. However, some Indians did accept Christ as Saviour.

An Indian proclaims his resistance to white settlers

Even with the missionaries' work, the Indians and the white settlers did not understand each other's ways. The Indians believed that the land belonged to everyone. Most of the tribes did not use money, and they were not interested in becoming rich. The Indians believed that their ways were just as good as the white man's ways. The white man disagreed. Of course, these differences caused trouble.

The earliest colonists had had trouble with the Indians. The pioneers who went west also had trouble. They took over land that had been the Indians' hunting grounds for hundreds of years. The Indians did not want to give up this land, but the white men wanted to settle on it. Both the Indians and the white men were willing to fight for this land. And that is exactly what happened.

The Trail of Tears

In the southeastern United States lived the Cherokee and four other Indian tribes. Before the War for Independence, a few white missionaries had lived among them. Later, as the frontier moved westward toward Indian territory, the settlers lived closer to the Indians. More missionaries went to the Indians and taught them about God and the Bible. They also taught them many of the white man's ways. These Indian tribes slowly changed their ways of living by copying the white settlers' habits and customs. The

Indians began to grow the same crops and build the same kinds of houses as the white people. They sent their children to school and to church. Because they lived like the white settlers, these Indians were called the **"Five Civilized Tribes."**

As years went by, the settlers began to take land belonging to these tribes. They wanted to grow cotton on the rich soil. A few of the planters, armed with rifles, used force to drive the Indians from their homes. The Indians pleaded with Congress for protection. Davy Crockett and some other Congressmen in Washington believed that the Indians' rights should be protected. However, many disagreed.

In 1834, Congress decided that the Indians would have to leave their homes and go to special lands west of the Mississippi River. Congress said that this territory, or **reservation,** would belong to the Indians "as long as the grass shall grow." The Indians accepted the government's decision and agreed to live by it. They gathered their belongings and families together to prepare for the move west.

The journey to their new home west of the Mississippi River was a terrible experience for the Indians. The United States government promised to provide food and supplies for the journey, but it failed to keep its promise. Much of the trip took place during the coldest winter months. The Indians traveled without proper clothing, and some had only one blanket for an entire family. Many times the food supplies were late or never arrived at all. However, the Indians believed in honoring their promises. They kept going even when the hardships were great. Before the journey was over, thousands of Indians died from smallpox and hunger. The Indians named this painful journey the **"Trail of Tears."**

After these Indians were gone, white families moved into their lands in increasing numbers. The United States continued to grow.

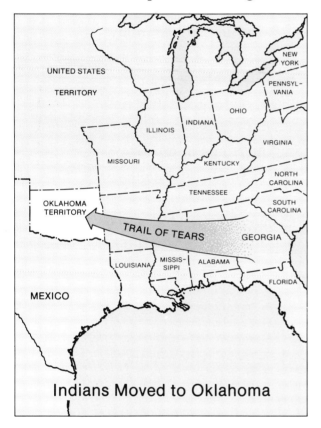

Indians Moved to Oklahoma

Sequoya

Sequoya, a Cherokee Indian, could not read, but he wanted his people to have the white man's secret of the "talking leaves." He decided to invent an alphabet. His plan was to draw a simple picture for each Cherokee word. Sequoya worked every moment he could, making thousands of drawings. His wife became angry because he neglected the house and garden, and she burned all his work.

Sequoya started over again, but this time he made symbols for the sounds in Cherokee words. He ended up with eighty-six symbols.

The new alphabet was a great help to the Indians. Cherokees who had not been able to learn English were able to read and write their own language in just a few days. Books and a newspaper were printed in this alphabet.

The Cherokee people considered Sequoya a genius. Today Americans remember his name because the giant redwood trees of the Pacific coast were named for him.

Things to know

1. The first Sunday school was started in _____.

2. _____ was a great American Sunday school missionary.

3. Preachers who traveled from town to town were called _____ preachers.

4. Religious services that lasted several days were called _____.

5. The best-known textbooks in pioneer schools were called the _____.

6. The Indian tribes that followed the ways of the white men were called the _____.

7. The terrible journey of these Indians to their new home in the West was called the _____.

Things to talk about

1. Why do you think so many of the first pioneers built their first buildings from logs?

2. What can you learn from the story in the McGuffey Reader?

3. Can a person believe in God and still not be saved?

4. Why was the idea of Sunday school so good for the pioneer towns?

5. Why did the pioneers enjoy camp meetings so much?

6. What can you learn from the example of Stephen Paxson?

7. Why do you think the men in Congress in 1834 decided that the Indians must give up their homes? Do you think this decision was right?

Things to do

1. Find out how a log cabin was built.

2. Learn the song "Brethren, We Have Met To Worship."

3. Write a play from Mr. Paxson's "peach-basket" story.

4. Start a Sunday school or Bible club in your neighborhood for children who do not go to church.

5. Find out how a missionary starts a work in an area where there is no church that believes the Bible.

6. Find some places in your city and state that are named after people. Find out why these people have been honored.

7. Add to your flag booklet.

CHAPTER 7

GROWING WESTWARD

Fur trading had been an important business in America since colonial days. Many men had come to America just to obtain furs and take them back to Europe. The fur trade continued to be profitable during the early 1800s even after the United States had become a nation. French, British, and American trappers and traders went farther and farther west to find the plentiful beaver, otter, fox, and other valuable pelts. During the long months in the wilderness, these men faced cold,

hunger, loneliness, and danger from fierce Indians. In spite of their hardships these determined men kept on. Their work helped open the far West for future settlers.

Fur Companies in the West

Fur companies from both the United States and Britain set up trading posts in the far West. John Jacob Astor was the president of the American Fur Company. In 1811 his men built Astoria, the first trading post in the Oregon

Beaver

Otter

Fox

Columbia River. Trappers from all over Oregon brought furs to the trading post at the fort. The furs were then shipped to countries as far away as England or even China.

Dr. McLoughlin was a wise man and a good leader. He directed his men to start farms, plant orchards, and raise horses and cattle. They built a flour mill and a sawmill. Dr. McLoughlin treated his workers and the Indians fairly, and they greatly respected him. They called him the "King of Oregon."

Meanwhile, the American Fur Company moved its headquarters to St. Louis. Their trappers, called "mountain men," worked alone or in pairs from fall until spring to get their furs. They often met Indians while trapping. Usually the Indians were friendly, but sometimes the trappers had to fight for their lives.

When summer came, the trappers took their furs to a **rendezvous.** This is a French word that means "a planned meeting." The trappers made their way over the Rockies to the Great Salt Lake. Indians also came by the hundreds from the surrounding area. There they met the agents from the American Fur Company, who bought their furs. The agents always brought new traps, gunpowder, food,

Territory. They sold the post to a British company during the War of 1812.

About 1820 the Hudson's Bay Company took over the fur trade in the Oregon Territory. Dr. John McLoughlin, the head of this British company, built Fort Vancouver on the

A rendezvous

and other supplies from St. Louis to sell to the trappers and the Indians.

The rendezvous lasted several weeks. It was a time for both business and pleasure. The trappers enjoyed sharing their experiences with other mountain men. Sometimes they held horse races and shooting contests. The Indians at the rendezvous always outnumbered the white men. They took part in the pleasure as well as the business. Often they traded their furs for guns and other supplies.

By the end of the 1830s fur trading had almost ended. Beaver and other animals were becoming scarce. Besides, the beaver hat had gone out of style.

Even though fur trading ended, something more than fur had come from the trapping. The mountain men had found passes through the mountains and trails leading westward. They had seen fertile valleys and rich forests beyond the Rockies. This information became more valuable to the new nation than the furs had been because it encouraged people to go even farther west.

Missionaries Go to Oregon

Often the first people to settle in a new region are missionaries. Such was the case with the Oregon Territory. After the fur traders the first real settlers were missionaries. The story begins in 1831 when four Indians from the Oregon country paddled over two thousand miles down the Missouri River to St. Louis. They had heard about Christianity and wanted to learn more about it. They went to Captain William Clark, who was the Superintendent of Indian Affairs, and asked that Christian teachers be sent to their tribes. A church magazine in the East printed their request. Among the first to answer this call were Dr. Marcus Whitman and his wife Narcissa.

The Whitmans left New York for Oregon in March, 1836. In Pittsburgh, Pennsylvania, Henry and Eliza Spalding joined them. Together the four young missionaries traveled to Missouri, where they met some of the Astor fur trappers. The trappers guided the missionaries as they continued west. Narcissa and Eliza were the first white women to cross the plains and mountains to the Pacific Ocean.

Fort Vancouver

The travelers reached Fort Vancouver in September. Dr. McLoughlin greeted them and provided them with a fine meal of roast duck, boiled pork, salmon, potatoes, vegetable soup with rice, bread and butter, tea, and apple pie. What a treat this meal was for people who had been living on dried buffalo meat for several weeks!

The missionaries were greatly impressed by the rich soil, the plentiful crops, the salmon fishing, and the beautiful landscape of Oregon. They often wrote to their families and friends in the East and encouraged them to come to Oregon.

The Whitmans built a mission at Walla Walla on the Columbia River. The Spaldings lived about four days' journey from them. The missionaries preached the gospel to the Indians and tried to teach them to obey the Bible. Dr. Whitman also spent much time treating sick and injured people.

The missionaries did not have much success in their efforts to win the

Fort Vancouver

Indians to Christ. Most of the white men that the Indians knew were wild and evil men. The Indians found it hard to understand love, honesty, and peace. To show them Christ, the missionaries determined to live as good Christian examples before them.

As the years passed, more and more settlers came to Oregon. The Indians realized that these settlers would take their hunting grounds. They became unfriendly to all whites, including the missionaries.

Their dislike of the white men grew stronger when in 1847 some settlers arrived in Oregon with measles. The disease spread throughout the Indian villages, killing almost half of the people. Although Dr. Whitman treated many of the sick, most died anyway. Some Indians even thought he had poisoned their people.

The Indians grew to hate the white man. One day two Indians came to the

Whitmans' home to see the doctor. No one knows exactly what happened, but Marcus, Narcissa, and twelve other whites were killed, and the mission was burned.

The Indians had hoped to scare away the white men with their terrible deeds, but they were not successful. The Whitmans were dead, but the message of the gospel was not stopped. The Indians frightened some settlers, but they could not keep their land from being taken by others who eagerly came west.

On the Oregon Trail

The news about the fertile land of Oregon had caused great excitement back East. Many farmers whose soil was "worn out" wanted to start over with this free, fertile land. Mill laborers who were out of work saw Oregon as an opportunity to own land and to make a good living. Men and women who wanted adventure were also eager to go west. Many families became pioneers and started for the Oregon Trail.

The Oregon Trail was long and hard. It started at Independence, Missouri, and followed the trail of the trappers along several rivers to the Continental Divide. The easiest place to cross was at the South Pass in what is now Wyoming. From there the trail led to the Columbia River and on to the Pacific.

The eager pioneers, traveling in trains of wagons hauled by oxen, journeyed from ten to twenty miles a day. They crossed the treeless plains

John
McLoughlin

Fort Hall

South Pass

Fort Bridger

The Oregon
Trail

Independence

Marcus and Narcissa
Whitman

and faced the hot, dry winds. As they forded rivers and streams, they sometimes faced the dangers of flood or quicksand. They endured heavy rainstorms and pounding hail. Besides these problems, they were often in danger of Indian attack.

A wagon train

The trip from Missouri to Oregon took from four to six months, so the travelers started in the spring. The rule of a wagon train was "Keep moving." If an ox became exhausted on the trail, the men shot it and replaced it with one from the herd that followed behind the wagons. Families often had to leave household goods along the trail to lighten the load in the wagons. Women wept about their lost treasures, but the wagon train kept moving.

The following description comes from a journal kept by Jesse Applegate during his journey on the Oregon Trail in 1843:

From six to seven o'clock is a busy time; breakfast is to be eaten, the tents struck, the wagons loaded, and the teams yoked and brought up in readiness to be attached to their respective wagons.

It is on the stroke of seven; the rushing to and fro, the cracking of the whips, the loud command to oxen, . . . confusion of the last ten minutes [have] ceased. Fortunately every one has been found and every teamster is at his post. The clear notes of the trumpet sound in the front; the pilot and his guards mount their horses, the leading division of wagons moves out of the encampment, and takes up the line of the march, the rest fall into their places with the precision of clockwork, until the spot so lately full of life sinks back into that solitude that seems to reign over the broad plain.

Oregon Joins the United States

When the first settlers went to the Oregon country, this land did not belong to the United States. Spain and Russia had each claimed it in the past. Great Britain still claimed it, but most of the people living there were Americans. The American settlers started the first government in Oregon.

While on the Oregon Trail, the pioneers had had to govern themselves. They had made rules and elected officers to enforce the rules. When they arrived in Oregon, they continued to rule themselves.

In 1843 a group of people met in the Williamette Valley near what is now Portland. These people represented all the settlers. They wrote an agreement that started like this: "We, the people

of the Oregon Territory, for purposes of mutual protection, and to secure peace and prosperity among ourselves, agree to adopt the following laws. . . ." This agreement was the basis of the government they set up.

Because the British still claimed Oregon even though most of the settlers were citizens of the United States, it looked for a while as if the two countries would fight over the land. However, neither one of the countries wanted another war, so in 1846 they signed the Oregon Treaty. This treaty set the boundary between the western United States and Canada where it is today. This added land helped the United States continue to grow.

Americans in Texas

One summer afternoon in 1821, Stephen Austin arrived in the small town of San Antonio. San Antonio belonged to Spain, but he had come

Stephen Austin

to make arrangements with the Spanish authorities to start an American colony in the area called Texas. While there, Stephen heard the news that the Mexicans had declared their independence from Spain. When the people heard of it, they went wild with excitement. Young men raced their horses through the streets, shooting their guns into the air and shouting, *"Viva la Independencia!"* ("Long live independence!") Stephen now realized that he must get his permission from the new Mexican government.

Look at the map to find the land belonging to Mexico in 1821. Few people realized how big and rich this land really was. Many years before, a few Spanish explorers had searched for gold and silver throughout this southwestern land. They had found Indian villages but not as many riches as they had hoped.

Before Mexico became free from Spain, Spanish families had come to the New World. They started large cattle ranches and towns such as San Antonio and Sante Fe.

Many Spanish priests had also come to the New World. They built missions along the way from Texas to California. They encouraged the Indians to accept the Roman Catholic religion and change their ways of living.

In 1821 the scattered ranches, towns, and missions were still there, but most of the land was wild and empty. It was the home of the Indians, the buffalo, and great herds of wild cattle and horses.

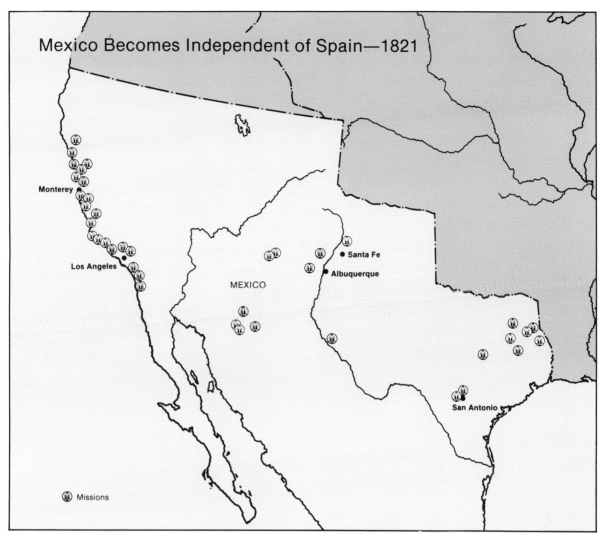

Mexico Becomes Independent of Spain—1821

Monterey

Los Angeles

MEXICO

Santa Fe

Albuquerque

San Antonio

🏛 Missions

The new Mexican government let Stephen Austin start a colony. In the next few years, he brought many families from "the States" into Texas. The Mexican government offered land to any American who would settle

there. At one time, a person could buy four thousand acres for thirty dollars!

Desiring cheap land, people from many parts of the United States poured into Texas. Some came in creaking wagons piled high with their household goods. Others came alone, walking along the trails, carrying knapsacks on their backs and rifles on their shoulders. Wealthy planters rode on horseback, followed by a long line of wagons and livestock.

Most of the settlers came from the southern states. The rich soil of Texas was just right for growing cotton, so the men built great plantations. They bought slaves to do the field work. Soon cotton became one of the most important crops on the new frontier.

Remember the Alamo

By 1835, nearly twenty thousand Americans lived in Texas. The Mexican government began to regret that it had invited the settlers to come there. They disliked the Americans' talk about making Texas a free and independent country. For several years trouble had grown between the settlers and the government.

Finally a Mexican army under General Santa Anna marched into Texas. The general boasted that he would drive the foreigners out of his land.

The settlers asked the United States government to let Texas become a state.

They said, "The Mexican government has ceased to protect the lives, liberty, and property of the people. . . . It has failed to establish any system of public education. . . . It has demanded that we deliver up our armies." However, the United States refused their request.

The Americans then declared that Texas was an independent country. The Texans adopted a constitution much like that of the United States. They decided that if they could not have a star on the United States flag, then they would have a "Lone Star" flag.

Hearing of this action, Santa Anna and his army hurried to San Antonio.

Top: The Lone Star flag of Texas
Bottom: The Alamo as it stands today

Davy Crockett   Jim Bowie

One hundred eighty-seven Texans fortified themselves inside a small nearby mission called the Alamo. Three thousand Mexicans surrounded the mission, and the fighting began.

The battle was hopeless for the Texans, but they refused to surrender. Several days passed. Then on March 6, 1836, at four o'clock in the morning, the Mexicans rushed into the mission from every side. Within a short time, they had killed every Texan. Among those killed were the frontiersmen Davy Crockett and James Bowie.

Sam Houston

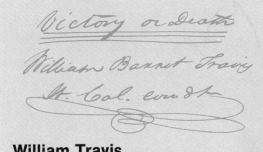

William Travis from the Alamo

I am besieged by a thousand or more of the Mexicans, under Santa Anna. . . . I shall never surrender or retreat. Then, I call on you in the name of Liberty, of patriotism and of everything dear to the American character, to come to our aid. . . . I am determined to sustain myself as long as possible and die like a soldier who never forgets what is due to his own honor and that of his country. Victory or death.

News of the defeat angered the people of Texas. Some fled to the United States for safety. Others joined Sam Houston, the leader of the Texan army. He promised to repay the Mexicans for the slaughter at the Alamo.

At first the struggle seemed hopeless. The Texans chased the Mexicans all over Texas. Then, after two months, Houston caught Santa Anna by surprise. The Texans attacked, shouting, "Remember the Alamo!" The Mexican army was defeated and Texas was free.

The people now made Sam Houston the first president of Texas. Stephen Austin became the secretary of state.

After a while the people of Texas again asked the United States government to allow them to join the United States. This time their request was granted, and Texas became a state in 1845.

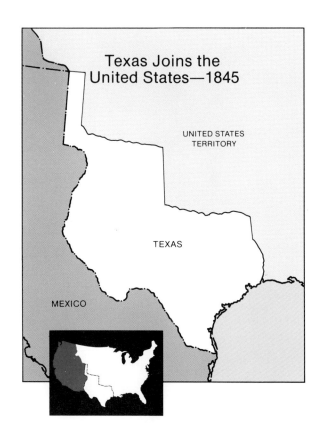

Things to know

Match the following people with their job.

_____ 1. John Jacob Astor

_____ 2. Dr. John McLoughlin

_____ 3. Marcus Whitman

_____ 4. Stephen Austin

_____ 5. Sam Houston

_____ 6. Santa Anna

a. Missionary to Oregon

b. "King of Oregon"

c. President of American Fur Company

d. First president of Texas

e. Leader of settlers to Texas

f. Mexican general

Things to talk about

1. Do you think it would be wise for a trapper to work alone all winter? Why or why not?

2. Imagine that you are living in 1836. Would you want to go to Oregon with the Whitmans and the Spaldings?

3. Why would a wagon train need laws and rules?

4. What do you think would be the best and the worst parts of a trip to Oregon by wagon train?

5. Why do you think Great Britain was willing to give up Oregon to the United States?

6. Why do you think Texas wanted to become a part of the United States instead of staying an independent nation?

Things to do

1. Write a report on salmon.

2. Find Astoria, Vancouver, Walla Walla, the Columbia River, and Portland on a map.

3. Find out about how far the Whitmans traveled to go to Oregon from New York.

4. Draw a picture of a wagon train.

5. Write a story about a day on the Oregon Trail.

6. Write a report on the Bowie knife.

7. Add to your flag booklet.

CHAPTER 8

ON TO CALIFORNIA

In the last chapter you learned that Texas was once part of Mexico. In 1846 the United States fought a war with that country. The map on the next page shows that California was a part of the land obtained at the end of this war.

In the early 1800s, American ships bound for Hawaii or China sometimes stopped at towns along the coast of California for fresh water and supplies. They sometimes traded manufactured goods for cattle hides from the ranches nearby. Except for this brief contact, few Americans knew about California. Only a small number of Americans were interested in going to California, since it belonged to Mexico and was so far away.

Jedediah Smith

Jedediah Smith was the first American to reach California by land. This trapper was said to be "half-grizzly bear and half-preacher." He always carried his Bible, and he sang hymns as he traveled the western mountains in search of furs.

By the 1830s a few brave men had gone to California and settled there. One of these was John Sutter. Mr. Sutter had come to America from Switzerland when he was a young man. First he traveled to Oregon and then to California. There he received land from the Mexican government and built a fort where the city of Sacramento stands today.

Sutter's Fort was the first settlement reached by those few people who left the Oregon Trail and went southwest to California. Mr. Sutter always welcomed the weary travelers. He gave them food and shelter and helped them when he could.

Mr. Sutter's fort was a ranch of about fifty thousand acres. He raised cattle, horses, and sheep. Outside the fort grew orchards, vineyards, and fields of grain. Within the fort were sheds, shops, and houses for workers.

To use the wood of nearby forests, Mr. Sutter decided to build a sawmill on the American River. He hired John Marshall to build and run it. The sawmill would provide lumber that was needed on the ranch or that could be sold to new settlers. By 1849 that sawmill was famous around the world, for gold had been discovered there.

Gold Rush Days

Marshall gave the following account of the discovery of gold:

> I shall never forget that morning. As I was taking my usual walk . . . my eye was caught by a glimpse of something shining in the bottom of the ditch. . . . I reached my hand down and picked it up. It made my heart thump, for I was certain it was gold. . . . I sat down and began to think right hard. . . .
>
> In a very short time, we discovered that the whole country was but one bed of gold. So there, stranger, is the entire history of the gold discovery in California.

The United States Expands to the West Coast

OREGON COUNTRY

LAND WON FROM MEXICO

A gold prospector and his tools

Mr. Marshall and Mr. Sutter decided to keep the news about the gold to themselves, but the secret got out. The editor of a newspaper in San Francisco published the news of the discovery. Immediately, men and women began panning for gold along California's rivers and streams. Hunters, trappers, and sailors helped spread the story. Soon the whole world knew that there was gold in California.

Gold fever! It infected people everywhere. Some towns in California and Oregon lost every man who was able to pan for gold. Hundreds of soldiers deserted their posts. Ships were left to rot in San Francisco harbor as the captains and crews hurried ashore to join the hunt for riches.

Easterners boarded ships in New York for the six-month journey "around the Horn" to California. In the spring of 1849 many wagon trains headed for the South Pass and turned toward California instead of Oregon.

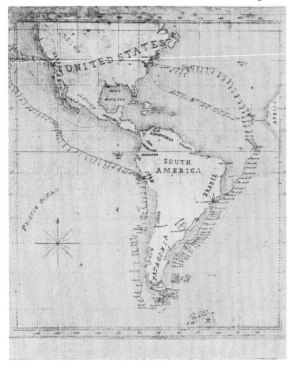

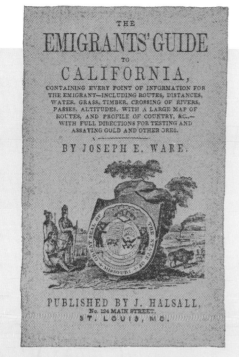

Advice to Gold Seekers

Never Travel on the Sabbath; we will guarantee that if you lay by on the Sabbath, and rest your teams, that you will get to California 20 days sooner than those who travel seven days a week.

—The Emigrants' Guide to California, *1849*

Guidebooks with advice to gold hunters were published in Europe as well as in the United States. Soon thousands of men from Germany, France, Ireland, and other countries flocked to the gold fields. The gold rush was on!

Life was rugged in California gold country. Mining camps of tents and small huts sprang up along the rivers and on the mountainsides near the gold fields. The camps had names such as Hangtown, Red Dog, and Rich Bar. Fighting, robbery, and murder were common in these camps.

Crime was especially serious in San Francisco. That town had no regular government, and the population grew from two thousand to twenty thousand in a single year. Some of the newcomers were wicked men who would do anything to cause trouble and to get money. Good citizens banded together to fight the criminals and to restore law

A gold mining camp

and order in their communities. These citizens called themselves **vigilantes**. Because of the concern of the city's good citizens, San Francisco became a safer place to live.

The gold rush lasted about ten years. During that time the prospectors found about 500 million dollars' worth of gold. Some men used the money from their gold to build homes and businesses. Others lost their money through drinking and gambling. The gold rush made millionaires of only a few; however, it made California and the western United States home for many.

Not everyone who went to California worked in the gold fields. Some made money by selling food and equipment to the miners. Miners sometimes paid a dollar for an egg and

fifteen dollars a week to sleep on a cot in a tent.

After the gold fields were exhausted, people found other riches in California.

A deserted mining camp

The fertile soil let them raise great crops of wheat in the valleys and fine fruit in huge orchards and vineyards. Farming became the leading industry of the state.

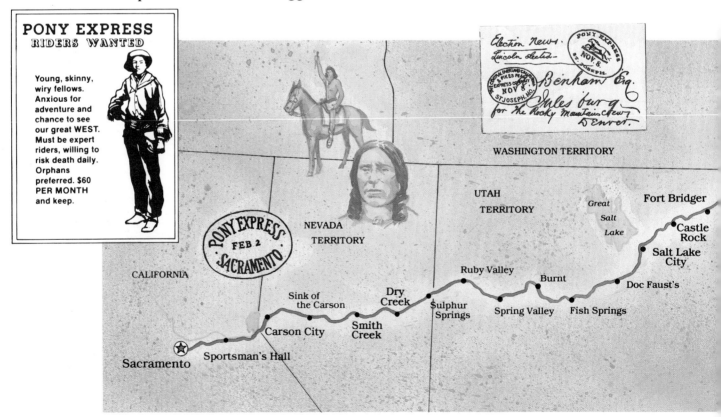

The Pony Express

Travel between the East and the West increased as a result of the gold rush. Stagecoach lines carried travelers to and from California. Coaches drawn by four or six horses carried mail and as many as nine passengers from Missouri to San Francisco. The coaches traveled night and day. They stopped every ten or fifteen miles at wayside stations to change horses and to let the passengers rest. The tiring trip took about twenty-five days and cost about two hundred dollars.

The stagecoach was a popular form of travel for passengers, but it was too slow for important mail. In 1860 a group of men organized the pony express. Racing through Nebraska, Wyoming, Utah, and Nevada, riders on horseback covered the distance from St. Joseph, Missouri, to Sacramento, California, in about ten days.

Only the bravest men and the best riders could work for the pony express. They rode over mountains, plains, and deserts in all kinds of weather. At any time they might have to fight off Indians and robbers.

Each man's route was about seventy miles long. He rode at top speed, stopping every ten or fifteen miles at a "swing station" to change horses. He would throw his saddlebags full of mail on a fresh horse and be on his way in about two minutes. A rider could make his run in about six hours if the trail were level.

The pony express was like a relay race. The mail was passed from rider to rider. Since mail was going in both directions, each man rode back and forth over the same route. The riders usually rode about four hundred miles each week.

Riders for the pony express were always ready to go. One day Jim Moore rode two regular routes westward to take a special rush message from Washington. When he reached the second station, he found special rush mail from California. The regular rider was not there, but Jim knew the mail had to go. After taking ten minutes' rest, he mounted a fresh horse and made the return trip east as well. It is said that he set the record for speed on this special run. Altogether he rode 275 miles in fourteen hours and forty-five minutes.

The pony express lasted only about a year and a half. When the first telegraph line to California was finished, the pony express was no longer needed. However, until electricity in wires outran the fastest horse, the pony express helped to bind our nation together.

"What Hath God Wrought"

Finley Morse and his brother Sidney were at the supper table. They, along with nine other brothers and sisters, listened carefully to their father. Jedediah Morse was a preacher and also a writer. He told the children about the printing of his latest geography book. Then he read them a draft of an article he wished to publish in the church magazine he edited. With a parent who was sometimes called "the Father of American Geography," mealtimes were times of happy, lively talk.

Years later, in 1832, Finley was at another supper table, this time with a medical doctor. Both men were on a ship returning from France. The talk turned to science. Morse again used his mealtime for learning. He asked the doctor whether surges of electrical current could travel over a long wire. The doctor answered that he thought they could. Morse's mind quickly saw a practical way to use this idea. He rushed back to his room. He began to sketch a crude device that he thought could be used to send messages. It would stop and start electrical surges that were sent over a wire. If each surge were a slightly different length, it could be used to communicate. This device could send messages long distances. Morse thought that perhaps with this idea, he would become what he had always wanted to be—"the means of helping others."

Finley Morse had attended grade school at Phillips Academy in Massachusetts. He then chose Yale for his college education. His life's dream was to become an artist, but of course he had to study other subjects, such as science. Even though he studied science, Finley really wanted to be a painter. He went to Europe to study painting. When he came back to America, he began to use his first name, Samuel. He tried to earn money by painting. But most Americans did not have money to pay for paintings. They were too busy building their country and trying to make a living. For several years Samuel hardly had money to feed his family. He and his brother Sidney invented a few machines, but they made little money. During this time Samuel also suffered the deaths of his youngest daughter, his wife, and his parents. Discouraged, he returned to Europe. It was on the return trip in 1832 that he began to work on his idea for the telegraph.

For four years Morse worked on his idea. He did not know much about recent scientific changes, nor did he have much mechanical ability. He did not have the money he needed to do experiments. But he was determined to be the first to invent a telegraph machine that worked. He knew that if he could get the first patent, he could make a lot of money.

Several people helped Morse. Scientists gave him advice. A young man named Alfred Vail became his helper. Vail's father gave them two thousand dollars for their work.

When the telegraph machine finally worked, Morse asked Congress for thirty thousand dollars to build a trial telegraph line from Baltimore to Washington, D.C. For over six years Congress said no. In 1843 Samuel was sure they would say no again. Sadly, he left the Capitol and went home. Imagine his surprise when the daughter of a friend who worked in the patent office brought him news of the vote. Both the House and the Senate had passed his bill at last! Morse was so happy at this good news that he told the girl that she could choose the first words he would send in his first message. She chose part of Numbers 23:23, which says, "What hath God wrought [brought about]!" Even though Samuel Morse had worked hard on his invention, it was God who should get the credit.

On May 24, 1844, the wire from the railroad depot in Baltimore to the Supreme Court chamber in the Capitol was ready. Morse and Vail had

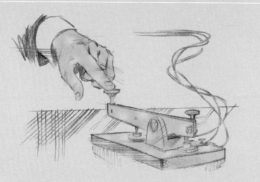

prepared for this day by writing a code for letters and numbers. Called the Morse code, it used dots and dashes. A dot was a short stroke on the telegraph key, and a dash was a long stroke. Using his new telegraph key, Morse carefully tapped out his message. At the same time, an operator in the Capitol listened and wrote down the letters and numbers meant by the dots and dashes. "What hath God wrought!" flew over the wire to Washington. The telegraph was successful.

People were so excited by this wonderful new invention that they came in large numbers to see it work. Soon they had found many good reasons for sending messages by telegraph, called telegrams. By 1844 all states east of the Mississippi except Florida had the telegraph. When the Mexican War began, the telegraph was used to send military messages. Reporters who traveled with the army used it to send news of battles back to their newspapers. Railroads began to use the telegraph to keep track of train traffic. They could tell trains when to stop and start so that they would not have accidents by being on the same track at the same time.

There was much confusion in the early days of the telegraph. Sometimes as many as twenty operators tried to send messages over the same wire. In 1856 a group called Western Union was started. It brought order out of the confusion and set up a good, working telegraph system.

By the end of the Civil War, there were over 200,000 miles of telegraph wires crisscrossing America. Not until the 1950s did the growing number of telephones all over the world lessen the use of the telegraph. Today the telegraph is sometimes used for business messages. In parts of the world where homes do not have telephones, messages are still sent to telegraph offices. Some missionaries you may know who serve in places like Africa or South America may use telegrams.

From Sea to Sea

The map below shows when the United States obtained the lands west of the Mississippi River.

You can see by this map that the United States had grown to be a large nation by 1860. It stretched from the Atlantic Ocean to the Pacific. It reached from Canada to Mexico and the Gulf of Mexico. This region was one great nation, but the people were not all alike.

Many of the people in the Northeast lived in cities and towns. Some worked in great mills that spun thread and wove cloth. Some worked in factories that produced furniture, clocks, glass, guns, tools, and other useful goods. Others in the Northeast were merchants,

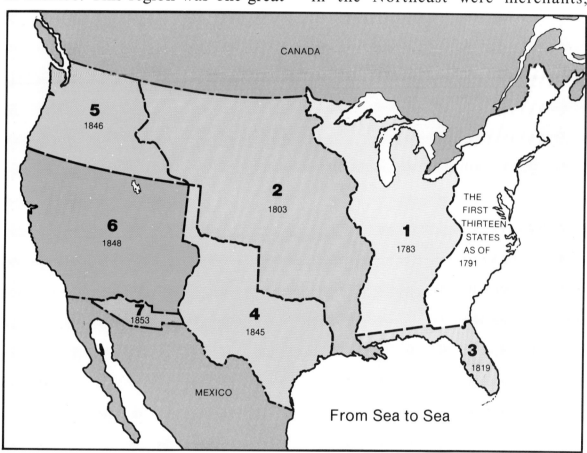

This map shows how the United States grew until 1859.

1. Britain gave this land to the United States.
2. Louisiana was purchased from France.
3. Spain gave this land to the United States.
4. Settlers in Texas fought Mexico to become free. Then they joined the United States.
5. Settlers in Oregon wanted to belong to the United States instead of Britain.
6. This land was won in the Mexican War.
7. This land was bought from Mexico.

shipbuilders, and fishermen. Of course, many were farmers.

Most of the people in the South lived on small farms. All members of the family worked hard to help earn their living. A few southerners lived on large plantations with many slaves to do the work.

Life in the West differed from that in both the Northeast and the South. Families in the West were busy building their homes and clearing land for farms. Most of them lived in constant danger from Indians. Their scattered villages and towns were simple and small.

The people of the different parts of the United States did not understand each other's problems. They were all Americans, but they did not all think alike. Their differences finally led to trouble.

Things to know

1. The land in California on which gold was discovered belonged to _____.

2. The town in California that grew very rapidly during the gold rush days was _____.

3. The gold rush lasted about _____ years.

4. A ship that traveled "around the Horn" to California traveled around _____.

5. The pony express was organized for the purpose of _____.

6. The pony express lasted about _____.

7. The pony express went out of business when a _____ was completed to California.

Things to talk about

1. Read I Timothy 6:10a. What did you read in this chapter about the gold rush that shows the truth of this verse?

2. Why is it so important that mail be carried quickly?

3. What were some things that had to be planned and arranged before the pony express could begin?

4. Do you wish you could have been a prospector for gold? Why or why not?

5. Do you wish you could have been a pony express rider? Why or why not?

6. Find out the years in which California and Oregon became states. Why do you think California became a state before Oregon?

7. Why were the prospectors for gold willing to pay such high prices for food and a bed?

Things to do

1. Read Psalm 19:9-10, Proverbs 16:16, and I Peter 1:7. What does the Bible say is more valuable than gold?

2. Draw a picture of a pony express rider and his horse.

3. Write a story about a day in the life of a pony express rider.

4. Look at the map on page 82 to see the ocean route "around the Horn."

5. Gold was discovered in other parts of the United States. Find out what you can about the gold rush to Colorado.

6. Read a book about the pony express.

7. Learn how to signal your name in Morse code.

8. Make a toy telegraph.

9. Add to your flag booklet.

A Divided Nation

THREE

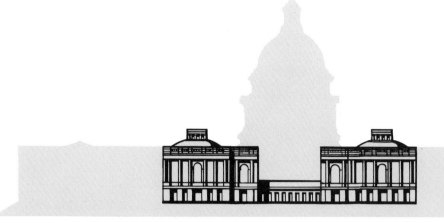

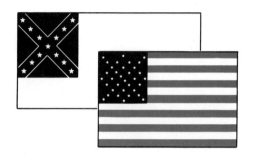

Two Flags   Congress made this the official flag on July 4, 1861. How many states were there at this time?

The southern states had a number of flags during the Civil War. The one shown here is called the "Stainless Banner." Soon after it was made, it covered the coffin of Stonewall Jackson, a brave southern general.

UNIT GOALS

- I will be able to describe how slavery began and increased in the United States.
- I will bc able to explain what the word *secede* means.
- I will be able to describe some events of the Civil War.
- I will be able to describe the lives of Abraham Lincoln, Robert E. Lee, Clara Barton, and Dwight L. Moody.
- I will be able to locate Fort Sumter, Gettysburg, Atlanta, Richmond, and Appomattox Court House on a map.

TIME LINE

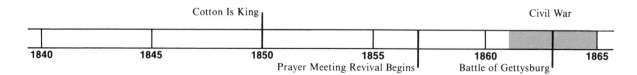

THE COMING OF WAR

Perhaps the saddest time in American history began in 1861. In that year the country went to war—this time against itself. The North and the South fought for four years in this war. Because it was fought between citizens, this war is called a **civil war.** The American Civil War is also sometimes called "The War Between the States." The disagreements that led to the war between two parts of the United States started many years before. We will go back to the days of the early colonists to see how one of the problems came about.

Slavery in America

The first English colony in America began in Jamestown, Virginia, in 1607. The first black slaves were brought to Virginia in 1619. At that time people in many parts of the world owned slaves.

As time went by, the southern colonies brought over more black slaves than the northern colonies.

Southern farmers needed workers, but few white settlers wanted to do the hard work on Southern plantations. Black slaves, however, could provide a permanent source of labor for the plantations. By using slaves, southerners made their farms prosper.

A slave family

The main products in the South were tobacco, rice, and indigo. These crops required a great amount of work to plant, tend, and harvest. Slaves did most of this work. The grain and other crops of the northern states did not require so much care. Therefore, slavery was not so common in the North.

At the time our Constitution was adopted, most people in the United States thought that all slaves should be freed. George Washington wrote in his will that all his slaves should go free after he died. Patrick Henry and Thomas Jefferson also did not think that slavery fit in with the ideas of freedom that were in the Declaration of Independence. These men were all from Virginia, a southern state. They believed the United States could prosper without slaves. In 1808 the United States government passed a law against bringing more slaves into the country. But a new machine changed things.

Eli Whitney and the Cotton Gin

When the United States became a nation, southern farmers raised some cotton, but it was not an important crop. The cotton **boll** contained the fiber and many sticky seeds. The fiber could not be used until the seeds were taken out, and the seeds had to be removed by hand. It took a person one whole day to prepare one pound of cotton. Unless this job became easier, cotton would never be an important crop. A machine to clean the cotton was what the farmers needed.

Above: A cotton field
Below: A cotton boll

Eli Whitney liked to make things. He made a violin when he was only twelve years old and had a business making nails when he was a teenager. Eli went to Georgia in 1793 when he was twenty-eight. He saw the need for a machine to clean the seeds from the cotton boll and decided to make one. In a few days he built the first **cotton gin.** This machine could clean cotton as fast as fifty men working by hand.

Eli Whitney and his cotton gin

The Growth of Slavery

Southern farmers and plantation owners saw that they could now make money by raising cotton. They knew that mill owners in the northern states and in England would buy their cotton to make cloth. If they could only grow more cotton! Instead of freeing their slaves, they chose to buy more.

Cotton plants need good soil and and are very hard on the land. When the cotton fields were "worn out," the planters left them and moved on to better land.

Many families moved south and west into the lands that became the states of Alabama, Mississippi, Arkansas, and Louisiana. This land was good for growing cotton, so they took their slaves with them. Remember that much of this land was the first home of the "Five Civilized Tribes" of Indians (see pages 64-65).

By 1850, many southerners depended on cotton for their living. To them cotton was "King," and the South the **"Cotton Kingdom."**

Few people in the South now wanted to free the slaves. They were needed more than ever. Most slave owners treated their slaves well. They wanted them to be strong and healthy so that they could work. Southern men wrote books and made speeches claiming that slavery was a good thing. They said that the slaves had food, clothing, and a place to live. They did not have to worry about losing their jobs. They were better off than if they had been in the jungles of Africa.

Most people in the North did not agree. They said that it was not right for one person to own another. They also pointed out that some masters did not treat their workers well. Some owners beat their slaves. They sometimes broke up families by selling the father, mother, or children to other slave owners. Books, magazines, and speeches in the North stirred the people against slavery.

GO DOWN, MOSES

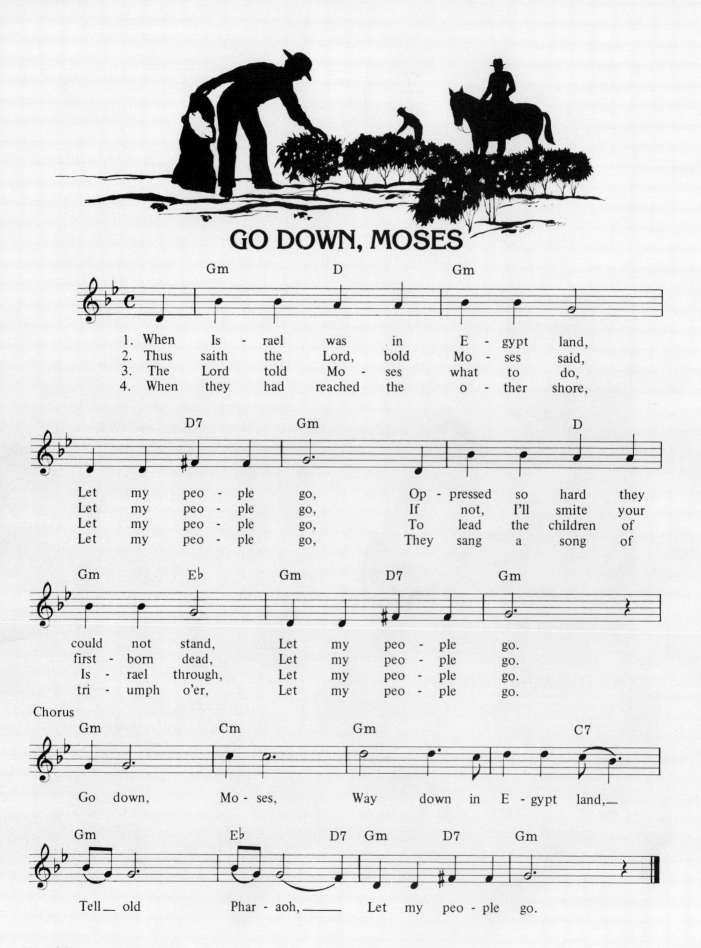

Gm   D   Gm

1. When   Is - rael   was   in   E - gypt   land,
2. Thus   saith   the   Lord,   bold   Mo - ses   said,
3. The   Lord   told   Mo - ses   what   to   do,
4. When   they   had   reached   the   o - ther   shore,

D7   Gm   D

Let my peo - ple go,   Op - pressed so hard they
Let my peo - ple go,   If not, I'll smite your
Let my peo - ple go,   To lead the children of
Let my peo - ple go,   They sang a song of

Gm   Eb   Gm   D7   Gm

could not stand,   Let my peo - ple go.
first - born dead,   Let my peo - ple go.
Is - rael through,   Let my peo - ple go.
tri - umph o'er,   Let my peo - ple go.

Chorus

Gm   Cm   Gm   C7

Go down,   Mo - ses,   Way down in E - gypt land,—

Gm   Eb   D7 Gm   D7   Gm

Tell_ old   Phar - aoh,_____ Let my peo - ple go.

A Prayer Meeting Revival

As problems in the nation grew, God used men and women throughout the country to help stir revival. America in the late 1850s needed God's help. The differences over slavery caused division and hatred. Also, business was poor, and many people had no work. However, many people still refused to turn to the Lord for help.

One man who wanted to influence others for God was Jeremiah Lanphier of New York City. He believed that God wanted him to start a prayer meeting. He held the first meeting at noon on September 23, 1857. Only six people attended that day, but the next week twenty came. Forty people met for the prayer service the third week. These Christians decided to meet every day instead of just once a week.

By the spring of 1858 Christians were holding twenty noon prayer meetings throughout New York City. Unsaved people began to attend, and many trusted the Lord for salvation.

Soon other Christians started prayer services in other large cities like Boston and Chicago and in dozens of smaller cities and towns. The services usually started at noon and lasted one hour. After a short song, the leader prayed. Then anyone present could have five minutes to give a testimony or a prayer request, to pray, or to lead another song. The meeting closed at one o'clock. Anyone who wanted help from God's Word stayed afterward.

As the months went by, the revival spread throughout the whole nation. Shopkeepers locked their doors during the noon hour to spend time in prayer. The front pages of newspapers carried stories of people's conversions. By the end of 1859, about one million people had been saved.

This great prayer meeting revival helped prepare the United States for the sorrow and hardships of the Civil War. It spread into the southern states and among the slaves. Because faithful Christians prayed, many people turned to Christ for salvation.

Battle Hymn of the Republic

Many historians think that the tune for the "Battle Hymn of the Republic" was written for a southern camp meeting about 1855. The words often sung to this tune were, "Say, brothers, will you meet us . . . On Canaan's happy shore?" Later, soldiers in the northern army sang the words, "John Brown's body lies a-moldering in the grave. . . . His soul goes marching on."

In 1861 Julia Ward Howe visited an army camp near Washington, D.C. She heard the soldiers singing "John Brown's Body" as they marched along. The melody ran through Mrs. Howe's mind the rest of the day, but she did not think the words had much value. Mrs. Howe awoke early the next morning and, finding "an old stump of a pen," wrote down the words to a poem to fit the tune.

Newspapers, magazines, and an army songbook soon published the new words for the song. President Lincoln was so pleased with the words the first time he heard them that he asked the soloist to sing the song again. Today many Americans consider the "Battle Hymn of the Republic" one of our greatest patriotic songs.

The North and South Disagree

The differences over slavery grew. Other differences between the North and South also grew. Many northerners lived in cities and towns and worked in factories or businesses. Most southerners lived on farms or plantations. The North depended on factories, while the South depended on farms. These differences kept the North and South from understanding each other. Finally the differences became so great that some southerners began thinking that the southern states should not be a part of the United States. They thought they should start a nation of their own. Most northerners felt that the southerners should not be allowed to start their own nation. They believed that for the United States to be great, all the states must be united.

One man who saw problems in breaking up the nation was Abraham Lincoln. He became well known throughout the country because of his speeches about slavery. He warned, "A house divided against itself cannot stand. I believe that this government cannot endure permanently half slave and half free."

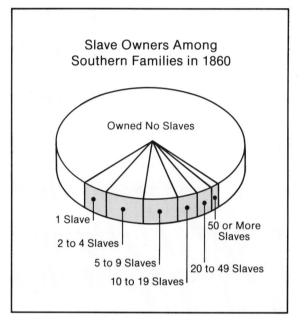

Slave Owners Among Southern Families in 1860

Owned No Slaves

1 Slave

2 to 4 Slaves

5 to 9 Slaves

10 to 19 Slaves

20 to 49 Slaves

50 or More Slaves

Mr. Lincoln was elected president of the United States in 1860. The southern states knew that he was not in favor of slavery. After his election

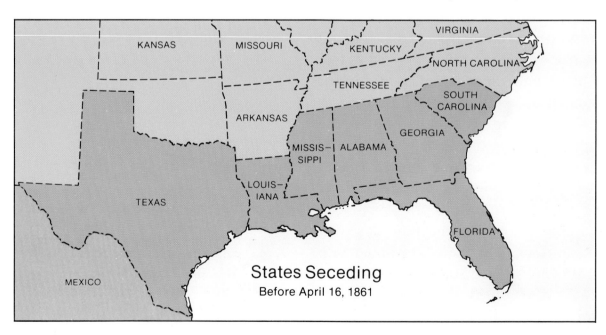

States Seceding
Before April 16, 1861

Jefferson Davis

they decided to leave, or **secede** from, the United States.

These states set up a new nation called the **Confederate States of America.** They elected Jefferson Davis to be their president. They chose Richmond, Virginia, as their capital city.

President Lincoln faced a hard problem. What should he do? As president, he believed it was his duty to preserve the **Union,** that is, the United States of America. He asked the

people of the nation to unite. He said, "We are not enemies, but friends. We must not be enemies. . . ." But his pleading was in vain, and the southern states refused to return to the Union. Mr. Lincoln knew that war would come.

Abraham Lincoln
(1809-1865)

Life was hard on the frontier. It was hard to clear the land and to build a house. It was hard to face the dangers of Indians and wild animals. But people did. They came by the thousands, and they bravely faced the hardships. They often said, "The cowards never started, and the weak died on the way."

Tom and Nancy Hanks Lincoln lived in a tiny log cabin in Kentucky during those hard frontier days. On the morning of February 12, 1809, Tom told a neighbor, "Nancy's got a boy baby." They named him Abraham after his grandfather.

Little Abe grew rapidly. When he was seven years old, he and his sister Sarah walked four miles a day to go to a little log school. It had a dirt floor and no windows. The students learned their lessons by saying them out loud over and over.

The teacher called on the students, one at a time, to recite the lesson. This kind of school was called a "blab" school.

The Lincoln family moved to Indiana in 1816. At first they lived in a pole-shed. This was a three-sided shelter made of poles, branches, brush, dried grass, and mud. They kept a log fire burning in the open side. The Lincolns slept on beds of dry leaves piled in the corners. They lived in the shed for over a year before they finished building their cabin.

In Indiana Abe and Sarah had a chance to go to another "blab" school for a few weeks. This time they had to walk eighteen miles each day. Tom Lincoln thought it was a waste of time to go so far, but Nancy wanted Abe to learn all he could.

After a while Nancy became very sick. As she lay dying, she stroked Abe's rough hair and told him to be good to his sister and father. Abe never forgot his pioneer mother. She had loved him and his sister. She had tried to teach them what was right.

About a year after their mother's death Abe and Sarah had a surprise. Tom Lincoln drove four horses and a wagon into their clearing. Out jumped his new wife, Sarah Bush Lincoln, and her three children. Sarah's first husband had died, and now the two families became one. Sarah soon grew to love her two new children. She had a special love for young Abe. She always encouraged him to learn, to work, and to be honest and brave.

Between the ages of eleven and seventeen Abe grew. His body grew. His mind grew. His interest in people grew. Abe was taller than most boys his age. He was also stronger. Almost every day he spent hours swinging an axe. He also cleared timberland, cut logs, split firewood, and built pigpens. One day he put his shoulders under a newly built corncrib and carried it where the owner wanted it. He did the same thing with a chicken coop.

Abe was also good in sports. He was the best wrestler in his county. He often

won footraces and contests of jumping, throwing the maul, and pitching the crowbar.

Like all young men on the frontier, Abe learned many skills. He worked as a carpenter, a well digger, and a butcher. He planted and harvested grain. He could skin and cure hides of deer and raccoons. He learned to work hard. But he preferred to read.

However, books were scarce in Indiana in those days. The Lincolns had a Bible and an old arithmetic book, which Abe read, but he wanted to read more than these. He was able to get *Aesop's Fables, Pilgrim's Progress, Robinson Crusoe,* and *The Life of George Washington.* Abe used to say, "The things I want to know are in books: my best friend is the man who'll get me a book I ain't read." He would work all day and then read by the light of the fire until midnight. He often read aloud. He liked to explain what he read to others. Explaining an idea to someone else made it clearer to himself. Abe went to school only a few months in all, but he kept reading and studying all his life.

Abe liked people. He laughed at the "yarns" his neighbors told and joked with them. When he had a chance, he listened to the talk of the old men of the town and to the sermons the preacher preached. While he worked, he would think about what he had heard.

When he was sixteen years old, Abe worked on a farm near the Ohio River. Part of the time he ran a ferryboat across the river. One day he took two men out to a steamboat. They each gave him a half-dollar. Abe felt rich. The most money Abe had ever earned before this was thirty-one cents a day for butchering hogs. Then one of the half-dollars slipped into the river. Abe quickly realized that a person can lose money faster than he can earn it.

Abe met all kinds of people at the ferry. He talked with settlers, land buyers, preachers, traders, hunters, peddlers, teachers, and politicians. He tried to learn something from each one.

When Abe was nineteen, he and another man took a flatboat loaded with farm produce down the Ohio River to the Mississippi and on to New Orleans. They traded potatoes, bacon, hams, apples, and flour for cotton, tobacco, and sugar. They sold the flatboat and returned home on a steamer. Abe saw many new sights in New Orleans, including his first look at slaves. Some were chained together into gangs headed for the cotton fields. Some were chained in the market waiting to be sold.

Abe had many things to think about on the long journey home.

The Lincoln family moved to Illinois when Abe was twenty-one. At first he helped his father clear land and build a house. Then he left home and went to New Salem, Illinois, to work in a small store. One day Abe made a mistake of a few cents in a woman's change. That night after he had closed the store he walked a long way to return the money to her. Abraham Lincoln was an honest man. People called him "Honest Abe."

Abe held many jobs while he was a young man. He was a soldier during an Indian war but saw no fighting. He and a friend opened a store, but it was not a success. His partner died, and Abe had to pay all the store's debts. It took him several years, but he paid every cent they owed. Abe was appointed the postmaster of New Salem. He also learned to survey land and earned money by splitting rails.

As the years went by, many people learned about Abraham Lincoln. They liked his kind ways. They enjoyed his plain talk and his funny stories. Many people asked Mr. Lincoln to settle arguments for

Abraham Lincoln's home in Springfield, Illinois

them. Two friends once asked him, "Mr. Lincoln, how long should a man's legs be?"

Mr. Lincoln looked at the men. One man had very long legs. The other had very short legs. Mr. Lincoln thought for a minute. "Well, now," he answered, "I would say that a man's legs should be exactly long enough to reach from his body to the ground."

The people trusted him so much that they sent him to help make the laws for the state of Illinois. While serving his state, Lincoln decided to become a lawyer. He borrowed law books and studied them whenever he could. Sometimes he would walk twenty miles to borrow a book. He moved to Springfield, Illinois, and opened a law office there.

Abraham married Mary Todd when he was thirty-three. They had four sons, but the second one died at the age of four. The family lived in a small, comfortable house in Springfield.

Mr. Lincoln became a successful lawyer. The people voted to send him to Washington to help make the laws there. At this time slavery was causing great trouble between the northern and southern states. Lincoln remembered seeing the slave markets in New Orleans. He believed that slavery was evil and should not spread throughout the United States.

Abraham Lincoln gave many speeches against slavery. The speeches were printed in newspapers all over the country. Because

of this many people came to know Abraham Lincoln. In 1860 he ran for president of the United States. During the campaign, Mr. Lincoln received a letter from a young girl in New York.

Hon A B Lincoln
Dear Sir

My father has just come home from the fair and brought home your picture. . . . I am a little girl only eleven years old, but want you should be President of the United States very much so I hope you wont think me very bold to write such a great man as you are. Have you any little girls about as large as I am. . . . I have got four brother's and part of them will vote for you anyway and if you will let your whiskers grow I will try and get the rest of them to vote for you you would look a great deal better for your face is so thin. All the ladies like whiskers and they would tease their husband's to vote for you and then you would be President. My father is going to vote for you and if I was a man I would vote for you to. . . .

I must not write any more answer this letter right off

Good bye
Grace Bedell

Many people must have agreed with Grace, because Mr. Lincoln won the election.

After the election, Mr. Lincoln and his family went to Washington on a train. They made many stops to greet people along the way. In Westfield, New York, the new president asked to meet Grace. He lifted her up in his arms, kissed her, and showed her his newly grown beard.

The Civil War began in the spring of 1861. President Lincoln did not want a war, but he was determined to keep the United States together. He did not think of the people of the southern states as enemies, but he could not let them start a separate nation.

Abraham Lincoln had a difficult job during the war. He had to persuade men to join the army to fight. He had to get money to pay for the war. He had to encourage the northern people to keep on fighting, especially when they lost battles. He had little time to rest.

President Lincoln was often sad as well as tired. For hours each day, he saw people who came to call. He tried to help them with their problems. His visits to the army hospitals caused his heart to ache. He found some joy in playing with his little boy Tad. Late at night he sometimes found peace by reading the Bible.

President Lincoln felt great joy when the war ended on April 9, 1865. He said the soldiers of the southern army should not be punished but should be allowed to return to their homes. He wished to forget the past.

On April 14, Mr. Lincoln and his wife went to a play in Ford's Theater in Washington. About ten o'clock a shot rang out. An actor named John Wilkes Booth had shot the president in the head. Friends took Mr. Lincoln to a nearby house and called the doctor. The wound was so bad that nothing could be done. Abraham Lincoln died at 7:22 the next morning.

A train carried Mr. Lincoln's body back to Illinois to be buried. Thousands of people lined the tracks as the train traveled slowly westward. The whole nation mourned the loss of one of the greatest presidents the United States has ever had.

Robert E. Lee
(1807-1870)

Robert E. Lee was born into one of the finest families in the United States. The Lees had come to Virginia in its early days and had always taken an important part in leading the colony. Two Lees had signed the Declaration of Independence when the thirteen colonies became the United States. Robert's father, General Henry Lee, had been a brave soldier in the War for Independence.

Robert was the youngest in his family. He had three brothers and two sisters. His family lived in a large home called Stratford. It was near Mount Vernon, where George Washington had lived. The family went to the church that President Washington had attended before he died. It is no wonder that George Washington was young Robert's hero. Robert decided that he too would be brave and honest. He

made up his mind that he would always tell the truth and do what was right.

After a while the Lee family moved so that they would be nearer good schools. All of the sons did well at school, but Robert did the best of all. His favorite subject was arithmetic. He was good in sports too. He was a leader in the schoolroom and on the playground. His teachers praised him, and the students liked him.

Sadness came to the Lee home because both Mr. and Mrs. Lee became sick. When Robert was eleven, his father died. The oldest sons were away, so Robert became the "man of the house." He often gave up good times with his friends so that he could care for his home and be with his mother.

One day Mrs. Lee told Robert he must decide what he would do when he grew up. "I have already decided," Robert said. "I want to be a soldier."

When Robert was eighteen, he went to West Point Academy to be trained as an army officer. He studied hard there for four years. West Point had many rules. Robert carefully obeyed them and never got a mark for bad conduct.

Mrs. Lee lived just long enough to hear of Robert's graduation. Robert's first job in the army was as an engineer. During peacetime, engineers planned forts and did other useful work. In wartime they built roads and bridges. They studied the

land where battles would be fought and guided the movements of the armies.

Two years after Robert left West Point, he married Mary Custis. Mary was Martha Washington's great-granddaughter. The young couple lived in Mary's beautiful home, called Arlington, across the river from Washington, D.C.

Robert E. Lee was a soldier for almost twenty years before the United States fought a war. During those years, he served his country in many places. One time floods along the Mississippi River caused great danger to the city of St. Louis. An engineer was needed to plan a way to control the water, and someone suggested Captain Lee for the job. "He is young," said a general, "but if the work can be done, he can do it." Robert built high walls along the dangerous parts of the river. These walls kept the river within its banks.

In 1846 the United States went to war with Mexico. Captain Lee had studied war from books. Now he had a chance to learn by experience.

Robert spent almost two years in Mexico. While there, he was often in danger, but he always did his duty. One day Captain Lee was looking for a good route for the army to follow to attack the Mexican army. Suddenly he heard voices. He dropped to the ground in some bushes and lay quietly behind a big log that was near

a spring. The voices belonged to Mexican soldiers who were coming to the spring for a drink. Captain Lee lay as still as he could. More enemy soldiers came, and some even sat on the log and talked. Lee dared not move even though insects bit him and crawled over him. All day long the Mexicans came and went. When one soldier stepped over the log, he missed stepping on Lee's leg by inches. At last night came and the last enemy soldier returned to his camp. Captain Lee was safe.

On another night before a battle, Lee said that he would carry an important message to his general. Heavy rain was falling, and the way was rocky and dangerous. His only light was lightning flashing across the night sky. After Robert delivered the message, he led troops back over the rocks to attack the enemy. He did not rest until the battle was won a day later. He proved that he was determined to do his duty. Later his general wrote that Lee was "the very best soldier I ever saw in the field."

Although he was a good soldier, Captain Lee did not enjoy fighting. He thought often of his family at Arlington. He wrote to his son, "You have no idea what a horrible sight a field of battle is." After one battle he wrote again, "I wondered, when the musket balls . . . were whistling over my head in a perfect shower, where I could put you, if with me, to be safe." Captain Lee rejoiced as he returned home after the Mexican War was over.

Before long Robert E. Lee was sent to take charge of the officers' school at West Point. Later he became a colonel and was sent to Texas. Wherever he went, he worked hard and did what was right. He once wrote to his son, "Duty is the sublimest word in our language. Do your duty in all things. . . . You cannot do more; you should never wish to do less."

Then came the spring of 1861. Fort Sumter was attacked, and President Lincoln asked Robert E. Lee to take charge of the army of the United States. Colonel Lee had a hard choice to make. He loved the United States. He did not want to see any state secede, and he did not believe in slavery. In fact, he had already freed all the slaves at Arlington. Yet Virginia was his home, and his family was there. Sadly, Lee gave up his position in the United States Army and took command of the Virginia troops. Later he became the general of the whole southern army.

General Lee was a great leader and a great man. When he rode by on his gray horse, Traveler, the southern soldiers cheered. He lived in a tent and ate plain food just as his men did. He was always kind and unselfish. He wanted his men to fight like gentlemen. Although he fought against the Union soldiers, he said, "I have never seen the day I did not pray for them."

General Lee and his soldiers fought bravely throughout the war. Many times they held off a larger army, but they lost many men. As the war went on, artillery supplies ran short, and often soldiers went hungry. Finally the South could fight no more. "I would rather die a thousand deaths than surrender," the weary general said, but he knew that he must. And so the war ended.

After the surrender General Lee rode back to his men. His heart ached at the sight of the weary and wounded soldiers. They crowded around to be as close to him as they could. Some sobbed aloud. "Men,"

Lee said, "we have fought through the war together. I have done my best for you. My heart is too full to say more." And slowly the gray-haired gentleman in a gray uniform rode away.

Later General Lee became president of Washington College in Virginia. He received many honors. The name of the school where he worked was later changed to Washington and Lee University. Above all, he wanted his students to be good citizens of the United States.

As Lee grew older, his health began to fail. One night in October, 1870, as he stood at the table to bless the food, his voice stopped and he collapsed into his chair. Robert E. Lee died a few days later.

Arlington now belongs to the people of the United States. It is furnished as it was when Lee lived there. Many people visit the house every year. Around the house is Arlington National Cemetery, where many soldiers are buried. The Tomb of the Unknown Soldier is there. Arlington Cemetery helps us to remember the great southern gentleman, Robert E. Lee, and the men who gave their lives in different wars for our freedom.

Things to know

Part I.

Match the following years and events.

1. _____ 1619   a. Law forbidding the bringing of slaves into the U.S.

2. _____ 1793   b. Cotton gin was invented

3. _____ 1860   c. First black slaves brought to Virginia

4. _____ 1808   d. Prayer meeting revival began

5. _____ 1857   e. Abraham Lincoln was elected president

Part II.

Complete the following sentences.

1. The purpose of the cotton gin was to _____.

2. Many cotton farmers moved west because _____ and _____.

3. The city in which the prayer meeting revival started was _____.

4. The word *secede* means _____.

5. The southern states called their new nation _____.

Things to talk about

1. Why were there more slaves in the southern states than in the northern states?

2. Do you think that slavery goes along with the ideas of the Declaration of Independence? Why or why not?

3. Do you think that President Lincoln was right when he decided to fight to prevent the southern states from leaving the Union? Why or why not?

4. How was the prayer meeting revival different from most revivals that churches have?

5. Compare the arguments for and against slavery. Which are the most important?

6. What does the word *Union* mean?

7. Some New England states had great mills that made cotton cloth. How did they depend on slavery?

Things to do

1. Find out how linen and cotton fabric were made in the early 1800s.

2. Memorize "Dixie" and the first and last verses of the "Battle Hymn of the Republic."

3. Read a book about Abraham Lincoln.

Abraham Lincoln Review

1. Give the dates of Lincoln's birth and his death. How old was he when he was killed?

2. Describe Abraham Lincoln's feelings about learning. Do you feel the same way as young Abe did? Why or why not?

3. How did Nancy Hanks Lincoln and Sarah Bush Lincoln influence Abe's life?

4. List the different jobs Mr. Lincoln had before he became president.

5. What was President Lincoln's attitude about the people of the southern states?

6. How was President Lincoln killed?

Robert E. Lee Review

1. How was Robert E. Lee's early life different from Abraham Lincoln's?

2. How do you think Robert felt about learning? Compare his attitude and Abraham Lincoln's attitude.

3. Describe some of Lee's activities before the Civil War began.

4. What does Lee's statement about duties (p. 107) mean to you? Do you agree with him? How is his statement similar to Colossians 3:23?

5. Why was Lee's decision at the beginning of the Civil War so difficult? Do you think you would have made the same decision?

6. Why did Lee's soldiers love him so much?

7. Every year thousands of people visit Arlington. What do they go there to see?

CHAPTER 10

THE CIVIL WAR

In the harbor of Charleston, South Carolina, lies a small island. Fort Sumter, a United States fort, stood on this island. Each day the flag, "the Stars and Stripes," flew proudly over the fort. After the South seceded, the soldiers in the fort stayed loyal to the Union, even though they were in Confederate territory. President Lincoln wanted to take care of the men in Fort Sumter because he knew that they were running out of supplies. But he also knew that if he tried to send them supplies, the Confederates might attack. Finally Mr. Lincoln decided that the men must have supplies. The Confederates did not like his decision. In fact, they wanted Fort Sumter for themselves.

On April 11, 1861, Confederate leaders told the United States soldiers to leave Fort Sumter and give it to them. Major Anderson, the commander of the fort, refused. At 4:30 on the morning of April 12, a flash of light lit the sky above the harbor. Then came the boom of a cannon. The first battle of the Civil War had begun.

Throughout the day the people of Charleston crowded into the streets and looked toward the harbor to see what was happening. They watched as the cannons and the guns around the harbor fired again and again at the fort. Shots hit the fort. Cannonballs made large holes in the walls. The guns of the fort shot back, but their shots did little harm.

The battle went on. One cannonball hit the flagpole. The people of the city shouted, "Bring down the flag!" The guns fired again and again. Soon the flag came down. The people watching cheered, but their cheers soon stopped. A soldier in the fort caught the flag as it fell and nailed it back up again. This time the soldiers in the fort cheered.

As the day ended, a heavy rain began to fall. The Confederate general asked Major Anderson to give up the fight, but he refused.

By noon the next day the ammunition in the fort was almost gone. The soldiers could fire only one gun every ten minutes. They had no food. A fire had started, and smoke filled the fort. Major Anderson knew he would have to surrender, so he raised a white flag.

The inside of Fort Sumter

The Confederate general let Major Anderson lower the United States flag and take it with him when the soldiers left the fort. The Confederate flag was soon raised in its place.

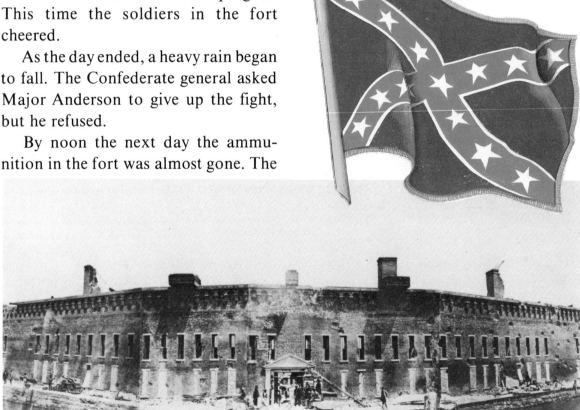
Fort Sumter in April, 1865

The United States vs. the Confederate States

NEW HAMPSHIRE   MAINE
VERMONT
MASSACHUSETTS
NEW YORK
RHODE ISLAND
CONNECTICUT
PENNSYLVANIA
NEW JERSEY
DELAWARE
MARYLAND
MINNESOTA
WISCONSIN
MICHIGAN
IOWA
OHIO
INDIANA
ILLINOIS
WEST VIRGINIA
VIRGINIA
OREGON
CALIFORNIA
KANSAS
MISSOURI
KENTUCKY
NORTH CAROLINA
TENNESSEE
SOUTH CAROLINA
ARKANSAS
GEORGIA
MISSISSIPPI   ALABAMA
LOUISIANA
TEXAS
FLORIDA

Union States
Confederate States
Territories

Look at the map above to see which of the southern states seceded from the Union after the surrender of Fort Sumter. (The people in the western part of Virginia did not want to secede. In 1863 they formed a new state called West Virginia. It remained loyal to the Union.)

When President Lincoln heard the news about Fort Sumter, he asked the nation for 75,000 men to fight to save the Union. The Confederate president, Jefferson Davis, called for 100,000 volunteers. Both sides began training their armies.

The War Years

At first the South won many battles. It had good officers, and they were fighting on their own land. But the North had bigger armies, more money, more supplies, and more ships. It had more railroads than the South. These

A bridge later destroyed during the Civil War

advantages allowed the North to provide for its men better than the South could.

The war went on month after month. The North fought to save the Union and to end slavery. The South fought for the right to leave the Union and to start a new nation. Men in both armies were brave and fought well.

Life in a Union Army Training Camp

We are in a field . . . on the side of a hill, near the top. . . . A blanket spread on the ground is our bed, while another spread over us is our covering. A narrow strip of muslin, drawn over a pole about three feet from the ground, open at the both ends [is our tent], the wind and the rain . . . beating in upon us, . . . and creeping things crawling over us, and . . . great hungry mosquitoes biting every uncovered inch of us. . . .

. . . We each get a piece of meat and a potato, a chunk of bread and a cup of coffee with a spoonful of brown sugar in it. . . . We make quick work of washing dishes. We save a piece of bread for the last, with which we wipe up everything, and then eat the dish rag.

—Lawrence Van Alstyne
128th New York Volunteer
September, 1862

Red Runs the River   Unusual Films

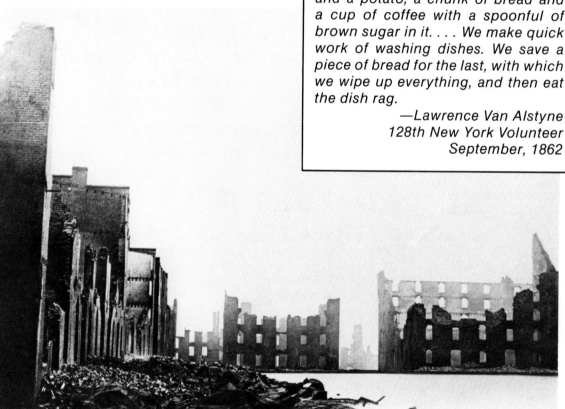

Richmond, Virginia, at the end of the Civil War

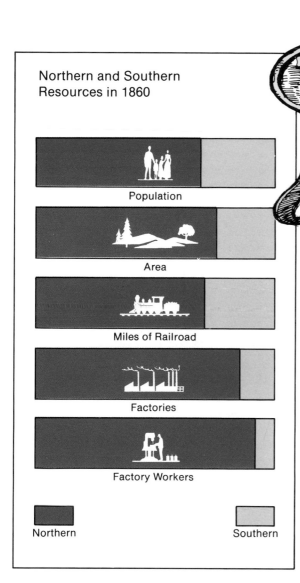

Northern and Southern Resources in 1860

Population

Area

Miles of Railroad

Factories

Factory Workers

Northern

Southern

Red Runs the River   Unusual Films

Civil War artillery at Richmond, Virginia, in 1865

The Blue and the Gray

The armies of both sides were made up of men of all ages, but many of them were between sixteen and twenty-five years old. These quotations from letters show that the soldiers were ordinary men who considered their duty to their country more important than their own comfort and desires.

Shiloh

Vicksburg

Billy Yank

The Union soldiers wore blue uniforms that were supplied by the government. They carried a Springfield rifled musket. These soldiers were called "Yankees" by the Southern people.

Johnnie Reb

The official color of the Confederate Army was gray. The soldiers often carried English-made Enfield guns. The men were called "Rebels" by the Northerners.

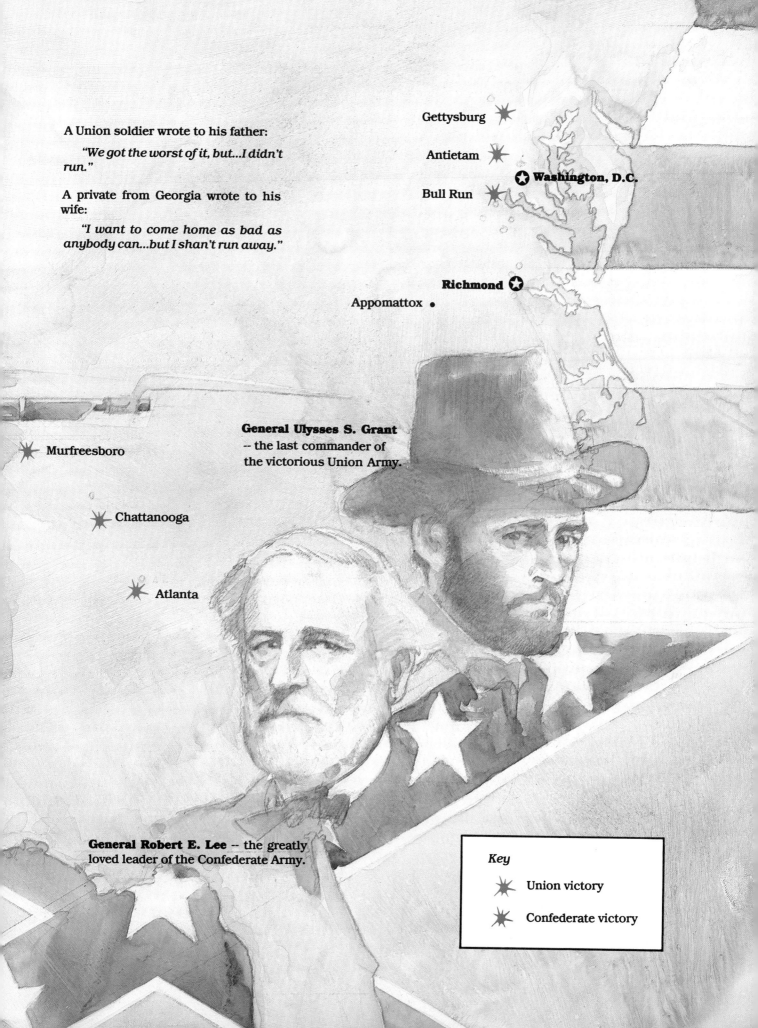

A Union soldier wrote to his father:

"We got the worst of it, but...I didn't run."

A private from Georgia wrote to his wife:

"I want to come home as bad as anybody can...but I shan't run away."

Gettysburg

Antietam

⭐ **Washington, D.C.**

Bull Run

Richmond ✪

Appomattox •

Murfreesboro

General Ulysses S. Grant -- the last commander of the victorious Union Army.

Chattanooga

Atlanta

General Robert E. Lee -- the greatly loved leader of the Confederate Army.

Key	
✴	Union victory
✴	Confederate victory

One of the most terrible battles of the Civil War was fought in 1863 at Gettysburg, Pennsylvania. Fierce fighting raged for three days until General Robert E. Lee and the Confederate Army retreated into Maryland. The Union soldiers and the townspeople spent the Fourth of July caring for the wounded and burying the dead. In all over 43,000 men were killed, wounded, or missing.

The great burial ground at Gettysburg was made a national cemetery to honor the men who gave their lives there. President Lincoln was asked to make a speech at the dedication of the cemetery. The main speaker gave a long speech lasting over two hours. Then Mr. Lincoln arose. He looked tired and sad. He was sad about all the men who had died in the war. The president spoke slowly for only five minutes. Later he thought that his simple message had not been a good one. Few people today have read or heard the long speech that the other man gave, but millions of Americans have memorized Lincoln's famous Gettysburg Address.

For four long years war divided the American people. Both sides suffered many hardships, but the South suffered more. Most of the battles were fought there. Many farms, homes, and crops were destroyed. Railroads, bridges, and buildings were also destroyed, and food and clothing were in short supply. The southerners still fought bravely, but the hardships became too great. Finally the South could not fight any more.

Lincoln's Gettysburg Address

Four score and seven years ago our fathers brought forth on this continent, a new nation, conceived in Liberty, and dedicated to the proposition that all men are created equal. Now we are engaged in a great civil war, testing whether that nation, or any nation so conceived and so dedicated, can long endure. We are met on a great battle-field of that war. We have come to dedicate a portion of that field, as a final resting place for those who here gave their lives that that nation might live. It is altogether fitting and proper that we should do this. But, in a larger sense, we can not dedicate—we can not consecrate—we can not hallow—this ground. The brave men, living and dead, who struggled here, have consecrated it, far above our poor power to add or detract. The world will little note, nor long remember what we say here, but it can never forget what they did here. It is for us the living, rather, to be dedicated here to the unfinished work which they who fought here have thus far so nobly advanced. It is rather for us to be here dedicated to the great task remaining before us—that from these honored dead we take increased devotion to that cause for which they gave the last full measure of devotion—that we here highly resolve that these dead shall not have died in vain—that this nation, under God, shall have a new birth of freedom— and that government of the people, by the people, for the people, shall not perish from the earth.

Abraham Lincoln

November 19, 1863.

The End of the War

On April 9, 1865, General Lee surrendered to General Ulysses S. Grant in a house in a little town called Appomattox Court House, Virginia. This was a time of victory for General Grant, the leader of the Union Army, but he was not really happy. He said he was "sad and depressed at the downfall of a foe who had fought so long and valiantly."

General Grant let the southern soldiers take their horses and mules home. They would need them to rebuild their farms and businesses. He also let the officers keep their swords.

After signing the surrender papers, General Lee mounted his horse and rode away. The northern soldiers began to cheer, but General Grant ordered them to be silent. "The war is over," he said. "The rebels are our countrymen again."

The war had settled the big problem: the southern states were to stay in the United States. The problem of slavery was also settled. During the war

Appomattox Court House

President Lincoln issued the **Emancipation Proclamation.** This statement said that the slaves in the Confederate States were "forever free."

After the war Congress made three additions, or **amendments,** to the Constitution. These amendments promised freedom to all men, made them citizens, and gave them the right to vote. These changes were for black men as well as white.

Rebuilding the Nation

The Civil War had ended, but the nation's differences were not forgotten. The southerners saw their ruined homes and land and found it hard to forgive the "Yankees." Many northerners thought the "Rebels" should be punished.

President Lincoln was relieved when the war ended. Earlier he had begged the northern people to have "malice toward none" and "charity for all." He asked them "to bind up the nation's wounds: to care for him who shall have borne the battle, and for his widow, and for his orphan—to do all which may achieve a just and lasting peace." But they did not follow his advice.

The years after the war were hard for the South. Selfish men from the North took advantage of the weak South. They tried to control the new southern governments and made the people pay heavy taxes. Often they spent the money from these taxes instead of helping the South rebuild. They made white southerners pay especially high taxes, and many had to sell their land to pay the taxes. The actions of these northerners made it even harder for the southerners to forgive them.

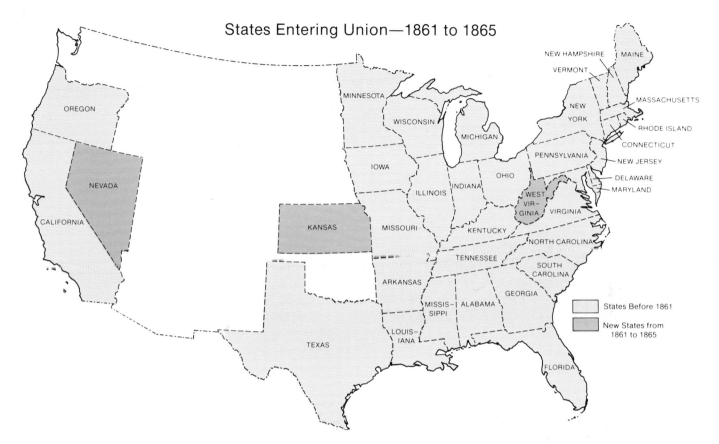

States Entering Union—1861 to 1865

OREGON

NEVADA

CALIFORNIA

MINNESOTA

WISCONSIN

MICHIGAN

IOWA

ILLINOIS | INDIANA | OHIO

KANSAS

MISSOURI

KENTUCKY

TENNESSEE

ARKANSAS

MISSIS- | ALABAMA
SIPPI

LOUIS-
IANA

TEXAS

NEW HAMPSHIRE | MAINE
VERMONT
NEW
YORK | MASSACHUSETTS
RHODE ISLAND
CONNECTICUT
PENNSYLVANIA | NEW JERSEY
DELAWARE
MARYLAND
WEST
VIR- | VIRGINIA
GINIA
NORTH CAROLINA
SOUTH
CAROLINA
GEORGIA
FLORIDA

☐ States Before 1861

▓ New States from
1861 to 1865

But slowly conditions changed. Southerners began to rebuild their land and take over their governments. Northerners left the South to return home or go west. Americans in both the North and the South worked to make the United States great. And in the West men and women from both parts of the country settled on the frontier.

Clara Barton
(1821-1912)

David Barton lifted his five-year-old sister, Clara, to the horse's back. "Hang on to the mane," he cried. David sprang onto another horse, and they galloped across the pasture. Little Clara laughed with joy.

"You rode well, Sister," said David. "You will be a fine rider."

Clara Barton was eager to learn. She lived with her family in Massachusetts. Her mother taught her to cook, sew, weave, make soap, and care for a garden. Her sisters taught her to read and study, and her brother Stephen taught her to like arithmetic. Her soldier father taught her to love her country. Clara once said, "I

THE CIVIL WAR 121

early learned that next to Heaven, our highest duty is to love and serve our country and honor and support its laws."

One day David was badly hurt by a fall from the roof of a new barn. Clara was only eleven, but she became his nurse. She gave him his medicine, read to him, and tried to make him cheerful and content. While nursing David every day for two years, she "almost forgot there was an outside to the house."

At last the doctor told David that he would soon be well. "You owe much to your sister's care," he said. "Clara is a real nurse."

When she was eighteen, Clara Barton began to teach school. She was only five feet tall, and many of her forty pupils were taller than she was. On the first day of class she stood before her class with a Bible in her hand. She instructed the students to turn to the fifth chapter of Matthew. Everyone took turns reading a verse from the chapter. Clara Barton had begun her teaching in the right way.

Clara enjoyed teaching and taught school in Massachusetts for about ten years. One day she heard about a town in New Jersey that needed a school. She went there and begged the leaders of the town to let her open one. But they said that the children were too wild to go to school. Clara said that she would teach for three months with no pay, so the men finally let her open the school.

The first students in this new school were six little boys that she found sitting on a fence by a road. As these boys spread the news about the school, her class grew to sixty students. Because Clara Barton was a good teacher, her school became popular. The next year she taught six hundred students! Clara had to work very hard. After a while she began to have trouble with her voice, and became so hoarse that she could not speak. Because of this illness, she had to give up teaching.

Miss Barton moved to Washington, D.C., and found a job in an office. She was working there when the Civil War began. One day Clara heard that soldiers from Massachusetts were coming from the battlefield to Washington on the train. She decided to meet them. Many of the men knew her, for they had been her students many years before. Now the men were tired, hungry, and dirty. Some were wounded. They had no baggage with them and no place to go, so they were sent to the Capitol Building.

Clara said, "These men need care. I will see what I can do to help them." She found other women to help her get supplies of food, medicine, and soap. They tore up sheets to be used for towels and bandages. Then they cooked for the men and bandaged their wounds. They made the soldiers as comfortable as they could.

Clara Barton kept helping soldiers as the war went on. Every day wounded men were brought by boat to Washington, and every day Clara met the boats. She gave the men food and medicine, helped bandage their wounds, and wrote letters for them.

Clara wrote a letter to a newspaper, asking people to give supplies to help the soldiers. In response, many sent boxes of food, bedding, bandages, clothing, and

other useful items. Others sent money. Soon Clara had to rent a place to store the gifts.

As the fighting went on, the number of wounded men increased. At the battlefield the army had no way to care for these men. Many died before they could get help. Clara's heart ached as she thought about this problem.

"I must go to the battlefield," she thought. "I could bandage the men to stop the bleeding and give them medicine. I could save many lives."

Clara told her old soldier father of her plan. He listened quietly until she had told him all about her idea. "If you believe this is your duty, you must go to the front," he said. "You need not fear harm. Every true soldier will respect and bless you."

At first Clara could not get permission to carry out her plan. "The battlefield is no place for a woman," the army officers said. "It is full of danger."

But Clara did not give up. "I am the daughter of a soldier; I am not afraid of the battlefield."

After a few months Clara Barton went to see a gruff, busy man named Major Rucker. When he asked Clara what she wanted, she suddenly began to cry. At last she was able to make her request. She told him about the supplies she had stored and about the work she wanted to do. Major Rucker agreed to help her. He gave an order giving Clara the use of wagons as well as men to load them. "Here is your permit to go to the front," he said. "May God bless you."

For three years Clara went from one battlefield to another, caring for the soldiers. No one could stop her from doing her duty. Once she worked for five days and nights with only three hours of sleep. Because of her tireless help, the men named her the "Angel of the Battlefields."

At last the war ended. Families eagerly waited for their loved ones to return, but many were disappointed. Parents wondered what had happened to their sons. Wives received no word from their husbands. Clara Barton wanted to help these families.

After hearing about her desire, President Lincoln wrote Clara a letter. He encouraged her to start this new work. It was a big job. Miss Barton gathered the names of men who had died. She put the lists in newspapers all over the country.

She also wrote thousands of letters to families to tell them what had happened to their men. This task took four years to finish.

Clara was very tired when her war work was finished. Her doctor suggested that she go to Europe to rest. While she was there, she heard about the Red Cross Society. This group helped care for sick and wounded soldiers just as she had done in America.

A war was going on in Europe, and Clara decided to help the Red Cross Society. Soon she was nursing the sick and feeding the hungry again.

When Clara returned home, she decided to start an American Red Cross. No one seemed to want to help her, but Clara had made up her mind to do it. She talked to the president of the United States. She wrote a booklet telling what the society would do. She made speeches and wrote letters to important men and women, trying to gain their support. At last, in 1882, the American Red Cross was formed. Clara Barton was chosen to be its first president. She held this office for twenty-two years.

Clara thought that the American Red Cross should help people in times of peace as well as during war. After disasters such as storms, floods, or fires, her workers helped those who were injured or in need. Clara and the Red Cross were always ready to help needy people.

Clara Barton died when she was ninety-one years old. She had spent her life helping people. She is remembered as one of the greatest citizens of our country.

Dwight L. Moody
(1837-1899)

Dwight was tired. Cutting broom corn was a hard job, and he had been working since morning. But he had almost finished the field, and the eight-year-old knew his mother would be pleased with the money he had earned.

The Moody family lived in Massachusetts. All the Moody children learned to work when they were young. Their father had died when Dwight was only four. Mrs. Moody taught her nine children to trust the Lord for their needs, but she also expected them to work.

Some time later Dwight agreed to work for a neighbor family. They gave him his meals for his pay. But the boy did not like the way things turned out. "Mother," Dwight said, "I am not going to work for that man any longer."

"Why not, son? You can do the work all right, can't you?" Mrs. Moody was puzzled. Dwight had been pleased to get the job. "Are you getting enough to eat?" she asked.

Dwight answered, "I guess I get enough, Mother. But do you know what I've had for the last nineteen meals? Cornmeal mush and milk. That's all! Meal after meal! I'm tired of it. I'm not going back!"

Mrs. Moody sighed. She knew how he felt. "Dwight, you promised to work all winter. You must keep your promise. You must keep every promise you make even when it is hard or unpleasant. God expects us to keep our word."

Mrs. Moody taught her children to do what they said they would do. She taught them to obey. She taught her children to be kind and to help each other. And she did not allow them to complain or to find fault with their friends. Mrs. Moody was a good mother.

Dwight was not happy living on the farm. He did not like to chop wood or work in the fields. He was tired of being poor. He wanted to go to Boston where he thought he could earn a lot of money.

One day when Dwight was seventeen, an older brother gave him five dollars. Dwight believed that this was his chance. He told his family good-by and took a train for Boston. Dwight's uncle, Sam Holton, had a shoe store in Boston, but Dwight did not ask him for a job. He wanted to get a job on his own.

For a week the young country boy hunted for work, but no one would hire him. He ran out of money, and he was hungry. To make matters worse, he got a big boil on the back of his neck that hurt every time he moved his head. He missed home and felt discouraged. Finally he went to his uncle and asked for a job in the shoe store.

Mr. Holton thought it over. He did not like his nephew very much because the boy was bold and liked to have things his own way. At last his Uncle Sam told Dwight he could have a job if he would make three promises. First, he must do his best. Second, he must ask about things he did

not understand. Third, he must go to Sunday school and church every Sunday. Dwight agreed.

Dwight had gone to church almost every Sunday of his life, but he was not a Christian. He knew about God, but he had never asked the Lord Jesus to be his Saviour. One day his Sunday school teacher in Boston decided to tell Dwight that he needed to be saved. He went to the shoe store and found the young man in the back, wrapping up shoes. The man reminded Dwight that Christ loved him. He told him that the Lord wanted Dwight to love Him too. He asked Dwight if he wanted to be saved. In a few minutes, Dwight gave himself and his life to Christ.

Dwight worked hard in the shoe store and was soon the best salesman there. He enjoyed talking to the customers. He knew that he could persuade them to buy boots and shoes. But Dwight did not always like his uncle's way of doing things. He wished he could run the store himself.

In those days many people talked about going west. Dwight listened and thought about it. At last he made up his mind and told his uncle he was leaving. Dwight went to the train station, bought a ticket to Chicago, and got on the train.

Two days after Dwight reached Chicago he found a job in another shoe store. On the first Wednesday night in Chicago, he went to a prayer meeting. He quickly made many friends there.

Dwight did not forget that he had given his life to the Lord. He worked as hard for the Lord on Sunday as he did for himself during the week. His special job was bringing children to a mission Sunday school that was held on Sunday afternoons.

Three years passed. Now almost a thousand children came to his Sunday school. Most of them were very poor. They all loved Mr. Moody. He understood them because he had been poor too.

One Sunday afternoon Abraham Lincoln visited Moody's class. He heard the

songs and prayers. He told the children, "I was once as poor as any boy in this school, but I am now president of the United States. If you will attend to what is taught you here, some of you may yet be president of the United States."

Dwight L. Moody was busy at work and church, but he had a problem. He was a good salesman, and he wanted to become rich. He was also a Christian and wanted to work for the Lord. Both jobs needed all his time. He had to decide which was the more important. A sick man helped him decide.

Mr. Hibbert, a fellow teacher, was too sick to teach his Sunday school class any more. He asked Moody to go to visit each of his pupils with him before he died. He wanted to ask each one to become a Christian. Moody did not want to go, but he thought he should help his friend. The two men went from one house to another. Mr. Hibbert begged the young people to accept the Lord as their Saviour. Almost everyone they visited was saved.

Now Dwight L. Moody knew what he was going to do. After that time of witnessing, he knew that he would rather see people saved than be the richest man in the world. The next day he quit his job. He chose to work for God every day.

Then in April, 1861, the Civil War began. Now Moody had another choice to make. Should he join the army? He agreed with President Lincoln that the southern states should not be allowed to secede, and he thought slavery was wrong. But he did not think he could kill a person. Besides, he had promised God that he would work for Him.

Some friends made a suggestion. Why not take the Word of God to the soldiers? Who needed to hear the gospel more than men who were going into a battle or men who were wounded and perhaps dying? His friends promised to raise the money he would need if he would go.

So Moody went to the soldiers. He preached in army camps, in prison camps,

in hospitals, on trains, and on boats. He took a trip on a boat down the Tennessee River. Four hundred fifty men were on the boat. Many of them were badly wounded. Moody made up his mind that he would not let a man on the boat die without telling him of Christ and heaven. He went from man to man. He gave each one a drink of water and told him about the Lord.

Nine times Moody went to the battlefields. He knelt beside the wounded men and told them of Christ.

"Chaplain, help me die," a soldier whispered. He had been wounded in a battle in Tennessee. "I've been fighting Christ all my life."

Moody gave him many verses from the Bible, but the man did not understand. Then Moody read the story of Nicodemus in the third chapter of John. He came to verse fifteen: "That whosoever believeth on him should not perish, but have eternal life."

The soldier lifted his hand. "What's that? Is it true? Read it again. That's good! Won't you read it again?"

Moody read the verse three times. The man smiled. Now he understood and believed God's Word. Now he was ready to meet his Saviour.

Mr. Moody also went to a camp near Chicago where prisoners from the southern army were held. Hundreds of these men were saved as they listened to God's Word.

At last the war ended. Moody had done a good work. He had shown men from both the North and the South how to get ready to meet God.

One night Moody heard a preacher say, "The world has yet to see what God can do with one man wholly committed to Him." Moody could not get the words out of his mind. Before he went to sleep that night, he told God that he would be that man.

Dwight L. Moody spent the rest of his life working for the Lord. He met a singer named Ira Sankey and asked him to work with him. Together they gave the gospel to all who would listen.

Moody, Sankey, and their wives went to England and Scotland to hold gospel meetings. Their American ways were strange to the people there. Moody did not always use good grammar, and Sankey sang solos in the meetings. No one else did that in English churches. Crowds of people came to hear the "crazy Americans." About two million people attended the services in London. Thousands accepted the Lord Jesus as their Saviour.

Moody and Sankey continued to hold gospel meetings when they came back to the United States. They went from north to south, and from east to west. Crowds came to hear them. In these meetings many people received Christ as Saviour.

Moody was very interested in young people, so he started a school for girls and then a school for boys in his hometown of Northfield, Massachusetts. In Chicago he started a Bible school to train young men and women to serve God.

Dwight L. Moody died when he was sixty-six years old. He showed the world what God could do through a man who was wholly committed to Him.

Things to know

Part I.

Match the following men and phrases.

1. _____ Abraham Lincoln
2. _____ Robert E. Lee
3. _____ Jefferson Davis
4. _____ Ulysses S. Grant
5. _____ Eli Whitney

a. President of the United States during the Civil War

b. Invented the cotton gin

c. General of the Confederate army

d. General of the Union army

e. President of the Confederate States during the Civil War

Part II.

Complete the following sentences.

1. The Battle of Gettysburg took place in the state of _____.

2. The speech President Lincoln made at the cemetery at Gettysburg is called the _____.

3. The surrender of General Lee to General Grant took place in the state of _____ in the year _____.

4. The _____ declared that the slaves in the Confederate States were free.

5. The amendments to the Constitution that were made after the Civil War guaranteed all men _____, _____, and _____.

Things to talk about

1. What were some of the advantages for the North during the Civil War?

2. Southerners were bitter and angry after the Civil War much longer than northerners were. What do you think caused this feeling?

3. Why is a flag important to a nation?

4. Why is it important to have special parks and markers established to show where battles and other historical events have taken place?

Things to do

1. Draw pictures of "Billy Yank" and "Johnny Reb."

2. Find these places on a map: Fort Sumter, Gettysburg, Washington, D.C., Atlanta, Richmond, Appomattox Court House.

3. Memorize the Gettysburg Address.

4. Make a graph showing the number of men who died during the Civil War. Give the number of battle deaths as well as deaths from disease, starvation, etc. for each side.

	Battle deaths	Deaths from disease, starvation, etc.
North	140,000	225,000
South	75,000	90,000

5. Find out when and why Memorial Day was made a holiday. How do you celebrate Memorial Day?

6. Add to your flag booklet.

Clara Barton Review

1. List some "keys to character" that can be seen in Clara Barton's life.

2. How did Clara help the soldiers in Washington, D.C.?

3. Why did Miss Barton want to go to the battlefield?

4. How did Clara help families after the Civil War ended?

5. Where did Clara Barton hear about the Red Cross Society?

6. What is the purpose of the Red Cross Society?

Dwight L. Moody Review

1. What are some Bible truths that Mrs. Moody taught her children?

2. Why did D. L. Moody leave his home and go to Boston? Why did he leave Boston and go to Chicago?

3. How did Dwight's willingness to work hard help him throughout his life?

4. Do you think Mr. Moody made the right decision about his work during the Civil War? Why or why not?

5. List some ways Moody worked for the Lord after the Civil War.

6. What does being "wholly committed" to God mean?

A Developing Nation

FOUR

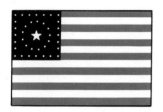

A Great Flag   This flag was first flown on July 4, 1877. Try to find out what state the thirty-eighth star represented.

UNIT GOALS

- I will be able to name some ways that the railroad changed life in the West.
- I will be able to tell what caused the wars in the West between the Indians and the white men.
- I will be able to describe a cattle drive.
- I will be able to describe life on the prairie.
- I will be able to explain how mass production changed life in the United States.
- I will be able to name some great inventors and tell what they invented.
- I will be able to locate these cities on a map: Sacramento, California; Omaha, Nebraska; Abilene, Kansas; Chicago, Illinois; Philadelphia, Pennsylvania; Dayton, Ohio; Tuskegee, Alabama.
- I will be able to locate these countries on a map of Europe: Germany, Italy, Ireland, Norway, Czechoslovakia.

TIME LINE

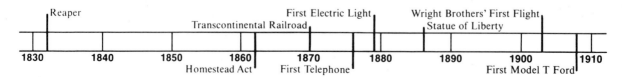

CHAPTER 11

RAILROADS TO THE WEST

There were thirty-four states in the United States at the end of the Civil War. How many of these were west of the Mississippi? (See page 121.)

Miles of plains, deserts, and mountains stretched between the states of California and Oregon and the settled parts of Texas and Missouri. The only way to get to the far West over land was a long, hard trip by wagon or stagecoach. The ocean journey around South America was also long and often unpleasant.

Thousands of miles of railroad covered the eastern United States, but these reached only as far west as Omaha, Nebraska. Americans dreamed of a railroad that would reach from the Atlantic Ocean to the Pacific.

To make that dream come true, Congress voted in 1862 to give money and land to two companies to build the railroad. The Union Pacific Company built westward from Omaha. The Central Pacific Company built eastward from Sacramento, California.

The Union Pacific Company

The Union Pacific men worked rapidly as they laid 1,086 miles of track over the wide plains. Few trees grew on the prairies, so the railroad ties came from the forests of Minnesota, Michigan, and other states. The iron rails were made in the mills of Pennsylvania. The ties and rails were brought west on train cars traveling the newly laid tracks. Many of the workers were Irishmen who had left their homeland because of a famine there.

The crews used picks, shovels, horse-drawn scrapers, and plows to level the ground for the track. Then they laid the wooden ties. Next the "iron men" laid the rails. At a signal from the foreman, five men on each side grabbed a rail. "Down," shouted the foreman, and the men placed the rail on the ties. The "spikers" fastened the rail in place. They struck three blows to each of the ten spikes they put in the rail. A good crew sometimes laid six miles of track in one day.

A crew laying track

The prairie Indians watched the railroad builders with fear in their hearts. They were afraid that the white man would take their land, and they were right. The United States government had made treaties with the

Indians that promised that they could keep certain hunting grounds, but the railroad companies often ignored the treaties. If the builders wanted to use some Indian territory, they did. The government, instead of enforcing the treaties, sent soldiers to guard the building crews when the Indians tried to drive them off their land.

The Central Pacific Company

The men of the Central Pacific laid 689 miles of track. They had plenty of timber from the forests in the West, so they made their own ties. Their rails, locomotives, and cars came from the East, fifteen thousand miles "around the Horn."

One of the problems of the Central Pacific Company was labor. Where could they find the thousands of workers who were needed for the hard and dangerous work of railroad building? The president of the company heard that there were plenty of workers in China who needed jobs. He sent messages there, and soon thousands of Chinese men made their way to California. They hoped to make good wages and send money home to their families.

The Chinese were good workers. They were orderly, peaceful, and dependable. They worked many hours every day and needed little food. No job was too difficult or too dangerous for them to do.

The Central Pacific Company had another big problem. The route of their track lay through mountains. They could not lay track as fast as the Union Pacific Company working on the flat prairie. The work went slowly. The men blasted roadbeds in the rock. They dug tunnels and built bridges. They sometimes worked from wicker baskets hanging down the side of a cliff.

Railroad surveyors working on the side of a cliff

Explosions and accidents took the lives of hundreds of men, but the company did not quit.

In winter, snow fell steadily in the high mountains, forming drifts as deep as one hundred feet. Snow slides swept away whole sections of track and buried crews of builders, but still the work went on. Ten thousand Chinese laid the rails mile by mile, steadily eastward, and finally the railroad reached the plain.

When the Irish crews on the Union Pacific heard that the Central Pacific crews had reached level land, they speeded up. After a while they were laying seven miles of track a day. The Central Pacific boss said that his Chinese workers could beat the Irish. One day they laid ten miles of track. No Union Pacific crew ever beat that record.

The Railroad Is Completed

Finally, on May 19, 1869, the two companies met at Promontory Point, Utah, near the Great Salt Lake.

The completion of the transcontinental railroad at Promontory Point, Utah

The railroad companies celebrated when the track was completed. A train from the East and one from the West brought officials of the railroad companies and their friends to watch the laying of the final rail. Irish and Chinese workers gathered in a crowd. Pioneers came in wagons and on horseback to join the crowd. Bands played and speeches were made. Finally the president of the Central Pacific Company came forward. The last tie was put in place. Spikes of silver and other metals were driven into it. Then the president took a silver-headed hammer to drive in the last spike, which was made of solid gold. An inscription on the golden spike read, "May God continue the unity of our country, as this railroad unites the two great oceans of the world."

Then engines from the East and the West slowly moved forward until they

America the Beautiful

Katherine Lee Bates was excited as she traveled to the top of Pike's Peak in 1893. Although this Massachusetts schoolteacher had visited Europe, she had never been in the western part of her own country before. At the top, Miss Bates looked about. Such a magnificent sight! Mighty, rugged, snowcapped mountains and tree-filled valleys rose and dipped before her. Vast, flat plains stretched eastward toward Kansas. This marvelous view filled her with a love for America that she had never felt before. Back in her room that evening, she wrote the words to "America the Beautiful."

Two years later a magazine published Katherine's poem. After reading her stirring poem, several people were inspired to write music for it. Samuel Ward wrote the melody that we now sing. This song has become one of America's best-loved patriotic hymns.

1869. **May 10th.** 1869.
GREAT EVENT
Rail Road from the Atlantic to the Pacific
GRAND OPENING
OF THE
Union Pacific
PlatteValleyRoute.
PASSENGER TRAINS LEAVE
OMAHA

10 MILES OF TRACK, LAID IN ONE DAY APRIL 28TH 1869

Promontory Point
Blue Creek
Corinne
Ogden
Devil's Gate
Bear River City
Echo
Wasatch
Great Salt Lake

Dutch Flat
Cape Horn
Cisco
Emigrant Gap
Sacramento
Central Pacific

Fort Sanders
Laramie
Sherman Summit
Cheyenne
Julesburg
North Platte
Fort Kearney
Council Bluffs
Omaha
Union Pacific

Ted Judah,
Father of the
Central Pacific

Golden Spike

touched. The great transcontinental railroad was complete.

Telegraph wires carried news of the great event to the rest of the country. Bells rang and cannons roared in New York and San Francisco. Whistles blew in cities across the nation. People celebrated because the railroad was finished. The East and the West were united.

The railroad caused many changes in the West. Families bought land along the railroad and started farms. Towns sprang up, and schools and churches were built.

The End of the Buffalo Herds

Much of the new railroad crossed the prairie. The prairie was the home of vast herds of buffalo. One herd was twenty miles wide and sixty miles long.

The Union Pacific Company hired buffalo hunters to provide meat for their crews. Bill Cody was the most famous of these hunters. In just eighteen months, Cody killed over four thousand buffalo. Railroaders made up a song about him:

Buffalo Bill! Buffalo Bill!
Never missed and never will.
Always aims and shoots to kill
And the company pays his buffalo
bill.

Buffalo hunting became popular after the railroad was finished. Some men hunted for sport, but others hunted buffalo for money. Buffalo skins were used to make lap robes. It became fashionable in the East to use buffalo robes to keep warm when riding in a carriage or a sleigh. A hunter could easily sell all the hides he could get.

Some men hunted from horseback, and some from slow-moving trains. When one buffalo was killed, others would crowd around it as it lay on the ground. The hunter then killed these

A herd of buffalo on the plains

animals too. A hunter with a good rifle sometimes killed dozens of buffalo in an hour.

Ten years after the railroad was completed, nearly all the buffalo were gone. In some places, buffalo bones were stacked in piles higher than houses. These bones were shipped back East, where they were ground up and used for fertilizer.

Wars with the Indians

The destruction of the buffalo herds caused great hardship for the Sioux, Cheyenne, Apache, and other Indian tribes. These Plains Indians depended on the buffalo for their food, clothing, and shelter. The Indians used every part of the buffalo and did not waste it. They thought the white man wrong to kill the buffalo just for the hide or just for sport. To protect their way of life, the Indians fought the white people.

The Indian warriors attacked wagon trains, stagecoaches, lonely farms, and small settlements. The settlers feared the sight of Indians in their war paint and the terrifying sound of their battle cry. The Indians attacked the buffalo hunters, killed many people, and burned many buildings. Soldiers, sent by the government to protect the settlers, built forts on the plains. From these the soldiers could attack the Indians. To give the Indians a place to live, the government set aside special lands called reservations. But the Indians wanted to remain where they were, on their own land.

There did not seem to be any way to prevent the wars that broke out

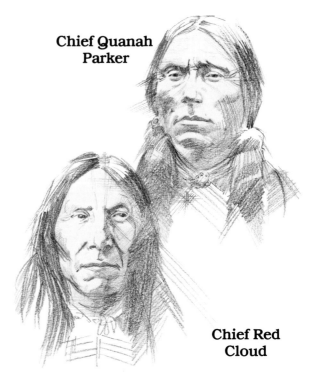

Chief Quanah Parker

Chief Red Cloud

between the Indians and the white men. Just as it was in the East in earlier years, the Indians and the white men did not understand each other. The Indians believed that the land belonged to everyone. Each person had a right to use what he needed. Indians did not have a desire to become rich. They were content when they had food, clothing, and a place to live. The white men thought the Indians were lazy, and the Indians thought the white men were greedy. Both sides believed that they were right, and both were willing to fight. Bitter hatred grew between the two groups.

After many battles, the Indians began to weaken. Most of their chiefs and warriors had been killed. The soldiers completely destroyed some Indian villages. They even killed the women and children. Indians from many tribes suffered from hunger and

Colonel George
Armstrong Custer

Chief Joseph
of the Nez Perce

Chief Sitting Bull
of the Sioux

Chief Satanta
of the Kiowa

cold. In 1876 two tribes of the plains, the Sioux and the Cheyenne, joined together to fight for their hunting grounds.

Lt. Colonel George Custer led a small army of about six hundred men

Chief Low Dog's Account of the Battle

They came upon us like a thunderbolt. I never before nor since saw men so brave and fearless as those white warriors. We retreated until our men got all together, and then we charged upon them. I called to my men, "This is a good day to die: follow me." We massed our men, and that no man should fall back, every man whipped another man's horse and we rushed right upon them. . . . The white warriors dismounted to fire. . . . They held their horses' reins on one arm while they were shooting, but their horses were so frightened that they pulled the men all around, and a great many of their shots went up in the air. . . . I did not see Gen. Custer. . . . We did not know . . . that he was the white chief.

August 18, 1881

Top: George Armstrong Custer
Bottom: "Custer's Last Stand"

into the Sioux territory in Montana to trap the Indian warriors. Custer ignored the scouts' report of the size of the Indian forces and attacked without waiting for reinforcements. This mistake cost him his life and the lives of his soldiers.

Custer's gravestone

Chief Joseph was a leader of the Nez Perce in Oregon. This tribe of Indians had been friendly to the white men since 1805, when they had helped Lewis and Clark in their expedition. In 1877 the United States government sent soldiers to force the Nez Perce to go to a reservation in Idaho. Reluctantly the chief decided to obey the soldiers and give up his land. Some of his people, however, became angry at this decision and killed over a dozen whites. Then Chief Joseph decided that his tribe of about five hundred people should try to escape into Canada. The soldiers pursued the Indians for four months. Finally, after many battles, Chief Joseph surrendered. The words he spoke when he gave himself up showed that he had no other choice.

> I am tired of fighting. Our chiefs are killed. The old men are all dead. . . . It is cold and we have no blankets. The little children are freezing to death. My people . . . have run away to the hills. . . . I want to have time to look for my children. . . . I am tired; my heart is sick and sad. . . . I will fight no more forever.

The Army moved Chief Joseph and his people to the Oklahoma Indian Territory. Chief Joseph never returned to his home in Oregon.

Indian reservations still exist in our country today. Some Indians who live on them still speak their tribe's language and follow the old Indian ways.

Things to know

1. The Union Pacific Company worked (in what direction?) _____ from Omaha. Many of their workers were _____.

2. The Central Pacific Company worked (in what direction?) _____ from Sacramento. Many of their workers were _____.

3. The two railroads met at _____.

4. Land set aside especially for the Indians is called a
_____.

5. _____ was the leader of the Nez Perce who surrendered to the whites.

Things to talk about

1. Imagine that you are a worker on the first railroad that crossed our country. Which company would you like to work for? Why?

2. Why was there such a great celebration when the first railroad across the United States was finished?

3. Why do you think the hunters were not careful to keep from destroying the buffalo herds?

4. Whom do you think did the greatest wrong—the Indians or the whites? Why do you think so?

5. Have you ever disliked someone because you did not understand him? How do you learn to understand people?

6. Is a way of life "bad" just because it is different from yours? How do we know if a way of life is good or bad?

Things to do

1. Think of a job you have to do. Plan a way to do it faster and better.

2. Look closely at a railroad track. Try to imagine what it would be like to build the track without our modern machines.

3. Show the route of the first transcontinental railroad on a map.

4. Draw and color a picture of an Indian chief.

5. Find out if there are any wild buffalo herds in our country today. If there are, where are they and where did they come from?

6. Find where the Indian reservations in the United States are located. Talk to or write to a missionary who works on an Indian reservation.

CHAPTER 12

CATTLEMEN AND FARMERS

When Columbus and other Spanish explorers came to North America, they brought many different animals with them: cattle, horses, sheep, and pigs. They used many of these animals for food. Some animals escaped from their owners, and some were left behind when the explorers returned home. These animals became wild and roamed about from place to place. As the years passed, great herds of wild horses and cattle grew up in the southwestern part of our country. These animals were free to anyone who could capture them.

Mustangs and Longhorns

The wild, roving horses were called **mustangs**. Mustangs were small, but they were tough and very quick. They could travel a long way without resting.

A herd of wild mustangs

They also had a good sense of direction and could tell when danger was near.

Most of the wild cattle in the Southwest were **longhorns**. These animals had horns that spread as much as seven feet from tip to tip. They had long legs, long tails, and long backs.

The longhorns could live through almost all kinds of weather. They

Longhorn cattle

would eat almost any kind of plant, so they could survive the hot, dry summers. They could smell water miles away. In the winter, the longhorns survived the freezing blizzards in an unusual way. When the snow began to fall, the cattle would turn their tails toward the storm and drift with the wind. Often they would simply walk out of the storm.

The longhorns were good fighters. Sometimes a pack of wolves attacked a herd. To protect their young from the fierce wolves, the cows bunched their calves into the middle of the herd. Then they formed a tight circle and faced the attackers. The wolves did not dare to approach this wall of sharp horns.

Early settlers in Texas captured wild cattle and started their own herds. By the end of the Civil War, there were about 3 million head of cattle in Texas. Their owners wanted to sell them to make a profit. People in the East wanted to buy the cattle for their meat and hides. Transportation was a problem for the cattle owners. They had to think of a way to get their herds to the East.

Cattle Drives

In 1867, Joseph McCoy, a young cattle buyer, had a plan. He knew that there was a railroad to Abilene, Kansas. He talked to the men in the railroad company and persuaded them to charge low rates to ship cattle on their railroad. Then he built cattle pens and loading platforms next to the railroad track. He sent word to Texas cattlemen that he would ship their cattle to Chicago and other cities if they would bring them to Abilene.

This plan suited the cattlemen. They rounded up the cattle they wished to sell and started the journey to Abilene.

The first herd driven to Abilene followed a trail that had been marked by Jesse Chisholm. Mr. Chisholm was an old storekeeper and trader who had used the trail when he traded with Indians in his younger days. This route became known as the Chisholm Trail.

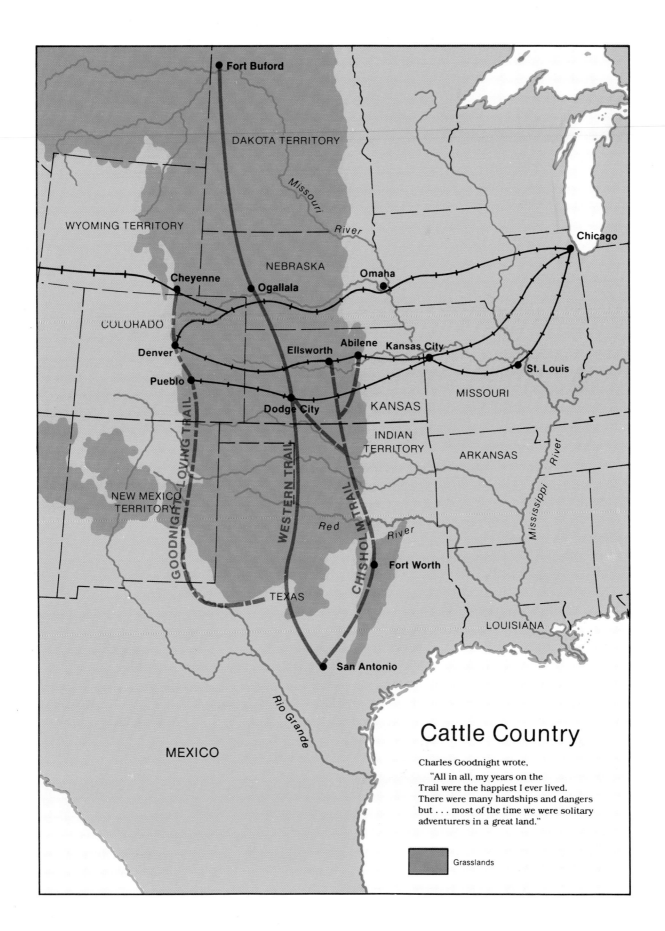

Fort Buford

DAKOTA TERRITORY

Missouri

River

WYOMING TERRITORY

NEBRASKA

Chicago

Cheyenne

Ogallala

Omaha

COLORADO

Denver

Ellsworth

Abilene

Kansas City

St. Louis

Pueblo

Dodge City

KANSAS

MISSOURI

INDIAN
TERRITORY

ARKANSAS

GOODNIGHT-LOVING TRAIL

WESTERN TRAIL

CHISHOLM TRAIL

NEW MEXICO
TERRITORY

Red

River

Mississippi River

Fort Worth

TEXAS

LOUISIANA

San Antonio

Rio Grande

MEXICO

Cattle Country

Charles Goodnight wrote,

"All in all, my years on the
Trail were the happiest I ever lived.
There were many hardships and dangers
but . . . most of the time we were solitary
adventurers in a great land."

Grasslands

Cattle driving was a great adventure, and many Texas boys were eager to "hit the trail." A **cattle drive** usually started in March and lasted about three months. A dozen men could manage a herd of 2500 cattle. With each herd went a trail boss, nine cowboys, a **horse wrangler,** and a cook.

The herd moved in a column about a mile long. The trail boss was in charge of the men and cattle on the drive. He rode ahead of the cattle to find water and good grazing grounds. He also took care of all the business of the drive.

The job of the cowboys was to protect the cattle from wild animals and Indians and to keep them from straying away. These were not easy jobs. The cowboys spent all day in the saddle and then kept watch at night in two-hour shifts. Sometimes when the cattle were restless, the cowboys sang to them. We still sing some of the old cowboy songs.

All cowboys dreaded a stampede. Most often, lightning caused a stampede. The lightning would frighten the herd, and the scared cattle would begin to run. If a stampede were not stopped, it might take days to gather the cattle together again.

Each man had from six to ten horses to use while on the trail. He had several horses ready in order to have a fresh mount when needed. The horses that were not being used stayed in a herd called a **remuda**. The horse wrangler's job was to take care of the remuda. He was usually a boy of about fourteen years of age.

Perhaps the most important man on the drive was the cook. He had to prepare good meals for a dozen men

Lively and rousing

CHISHOLM TRAIL

F

1. Oh,— come a-long boys— and— list-en to my tale,— I'll
2. With a ten dol-lar hoss— and a for-ty dol-lar sad-dle, I'm
3. Oh, it's ba-con and beans— most— ev-e-ry— day,— I
4. With my knees in the sad-dle and my hat— in the sky,— I'll

C7   Dm   F   Chorus

tell you of my trou-bles on the old Chis-holm Trail. Co-ma
a-rid-ing on the trail with the Tex-as cat-tle.
would-n't mind a change— to— prai-rie— hay.
still— punch— cat-tle in the sweet by and by.

Gm   C7   Dm   F

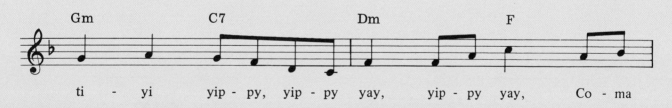

ti - yi yip-py, yip-py yay, yip-py yay, Co-ma

C7   F

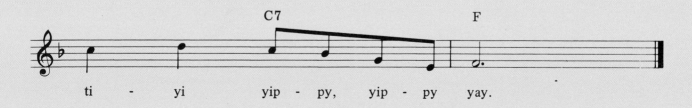

ti - yi yip-py, yip-py yay.

The Cowboy's Clothing and Tools

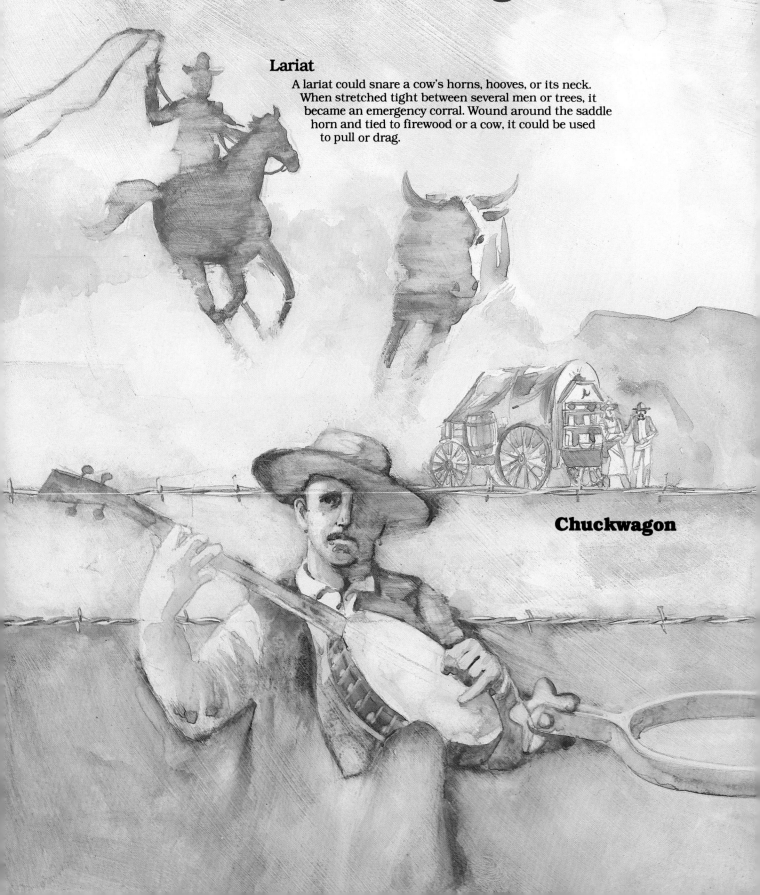

Lariat

A lariat could snare a cow's horns, hooves, or its neck. When stretched tight between several men or trees, it became an emergency corral. Wound around the saddle horn and tied to firewood or a cow, it could be used to pull or drag.

Chuckwagon

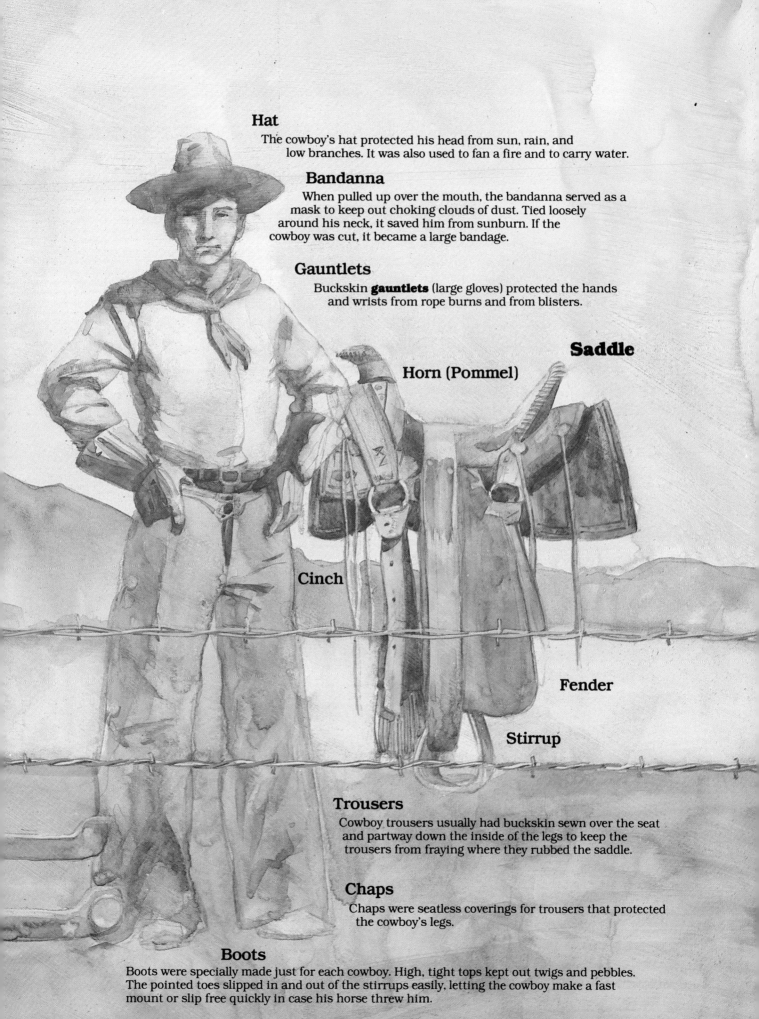

Hat

The cowboy's hat protected his head from sun, rain, and low branches. It was also used to fan a fire and to carry water.

Bandanna

When pulled up over the mouth, the bandanna served as a mask to keep out choking clouds of dust. Tied loosely around his neck, it saved him from sunburn. If the cowboy was cut, it became a large bandage.

Gauntlets

Buckskin **gauntlets** (large gloves) protected the hands and wrists from rope burns and from blisters.

Saddle

Horn (Pommel)

Cinch

Fender

Stirrup

Trousers

Cowboy trousers usually had buckskin sewn over the seat and partway down the inside of the legs to keep the trousers from fraying where they rubbed the saddle.

Chaps

Chaps were seatless coverings for trousers that protected the cowboy's legs.

Boots

Boots were specially made just for each cowboy. High, tight tops kept out twigs and pebbles. The pointed toes slipped in and out of the stirrups easily, letting the cowboy make a fast mount or slip free quickly in case his horse threw him.

every day, even when it rained. He carried all his supplies and equipment in a **chuck wagon.** The men ate biscuits, beans, bacon or beef, and dried apples at almost every meal. Sometimes the cook caught some fish or picked berries so that they could have a change of menu.

When the drive reached Abilene, the animals were loaded into railroad cars and shipped to eastern markets.

Raising cattle was a profitable business. It spread from Texas to other places where there was good pastureland. Look at the map on page 147 to find the land that was called "Cattle Country."

At first most of the cattle grazed on the **open range.** The open range was land that was owned by the government and was "open" to all who wanted to use it for pasture. Most of the open range was not fenced, and the cattle moved freely from place to place. And every year cowboys drove herds to Abilene, Dodge City, and other railroad towns on the way to market.

The End of the Cattle Drives

Many cattlemen decided to buy land from the government so that they would have their own grazing lands. They often fenced their pastures with barbed wire to keep their herds from roaming away. The fences also kept other cattle from mixing with their herds.

After the Transcontinental Railroad was finished in 1869, many more miles of railroad track were laid in the West.

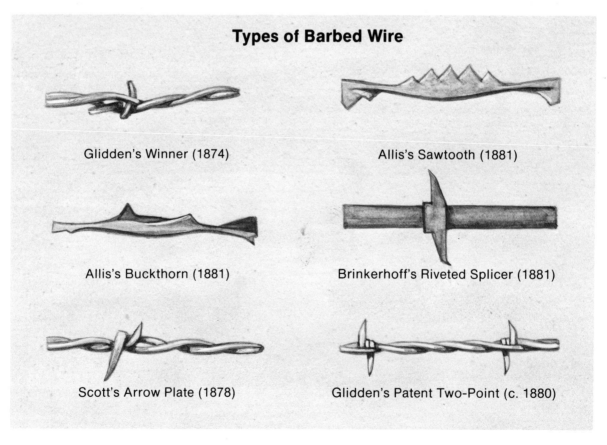

Types of Barbed Wire

Glidden's Winner (1874)

Allis's Sawtooth (1881)

Allis's Buckthorn (1881)

Brinkerhoff's Riveted Splicer (1881)

Scott's Arrow Plate (1878)

Glidden's Patent Two-Point (c. 1880)

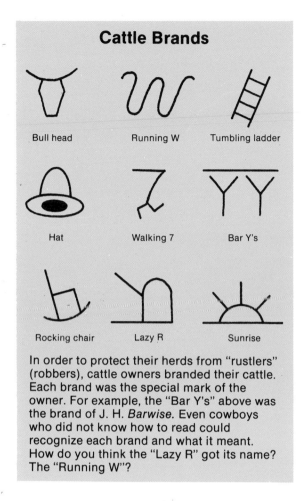

Cattle Brands

Bull head

Running W

Tumbling ladder

Hat

Walking 7

Bar Y's

Rocking chair

Lazy R

Sunrise

In order to protect their herds from "rustlers" (robbers), cattle owners branded their cattle. Each brand was the special mark of the owner. For example, the "Bar Y's" above was the brand of J. H. *Barwise*. Even cowboys who did not know how to read could recognize each brand and what it meant. How do you think the "Lazy R" got its name? The "Running W"?

Then the cattlemen did not have to drive their herds so far to ship them to market. The farmers who came after the railroads were built bought land and planted crops of wheat and corn. They also fenced their land.

As the prairie was fenced in, the days of the open range and the long cattle drives ended. The longhorns were replaced by cattle that produced more meat and were not so wild. Cowboys still rode horses and cared for cattle, but the excitement of the long drives was gone.

Life on the Prairie

Much of the land between the Mississippi River and the Rocky Mountains was prairie land. The pioneers described the flat, treeless prairie as a "sea of grass." Beneath the gently waving grass and bright flowers was rich black soil.

In 1862 the United States government passed the **Homestead Act**. This act offered 160 acres of government land free to anyone who would live on it and cultivate it for five years. The government hoped that the act would encourage people to settle the land. Much of this land was prairie land.

As the news of free land spread throughout the United States and Europe, thousands of families started West. After the Civil War ended and after the railroad was finished, even more came. Besides Americans, many people from Germany, Norway, Sweden, Russia, and other European countries went to the prairie.

The first homesteaders took land along the rivers and streams. Other homesteaders started farms along the railroads. Families that came later had to take whatever land was left.

Building a Home

One of the first jobs for the homesteaders was building a house. Very few trees grew on the prairie, so most houses were built of **sod**. The farmer plowed his grassy land in such a way that he cut long strips of sod. These strips were about eighteen inches wide and several inches thick. They were cut into pieces about three feet long. The homesteader built the walls of his house by laying these strips on top of each other like bricks. For the

A pioneer standing in front of a sod house

roof he first put down a framework of poles. He covered the poles with a layer of brush followed by a layer of long grass. He finished the roof by putting on a thin layer of sod. Flowers, grass and weeds often grew on the roof of a sod house.

Sod houses were good in several ways. In the first place, they did not cost much to build. Also, sod houses were cool in summer and warm in winter. The strong prairie winds could not blow sod houses over, and they did not catch on fire as wood houses often did.

Sod houses were hard to keep clean, however. Pioneer women fastened paper to the walls to keep pieces of sod from falling off. Insects and snakes often lived in the walls and in the roof. Because the roof always leaked and the sod held moisture like a sponge, it usually "rained" inside the house a day or two after it stopped raining outside. Because of this problem, homesteader wives sometimes held an umbrella over the food while they cooked.

Every pioneer family planted trees and a garden near their house and worked hard to keep these watered during the hot, dry summers. The fruit trees and garden provided food for the families. The long rows of other kinds of trees made a "windbreak" for the house and barn. They also provided shade and beauty in that treeless land.

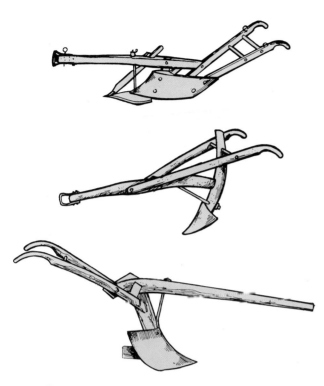

Three early pioneer plows. **Top:** A wooden plow invented by Thomas Jefferson. **Middle:** A shovel plow of the early 1800s. **Bottom:** The John Deere plow of 1837. This was the first plow used on the prairie.

Hardships on the Prairie

Life on the prairie had many hardships. Water was scarce, and pioneer families had to haul water from a stream or river until they dug a well. They used short-handled spades to dig the wells. As the hole became deep, the digger would place the dirt in a bucket. Someone above pulled the bucket up and emptied it. Sometimes they dug down two hundred feet before they found water. Early settlers had to draw water with a rope and bucket. In later years, farmers used pumps that were run by **windmills** to get water from their wells.

Fuel was also scarce on the prairie. Because there were so few trees, pioneer families rarely burned wood. The main fuel of the early settlers was "cow chips." These were the dried droppings of the cattle or buffalo. After farmers harvested their corn, they used cornstalks and corncobs for fuel. In an emergency, they burned twisted, dry grass. This made a hot fire, but the grass burned very quickly. Someone had to put fuel on the fire constantly.

The weather was another hardship the pioneers faced. Summers on the prairie were very hot, while winters were very cold. The wind rarely stopped blowing. Some summers passed with almost no rain, and all of the crops died.

Winter brought terrible blizzards. A prairie blizzard was not an ordinary snowstorm. The heavy snow was blown by winds so powerful that a person could not face them. It was almost

impossible for someone to find his way in the blinding storm. Farmers often stretched a rope from the house to the barn. They held on to the rope to keep from getting lost when they went out to care for their animals. Some blizzards lasted for days, during which the little sod houses would be completely covered by snowdrifts. Sometimes the families inside burned their beds, tables, and stools to keep their fire going so that they would not freeze to death.

Prairie fires were another problem. In the late summer and fall when the grass was dry, fires often started. A campfire, a burning wad from a gun, or perhaps lightning might cause a blaze. It would spread rapidly, burning everything in its way. Pioneer families tried to protect their buildings by putting a **firebreak** around them. They plowed a wide strip all the way around their property. Since there would be nothing on the ground to burn, the fire could not cross it.

Grasshoppers were a great problem for prairie farmers. Sometimes great swarms of these insects swept down on the land and ate almost every green plant in sight. The grasshoppers were sometimes inches deep on the ground. They would cover trees in such numbers that the limbs broke off from the weight of the insects. They even ate turnips and onions out of the ground, leaving only holes to show where the vegetables had been. Some people covered their gardens with blankets and sheets to keep the grasshoppers from eating the plants. The greedy grasshoppers ate the coverings first and then the plants.

The year 1874 was known as the Grasshopper Year because the insects

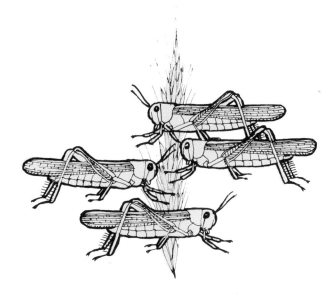

caused so much damage that year. The government gave large amounts of money to help the pioneer families. The next spring the government gave seed to the farmers who wanted to try farming again.

Some families could not face so many hardships. They gave up in despair. Others gave up because of illness or death in their families, while some ran out of money. These families sometimes had to leave their home-steads even before their five years were up.

Of course the hard times did not come all at once. Between the hard years were years when the harvests were large and the prices were good. Many families were willing to work, to live in their "soddies" and go without luxuries in order to keep their land. Some families had friends and relatives back East who helped them when times were bad. Most of the pioneer families helped each other when trouble came.

Year by year the number of families and farms increased. Towns with schools and churches sprang up. More railroads were built, making it easier to travel and to transport goods. By 1890 the prairie lands had all been made into states. The frontier days were over.

Notice the part of our country shown in white on the map below. Indian reservations were located in part of that land, so few white people went there. Part of the land was mountainous or desert. These and other problems prevented it from being settled as rapidly as the plains.

Use the map below and the map on page 51 to help you answer these questions.

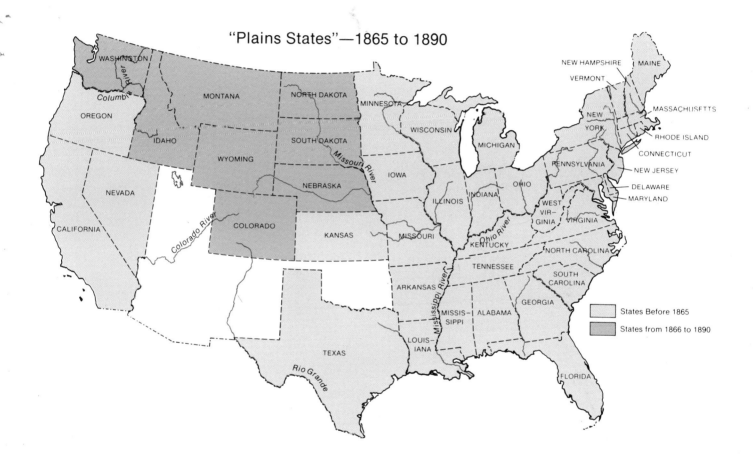

"Plains States"—1865 to 1890

States Before 1865

States from 1866 to 1890

1. Which states joined the Union between 1866 and 1890?

2. Through which states does the Missouri River flow?

3. Which states have the Mississippi River as a part of their boundaries?

4. How did the locations of Chicago and St. Louis help make them important cities?

5. How did Chicago and St. Louis help in the settling of the plains states?

Things to know

1. The wild cattle in Texas were called _____.

2. The wild horses in the Southwest were called _____.

3. One of the best-known routes for cattle drives was called the _____.

4. The boy who cared for the horses on a cattle drive was called the _____.

5. A cattleman _____ his cattle to show they belonged to him.

6. A _____ was a wild run by frightened cattle.

7. The Homestead Act offered 160 acres of land to anyone who would _____.

8. The wide, grassy plains that had few trees were called the _____.

9. The first home of many homesteaders was built of _____.

10. Four great problems for the prairie farmers were _____, _____, _____, and _____.

Things to talk about

1. How were the transportation problems of our nation solved? (See pages 13-14, 53, 71-73, 85-86, and 133.) Why is good transportation important to a nation?

2. Imagine that you lived in the days of the cattle drives. Would you like to "hit the trail"? Which job would you want?

3. Why is it important that we study about the "old days" of our country?

4. What is the hardest work you have ever done? Compare that to the hard things children who lived on the prairie did.

5. Why did the prairie farmers not build log cabins? Do you think they would have been better than sod houses?

6. What was the purpose of each part of a cowboy outfit?

Things to do

1. Learn the song "Chisholm Trail."

2. Listen to a record of cowboy songs. Are the words mostly sad or happy?

3. Find out what kinds of cattle are raised for beef today.

4. Visit a butcher to find out how beef is cut up to be sold.

5. Read the *Little House on the Prairie* books by Laura Ingalls Wilder.

6. Find out how a windmill works.

7. Make a collection of drawings of brands and what they are called.

8. Design a cattle brand for your family.

9. Study and draw a collection of different kinds of barbed wire.

10. List the states that were made from the prairie lands of the United States. Find out what their main farm products are now.

11. Write five questions that can be answered by examining the pictographs below.

GRAIN PRODUCTION IN THE PRAIRIE STATES IN 1980

Wheat   each symbol represents 50 million bushels

Kansas	⚇ ⚇ ⚇ ⚇ ⚇ ⚇ ⚇ ⅰ
North Dakota	⚇ ⚇ ⚇ ⚇ ⚇ ⅰ
Oklahoma	⚇ ⚇ ⚇ ⚇
Washington	⚇ ⚇ ⚇
Montana	⚇ ⚇ ⚇
Texas	⚇ ⚇ ⅰ
Minnesota	⚇ ⚇ ⅰ
Nebraska	⚇ ⚇

Oats   each symbol represents 10 million bushels

Minnesota	⚇ ⚇ ⚇ ⚇ ⚇ ⚇ ⚇ ⚇ ⅰ
South Dakota	⚇ ⚇ ⚇ ⚇ ⚇ ⚇ ⚇ ⅰ
Iowa	⚇ ⚇ ⚇ ⚇ ⚇ ⚇
Wisconsin	⚇ ⚇ ⚇ ⚇ ⅰ
North Dakota	⚇ ⚇ ⚇ ⅰ
Michigan	⚇ ⚇ ⅰ

Corn   each symbol represents 100 million bushels

Iowa	🌽 🌽 🌽 🌽 🌽 🌽 🌽 🌽 🌽 🌽 🌽 🌽 🌽 🌽 🌽 ⅰ
Illinois	🌽 🌽 🌽 🌽 🌽 🌽 🌽 🌽 🌽 🌽 🌽 🌽 ⅰ
Nebraska	🌽 🌽 🌽 🌽 🌽 🌽 ⅰ
Minnesota	🌽 🌽 🌽 🌽 🌽 🌽 ⅰ
Indiana	🌽 🌽 🌽 🌽 🌽 ⅰ

Rye   each symbol represents 1 million bushels

South Dakota	⚇ ⚇ ⚇ ⚇ ⚇
North Dakota	⚇ ⚇ ⚇ ⅰ
Georgia	⚇ ⚇ ⅰ
Minnesota	⚇ ⚇ ⅰ
Nebraska	⚇

CHAPTER 13

INVENTIONS

Americans like to invent things. They like to think of ways to make hard jobs easier. They like to make machines that can do work more efficiently. American inventions have helped to make our nation great.

Before 1776 Americans depended on England for most of their manufactured goods. When our nation became free, Americans began to want to make things themselves. A visitor to the United States in 1820 said that "the moment an American hears the word *invention,* he pricks up his ears."

Some inventions are the work of one man. For example, Walter Hunt sat in his New York shop one afternoon in 1849, twisting a piece of wire. In three hours he had invented the safety pin.

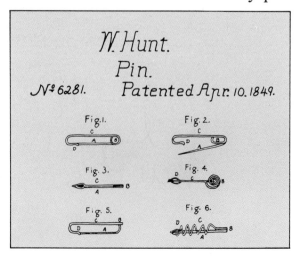

Other inventions, like the steamboat (see page 47), were the result of many ideas and took many years to develop.

Patents

After a person invents something, he applies to the government for a **patent.** A patent is a document that gives the patent holder the right to produce and sell the invention. No one else may build a patented item without permission from the owner of the patent. However, a person may sell his right to a patent if he wants to. Hunt sold his rights to the safety pin for four hundred dollars.

The first person in America to receive a patent was Joseph Jenks. He came to Massachusetts from England in 1643 to build an ironworks for that colony. His patent was for a water-powered mill. Later he built the first fire engine in this country. It was called an "Ingine to carry water in case of fire." He also designed the scythe that is still used today.

Scythe and cradle

Some inventions are large and complicated, while others are small and simple. Both kinds have been

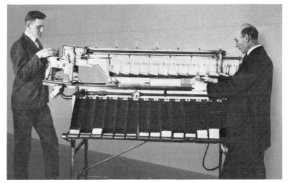
A machine to sort cards according to the information on them

important to the making of our country. The steel plow, barbed wire, and the windmill were perhaps the three most important inventions for the farmers who settled the Plains states. Of course, the railroad helped bring large numbers of people west. And without the Colt revolver and repeating rifle, the railroad could not have been built, for these guns were used to defeat the Indians.

Mass Production

Often inventions are valuable only if they can be made for a price people can afford to pay. **Mass production** usually makes this possible. Two ideas that are needed for mass production were developed in the United States. These are the ideas of **interchangeable parts** and the **assembly line.**

Interchangeable Parts

You have already read about Eli Whitney and his cotton gin (see pages 96-97). Soon after that invention, Mr. Whitney had a new idea that changed manufacturing in this country and

Eli Whitney

around the world. Until this time manufactured goods were made in small workshops. The workers made each part of the product by hand and then put the parts together. Because of this handcrafted method, no two articles were ever just alike.

In 1798 Eli Whitney made a contract with the government to make ten thousand guns. He said he could make them in two years. This seemed impossible because it took a man many days to make just one gun. But Mr. Whitney had a plan.

He planned that all the different parts of each gun would be exactly alike. If the parts were all alike, any part would fit any gun. The parts would be interchangeable. He just had to figure out a way to make the parts alike.

Mr. Whitney designed some machines and tools that would make the gun parts. One machine made the gun barrels, and others made the parts of the locks. Every gun barrel was the same as every other gun barrel. Every lock was the same as every other lock. This was also true of the other parts of the guns.

Mr. Whitney's idea was not a complete success at first. He was not able to make his machines as precise as he wished them to be, so the parts did not fit together as well as he had hoped. However, he was able to make fifteen thousand guns in two years after his machines were finished.

Other inventors used this idea of interchangeable parts. Samuel Colt used it to manufacture a gun he called

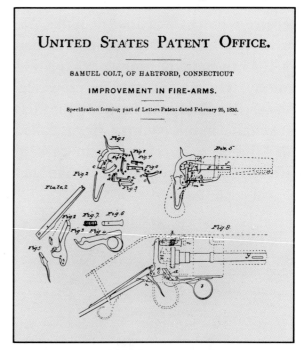

the revolver. Makers of clocks, stoves, locks, and farm tools were able to make their products more quickly using this method. This made the articles cost less. They could also be repaired more easily. By the 1850s the use of interchangeable parts had spread across the United States and to Europe.

It was called the American system of manufacture.

Assembly Line

Another important development in American manufacturing was the assembly line. These pictures show an early Ford automobile plant. Each worker added a part or did something to each car at his point on the assembly line.

Probably the first important use of the assembly line in the United States was about 1850. A meat packer in Cincinnati, Ohio, built a pork packing house to prepare the animals for market in an efficient way.

The man who showed the world the value of the assembly line was Henry Ford. The Ford Motor Company started making automobiles in 1903. Mr. Ford was determined to make good cars. He wanted them to be easy

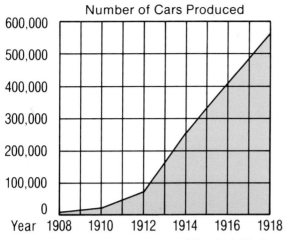

Number of Cars Produced

| 600,000 |
| 500,000 |
| 400,000 |
| 300,000 |
| 200,000 |
| 100,000 |
| 0 |

Year 1908 1910 1912 1914 1916 1918

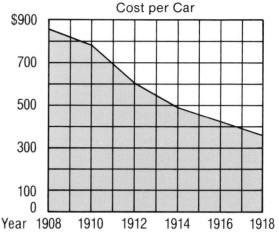

Cost per Car

| $900 |
| 700 |
| 500 |
| 300 |
| 100 |
| 0 |

Year 1908 1910 1912 1914 1916 1918

Model T Ford Touring Car

to drive, easy to repair, and cheap enough so that they would be easy to buy. After much study and work, he designed the car called the Model T Ford.

In 1908, the Ford Company sold almost six thousand Model T Fords.

They cost $850 each. But still Mr. Ford was not satisfied.

Mr. Ford and his partners tried to find ways to make a car in less time. The moving assembly line was the answer to their problem. They built a factory in which the cars were moved by conveyor belts and overhead cranes. Instead of twelve and one-half hours it took only one and one-half hours to put a car together. This quick process helped lower the price of the car.

The idea of the moving assembly line spread to factories all over the country. As other goods were manufactured more rapidly, their prices were lowered. Many people could buy things that they could not afford before.

The use of interchangeable parts and the assembly line made mass production in the large factories of our nation possible. These factories produce most of our cars, planes, furniture, clothing, tools, and household appliances. They prepare and

Boy working in a Massachusetts textile mill

package much of our food. They have made it possible for Americans to live more comfortably than most other people in the world.

Cyrus McCormick
(1809-1884)

Harvesting grain with a scythe was slow, hot, backbreaking work. The scythe was heavy. The stalks fell in all directions and had to be gathered into bundles to be threshed. Ripe grain had to be gathered within ten days, and good workers could harvest only two acres of grain a day. Certainly a reaping, or harvesting, machine was needed.

Cyrus McCormick decided he would build a reaper. Cyrus lived with his father, Robert McCormick, at Walnut Grove, Virginia. Mr. McCormick was a well-to-do Scotch-Irish farmer. He owned flour mills, sawmills, and a blacksmith shop. He invented a threshing machine and a blacksmith's bellows. He experimented with a harvesting machine but gave up the idea. Cyrus took his father's harvester and began to improve it.

In 1832 Cyrus was ready to show what his reaper could do. The first field he tried was rough and hilly. The clumsy machine bumped and jerked as it moved along. The owner of the field complained that it was damaging his grain and ordered Cyrus off his land. However, a neighboring farmer pulled down a rail fence and invited Cyrus to try the reaper in his field, which was level and smooth. That afternoon the reaper cut six acres of wheat, three times what a man did in a whole day.

The next year Cyrus cut all the grain on his father's farm as well as that of several neighbors. By this time, the machine had attracted attention throughout the

area. In 1834 Cyrus took out a patent on his reaper.

Obed Hussey built a reaper about the same time that Cyrus did. The two men often held contests to see whose machine was better. Many farmers watched these contests. Some liked McCormick's reaper; others preferred Hussey's machine. Hussey tried to sell his harvesting machine in the East where farms were small and the land was hilly and rocky. The machine was not very successful, so he sold his business.

Cyrus lost interest in the reaper for a while and went into the iron business. After a few years this business failed, so he again began to work with his reaper. In 1840 he sold two reapers. He sold six in 1842, twenty-nine in 1843, and in 1844 he built and sold fifty machines. He charged about one hundred dollars for each one.

In 1844 Cyrus McCormick took a trip that changed his life. He traveled through the western states of Ohio, Michigan, Illinois, and Indiana. There he saw wide, level fields where farmers were able to grow more grain than they could harvest. He decided to leave his home in Virginia and go west. Cyrus chose the small town of Chicago for the home of the manufacturing plant for his reapers.

Cyrus soon had a good business. He used interchangeable parts in his reapers. If a part on a reaper broke, the owner could order that part by mail. Usually he could replace the part himself.

Mr. McCormick hired salesmen to visit farmers and try to get them to buy reapers. He tried to make it easy to pay for the machines. He would let a farmer pay part of the price of the reaper and get the machine. The farmer paid the rest after the harvest was finished and the crop sold. Mr. McCormick also sent men out during the winter to help farmers get their machines ready for the next year.

By 1858 Cyrus McCormick was a millionaire. He did not like to spend money if he did not have to, but he was not a selfish man. He gave a great deal of money to D. L. Moody and others to help in the Lord's work.

As years went by, other people improved the reaper. Then farmers could plant and harvest even larger amounts of grain. Because there was so much grain, prices went down. Many more people could now afford to buy wheat flour and bread.

Some people think that the reaper helped the northern armies win the Civil War. Without the reaper, thousands of northern soldiers would have had to leave the army each summer to go home to help harvest the grain. Without the reaper, the North would not have had a good supply of food for their men and horses.

Today American farmers produce more grain than we can use. This grain is harvested by machines that are "descendants" of Cyrus McCormick's reaper.

Alexander Graham Bell
(1847-1922)

"Mr. Watson—come here—I want to see you."

Thomas Watson raced up the stairs, shouting, "I can hear you! I can hear the words!"

For a long time, Alexander Graham Bell and his helper had been trying to find a way to send the sound of a voice through a wire. At last they were successful.

Alexander Graham Bell was born in Scotland in 1847. As he grew up, he wished to do something great. For a while he thought of being a concert pianist or even a scientist. But after he finished school,

Alexander became a speech teacher like his father and grandfather.

Teaching deaf children to talk was Alexander's special interest, so he studied everything he could find about sound and how sounds were made. After visiting scientists who worked with sounds, he experimented with his own ideas. The telegraph, which carried sounds through wires by electricity, greatly interested him.

Then tragedy struck the Bell family. Alexander's two brothers died of tuberculosis. His parents were afraid that Alexander might catch the disease, so in 1870 they decided to leave Scotland and go to Canada. They hoped the climate there would be better for Alexander.

Soon after the family arrived in North America, Alexander was invited to Boston, Massachusetts, to teach deaf children. He lived with the family of one of his students, a little boy named George Sanders.

The Sanders family let Alexander use their cellar as a workshop. At night he experimented with sending sounds through wires. Mabel Hubbard was another of Bell's students. Her father became interested in Alexander's experiments also. He and Mr. Sanders encouraged the young teacher to continue his work with sound.

Alexander was working with two ideas. One was a multiple telegraph, a machine to send several messages at the same time over one wire. The other idea was the telephone, a way to send the sound of a voice over wire.

While Alexander taught, he studied and worked hard. He asked Thomas Watson to help him with his experiments. Mr. Hubbard and Mr. Sanders became Alexander's partners. They provided the money he needed to carry out his experiments.

Months passed, and Alexander's experiments showed that his ideas were good. He became more and more interested in the telephone as well as in his attractive deaf student, Mabel. This did not please Mr. Hubbard. He wanted Alexander to work on the multiple telegraph instead of the telephone, and he did not want the young teacher to marry his daughter.

Alexander did not know what to do, so in despair he gave up all his work for six months. Finally Mr. Hubbard agreed that Alexander and Mabel could become engaged. Alexander was overjoyed! He returned to his work and soon applied for a patent on the telephone, which he received on March 7, 1876.

In 1876 the great Centennial Exhibition was held in Philadelphia to celebrate our nation's one hundredth birthday. Mr. Hubbard arranged for Alexander to display his telephone there. The judges chose Sunday, June 25, to examine the exhibits on sound. Dom Pedro II, the emperor of Brazil, visited the exhibition hall at the same time. It was very hot in the exhibition hall and the judges wanted to leave before they had even seen Mr. Bell's telephone. Dom Pedro had met Alexander a few days earlier when he had visited the school for the deaf. Now the emperor insisted that everyone visit Mr. Bell's exhibit. Of course, everyone respected the emperor's desire.

Alexander explained how his invention worked. Then he went to a far corner of the hall. He sang into the mouthpiece that was connected by wires to a receiver. First a judge and then the emperor pressed the receiver to his ear. How excited they were when they heard the sounds! "I hear, I hear!" shouted Dom Pedro. People at the exhibition cheered, for Mr. Bell's telephone was a success. The next year the Bell Telephone Company was started.

Throughout his life, Mr. Bell continued to help deaf children. He met Helen Keller when she was a young girl and gave advice to her parents about how to teach her. Helen Keller later dedicated her autobiography to Mr. Bell. She wrote, "He is never quite so happy as when he has a little deaf child in his arms."

Alexander Bell greatly contributed to American society by giving us the telephone. His efforts to help others led him to develop one of the most useful instruments used by mankind today.

Thomas Alva Edison
(1847-1931)

Thomas Alva Edison was probably the greatest inventor of all time. He patented about 1,100 ideas during his lifetime. Among his most useful inventions are the electric light, the phonograph, the mimeograph machine, and the cement mixer. He improved the telephone, the typewriter, the electric-powered train, and the motion picture camera and projector.

Thomas Edison was born on February 11, 1847, the youngest of seven children. His family called him Alva or Al. His mother had been a schoolteacher, but she could not answer all the questions that little Alva asked. The young boy liked to find out things by experiments. He even tried to hatch some eggs by sitting on them. His investigations often got him into trouble. Once he fell into a canal and almost drowned. Another time he set fire to his father's barn "just to see what it would do." His parents punished him many times, but they could not keep him from being curious.

The Edison family moved from Ohio to Port Huron, Michigan, when Alva was seven. He became sick with scarlet fever and could not start school until he was

eight. Alva did not get along very well at the school. After three months his mother decided she would teach him at home. He became a good reader and was able to find answers to many of his questions. He liked to experiment to see if the books he read were right.

In 1859 a railroad opened between Port Huron and Detroit. Twelve-year-old Alva got a job selling newspapers and candy to the passengers. He got on the train at seven o'clock each morning and reached Detroit about ten. Alva usually went to the public library in the city and read until it was time to return to Port Huron. He reached home about nine-thirty at night.

One day Alva was late with his papers. He ran and leaped to the steps of the departing train. The brakeman grabbed him by the ears and hauled him on board. From about that time, Alva gradually became deaf. Perhaps the scarlet fever had already affected his hearing. In later years Mr. Edison wrote about the experience: "I felt something snap inside my head. . . . I haven't heard a bird sing since I was twelve years old."

One day when Alva was fifteen, he sat waiting at a train station. The station master's three-year-old son toddled onto the track in front of a train. In a flash Alva snatched the child to safety. The grateful father rewarded young Edison by teaching him how to send and receive telegraph messages.

In a few months Alva was able to get a job as a telegraph operator. He practiced until he could receive and send messages very rapidly. He also experimented with the telegraph machine to find ways to improve it.

Alva did not get along well with people, and he often changed jobs. He worked in Ohio and Tennessee, and also went to New Orleans, Boston, and New York. He was paid well, but he often went without proper food and clothing. He spent most of his pay for books and the materials he needed for his experiments.

When Edison was twenty-two, he decided to spend more of his time on his inventions. His first patent was for a vote-counting machine. He tried to sell it to Congress in Washington. He explained that it could count the votes quickly and that no one would be able to change his mind and then change his vote. The congressmen said, "It is the last thing on earth that we want here. Take the thing away." Edison decided that he would not invent anything unless it was useful and people would want it. After a few years, Edison built a laboratory at Menlo Park, New Jersey. He spent

Thomas Edison in his laboratory

nearly all of his time working there. He often worked twenty hours a day without stopping. Then he slept two or three hours and went back to work. He expected his helpers to work as hard as he did. He planned to turn out "a minor invention every ten days and a big thing every six months or so."

Edison is probably most famous for his invention of the electric light bulb. He and his men worked on this invention over a period of about two years. They spent much of this time trying to find the right material for the filament of the bulb. The filament, or wire, had to give off light when electricity passed through it. It also had to last for a long time without burning up.

At first Edison experimented with wires of various sizes and shapes, but none worked. The inventor wondered if carbon would work. One day Edison made a loop of cotton thread and placed it in a metal mold. He heated the mold for five hours. The thread turned black but did not burn up. It had been changed to carbon. This was what the inventor wanted, but the loop broke when he tried to take it out of the mold.

For three weeks Edison tried thread after thread. Finally, on October 19, 1879, he succeeded in placing the thread in a bulb. It made a good light! The bulb worked for forty hours before it burned

out. When news of this invention spread, Edison was called the "Wizard of Menlo Park."

However, cotton thread broke too easily. Something better was needed, so Edison and his workers tried every material they could think of. For example, they tried fishing line, tissue paper, coconut fiber, cork, and onion skin. They even tried leather, macaroni, and hairs from the beard of one of Edison's friends!

The final answer lay close at hand through all of the trials. It was in the bamboo rim of a palm leaf fan. The bamboo fibers were just right for Edison's lamp.

But there were many kinds of bamboo. Which was the best? Edison sent men to many parts of the world to collect samples. In all, they collected and tested about six thousand pieces of bamboo. Finally the inventor settled on bamboo from a plantation in Japan. A few wagonloads each year were enough for the millions of filaments that Edison needed.

The light bulb was just the beginning. Now the inventor had to plan a way to wire houses and to provide electricity so that the bulbs could be used. He invented the screw-in socket, the light switch, an electric meter, and many other devices. He arranged to have all of these made. In just three years, his first electric lighting system was ready. In 1882 Edison turned the switch that gave electric lights to eighty-five customers in New York City.

The electric lighting system did not work well at first, but Edison and his men kept improving it. In just a few years every large city in the United States had lighting systems. Edison even went to London to help set one up there.

At first the cost of making a light bulb was $1.25, but Edison sold them for forty cents. Later he was able to make a bulb for only twenty-two cents, but he still charged forty cents. He sold millions of bulbs, so he made a great deal of money. He used part of it to pay for the materials and labor needed for other inventions.

Over the years Thomas Alva Edison received many honors and awards for his work. Henry Ford was a close friend of Edison's. Ford wanted to do something special on the fiftieth anniversary of the invention of the light bulb. He had the laboratory at Menlo Park moved to a huge

Edison's laboratory

Henry Ford and Thomas Edison

museum called Greenfield Village in Dearborn, Michigan. Thousands of people still visit this laboratory each year.

Edison died in 1931 at the age of eighty-four. He had spent his life inventing things that helped make the United States the greatest nation on earth.

George Washington Carver
(1860?-1943)

"Oh! My baby! My poor sick little baby." Mary, a young slave woman, held her child close and rocked back and forth. The baby coughed and choked.

Suddenly the door of the tiny hut burst open. Masked men stormed into the room. They seized the mother, the baby, and four-year-old Melissa. In a moment they were all gone into the night.

Susan Carver wept for the kidnapped woman. Mary had been the Carvers' only slave, and she had been like one of their family. In the morning Mr. Carver went to a neighbor. He offered him a horse and forty acres of land if he would find Mary and her children and bring them back. In a few days the man returned. He handed the Carvers a damp and dirty bundle. "It's all I got. I don't know if it's alive or dead."

It was the baby. Mrs. Carver warmed the tiny body and tried to feed him some

sweetened milk. The child choked and cried a weak cry. "He's alive," said Moses Carver. "Keep the horse. You did the best you could."

Everyone called the baby "Carver's George." The sickly child grew slowly. He could not walk until he was almost three, and he stammered as he talked in his high, squeaky voice. The spindly boy stayed close to Mrs. Carver and learned to do household chores. He swept, washed dishes, and helped cook. He learned to wash and iron clothes and also taught himself to knit and crochet. He could sew as well as any woman.

George was very interested in nature. He was especially interested in plants. He spent hours in the woods and fields looking at ferns, flowers, grass, and grain. He even talked to the plants! He seemed to know what each plant needed in order to grow. Neighbors asked his help when their plants were not healthy. They called him the plant doctor.

George wanted to go to school. Mrs. Carver found an old spelling book and taught him the sounds of the letters. With this knowledge George learned to read. Mr. Carver taught him how to write his name and how to do a little arithmetic, but this did not satisfy George. He wanted to learn more and begged to go to school. Mr. Carver had to refuse because the school there did not allow black students to attend.

In 1875 George discovered a school for black children in a town about eight miles from his home. Although only about fifteen years old, George decided that he had to leave home and go there. Early one morning he set out with an extra shirt, a lunch, and a tearful good-by from the Carvers.

The next fifteen years were hard for the young man. He went from school to school, learning everything the teachers could teach him. He supported himself in any way he could. He cooked, cleaned, worked for a blacksmith, and worked in a greenhouse. He often earned his living by doing laundry. He farmed, picked fruit, and harvested grain. With his earnings he bought food and books so that he could go to school.

During these years George was always learning. He learned to paint beautiful pictures and to play the piano and the accordion. He discovered that he could sing. Above all, he learned about plants.

George entered a college in Iowa and graduated near the top of his class in 1894. The college gave him a job in the plant testing station. Soon George was well known for his work with plant diseases.

One day George received a letter from a man who had started a school in Alabama for black people. Booker T. Washington asked Mr. Carver to come to teach at Tuskegee Institute. George knew that there he would have a chance to help the Negroes in the South learn to become better farmers. Even though the slaves had

been freed, they knew little about farming. As slaves they had worked for a master. Now they needed help in learning how to farm.

Mr. Carver believed that God wanted him to go down to Alabama to teach black people. In just a few weeks, he packed all his belongings, told his friends good-by, and went to his new work.

The school at Tuskegee was new, but it did not have good buildings or much money. However, it did have students who wanted to learn and teachers who wanted to teach.

Mr. Carver loved his students, and he loved to teach. Together with his students, he built a laboratory where they tested many kinds of soil and fertilizer. He taught them what plants needed in order to grow properly. He taught them how to use their materials wisely and how to work hard.

Mr. Carver realized that many people could not come to school, so he decided to take a school to them. He hitched a mule to a wagon and traveled from town to town. He talked to anyone who would listen. He showed them how to improve their farms. He taught them to be clean and to eat good food.

The main crop of the South at that time was still cotton. Around 1892 disaster

struck when the boll weevil came into Texas from Mexico. These tiny insects destroyed the cotton crops. Slowly the weevils spread from state to state. The farmers did not know what to do.

Mr. Carver suggested that the farmers stop trying to grow cotton. He advised them to grow crops such as peanuts and sweet potatoes. Many farmers followed his advice, but then they asked him who would buy their crops. Mr. Carver realized that he must find a market for these products.

Mr. Carver believed that God helped him to find many uses for peanuts. He made peanut butter, peanut flour, and peanut candy. He pressed peanuts to get oil. He used the oil to produce margarine, soap, shaving cream, and cosmetics. From the red inside skins he made paper, and he used peanut shells in wallboard and imitation marble.

In a few years, factories were making products from peanuts. The farmers were able to sell all they could grow.

Mr. Carver kept on experimenting and found over three hundred uses for the peanut. He also discovered over one hundred ways to use the sweet potato. After experimenting with clay, Mr. Carver made beautiful dyes. He rediscovered a lovely blue dye that had been lost for years. His fame spread through this country and over the whole world.

George Carver did not take money for his discoveries. He did not think he deserved pay for the ability that God had given him. Thomas Edison offered Mr. Carver $100,000 a year to come to work for him, but George refused. He believed that God had called him to work at Tuskegee, even though his salary there was only $1,500 a year.

George Washington Carver worked at Tuskegee for more than forty years. He went there to help the black Americans, but he did much more than that. He made discoveries that have helped people everywhere.

The Wright Brothers

Wilbur (1867-1912)
Orville (1871-1948)

"Hello, boys! I've brought you something. Catch it!" Pastor Wright tossed the little gift to his sons. Orville and Wilbur reached for the toy. Instead of coming towards them, it rose to the ceiling. It fluttered for a moment and then fell to the floor. The boys eagerly examined their new toy. It was a small helicopter made of cork, paper, and bamboo. Its power came from twisted rubber bands. The boys played with the helicopter until it wore out.

Eleven-year-old Wilbur decided to build a helicopter. He wanted to make one bigger and better than the toy. Orville was only seven, but he helped. The boys were surprised that their bigger models did not fly well. If they were much bigger than the first toy, they did not fly at all. The boys wondered why. This was the beginning of their interest in flying machines.

All five children in the Wright family enjoyed reading. Wilbur and Orville especially liked to read the encyclopedia. Mr. and Mrs. Wright encouraged their children to think about what they read. They let them experiment to see if their ideas were right. When Orville was nine, he showed signs of becoming an inventor. He wrote in a letter to his father, "The other day I took a machine can and filled it with water then I put it on the stove. I waited a little while and the water came squirting out of the top about a foot."

The Wright family moved several times before finally settling in Dayton, Ohio. Pastor Wright received only a small salary, so the children had to earn their own spending money. One of Wilbur's jobs was folding a weekly church paper. He invented a machine to help him do this work. Orville liked to make kites. He sold them to his friends, who could not make them as well as he could.

When Wilbur and Orville were young men, they became interested in bicycles. The new safety bicycles with both wheels the same size were just becoming popular. Many adults as well as children rode them.

The two brothers decided to go into the bicycle business. At first they sold and repaired bicycles. Later they also built them. They sold their most popular model, the Wright Special, for eighteen dollars.

Wilbur and Orville never lost their interest in learning. They read everything they could find about scientific discoveries.

One day the young men read about a man who had built a glider, a flying machine without an engine. They read all they could about gliders and talked about how they could make one. They made a big kite and experimented with it. They watched birds fly. Finally they built a glider of their own.

The brothers knew that they needed a hill and good winds to fly their glider.

Orville and Wilbur Wright

They wrote to the Weather Bureau and found out that Kitty Hawk, North Carolina, met both of these requirements. In 1900 they took their glider there and tried it. It would stay in the air only a few seconds before it landed on the sand.

The next year the Wrights went back to Kitty Hawk to try a new and larger glider. It worked better, but the men thought of even more ways to improve it.

The brothers kept on experimenting. They built a wind tunnel, which was a long, narrow box with a fan that blew air through it. Then they built miniature gliders and tried them out in the box. They learned many things about flying in the wind from their experiments. Their third glider worked much better than the others.

Now Wilbur and Orville were ready to try building a flying machine with an engine. They had to build an engine that was powerful but not heavy. Then they had to design and make a propeller. It took them almost a year to get their airplane finished. They called it the *Flyer*.

The brothers went back to Kitty Hawk. On December 17, 1903, they were ready. Orville got into the machine and started

An early flight of the Wright Brothers' plane

the engine. Wilbur ran along at the side, holding one wing. The *Flyer* moved along the ground for about forty feet and then rose into the air.

How excited the brothers were! Their machine was flying! Five seconds! Ten seconds! Then the *Flyer* suddenly darted towards the ground. It landed in the sand about 120 feet from where it had taken off. It had been in the air twelve seconds.

The men made three more flights that day. The final one lasted fifty-nine seconds and covered 852 feet.

The Wrights went back to Dayton. They told the newspapers what they had done, but only a few carried the news about their flight. People did not believe it was possible to fly.

The brothers kept on building planes. They tried them out in a big pasture about eight miles from Dayton. Their flights became longer. In October, 1905, they flew over twenty-four miles in thirty-eight minutes and three seconds. But still the newspapers did not print their story.

The Wrights wrote to Washington and offered to build an airplane for the Army. They promised that their plane could fly at the amazing speed of forty miles an hour. In 1908 the government officials were finally convinced that an airplane could be useful. They paid the Wrights $25,000 for the first Army plane.

At last the accounts of the flying machine were widely published. People began to believe that flying was really possible. The Wrights formed a company to build and sell planes. They were successful, but Wilbur died in 1912 of typhoid fever. Orville did not want to continue the business, so he sold it in 1915.

Wilbur and Orville Wright were pioneers. They prepared the way for others to build and fly much better airplanes than they had produced. The brothers had read, thought, experimented, and worked. They had tried, failed, and tried again and again. Finally they had succeeded. We honor them as the inventors of the airplane.

Things to know

1. Match the following men with their accomplishments.

    ____ 1. Henry Ford   a. Invented the revolver

    ____ 2. Joseph Jenks   b. Received the first patent in this country

    ____ 3. Eli Whitney   c. Used the assembly line

    ____ 4. Walter Hunt   d. Invented the safety pin

    ____ 5. Samuel Colt   e. Thought of interchangeable parts

2. Explain mass production in your own words. What two ideas made mass production possible?

3. How did the use of interchangeable parts improve the products that were made?

Things to talk about

1. What are some small, simple inventions that you use each day?

2. What is something you wish someone would invent?

3. Do you think you could invent something? Why or why not?

4. Why do most people apply for a patent on their inventions?

5. How did the use of interchangeable parts lower the cost of manufactured goods?

6. How does the use of interchangeable parts make it easier to repair a product?

7. Have you ever worked on an assembly line to make things or to do a job at school, church, or home? If so, explain how it worked.

8. It has been said that the wheel is the greatest invention of all time. Do you agree? Why or why not?

Things to do

1. List what you think are the ten greatest inventions. Compare your list with those of your classmates.

2. Visit a factory to see how an assembly line works.

3. Find out what these men invented: Thomas Jefferson, Samuel F. B. Morse, Elias Howe, and C. L. Sholes.

4. Find out when the following were invented: typewriter, radio, television, automobile, calculator, and computer.

Cyrus McCormick Review

1. How did Cyrus McCormick's father help him to become an inventor?

2. Why was Cyrus McCormick's failure in the iron business really a help to him?

3. Do you think Chicago was a good choice for a place to manufacture harvesting machines? Why or why not?

4. In what ways did Mr. McCormick get farmers to buy his harvesters?

5. How did the reaper change the eating habits of the people of the United States?

6. How did Mr. McCormick serve the Lord?

7. How did the reaper help the North during the Civil War?

Alexander Graham Bell Review

1. Why did Alexander Graham Bell come to America?

2. Name some people who helped Mr. Bell in his work with the telephone. How did each one help?

3. Why is Helen Keller famous?

4. What were the first words spoken over a telephone?

Thomas Edison Review

1. List some inventions of Thomas Alva Edison.

2. List some character traits of Mr. Edison that helped bring about his success as an inventor.

3. Why do you think Alva did not get along very well with other people?

4. How did Henry Ford honor Mr. Edison on the fiftieth anniversary of the invention of the light bulb?

George Washington Carver Review

1. What happened to George Washington Carver when he was a baby?

2. What was George's attitude about learning?

3. What special talents did George have? What special problems did he have?

4. Why did Mr. Carver leave a good job in Iowa to go to teach in Alabama?

5. Why was Mr. Carver interested in experimenting with the peanut?

6. Do you think Mr. Carver was right when he decided he would not take money for his discoveries? Why or why not?

Wilbur and Orville Wright Review

1. What was Wilbur and Orville's attitude about learning?

2. Do you think that being poor was a disadvantage to the Wright brothers? Why or why not?

3. What are some "keys to character" that are illustrated in the Wright brothers' lives?

4. What is the main difference between a glider and an airplane?

5. How many years ago did the United States Army buy its first airplane?

CHAPTER 14

AMERICANS: PEOPLE FROM MANY LANDS

When the colony of Virginia was begun in 1607, there were about 600,000 Indians in the land that is now the United States. The Indians were **native** Americans. A native of a country is a person who was born in that country. The colonists were people from other lands. They were **immigrants.** An immigrant is a person who leaves one country and makes his home in another country.

Many of the immigrants who came to America were from Europe. The map on the next page shows many of the countries from which these immigrants came.

Taking a Census

Every ten years the government of the United States takes a count of the people in this country. This is called taking a **census.** Besides counting the people, the census takers try to find out what country each family has come from. They also collect other facts about the citizens of the United States.

The first census was taken in 1790. This was about the time our country adopted the Constitution and elected George Washington as the first president. At that time there were about 4 million people in the United States. About 3 million of these people were from families that had come from the British Isles (see the map below). Some people in the country were blacks who had been brought here from Africa.

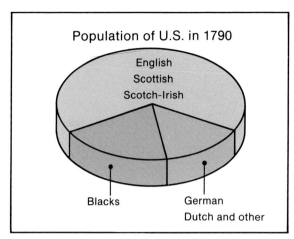

Population of U.S. in 1790

English
Scottish
Scotch-Irish

Blacks

German
Dutch and other

Most of the other people were from Germany, the Netherlands, France, or Switzerland.

For the next fifty years, families from these same European countries continued to trickle into the United

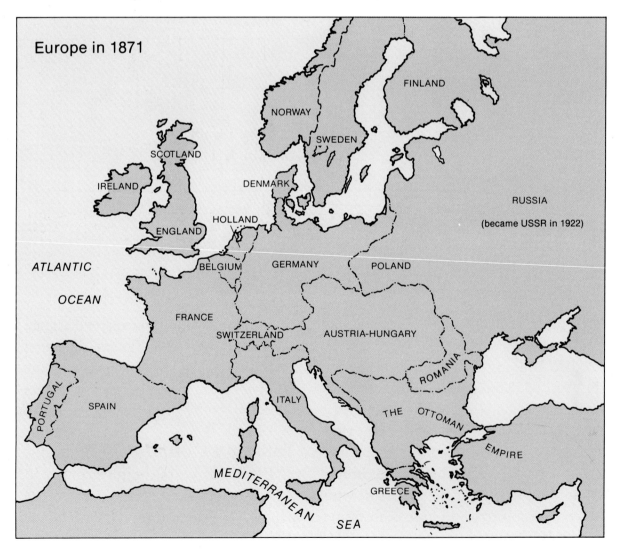

Europe in 1871

Immigration into the United States

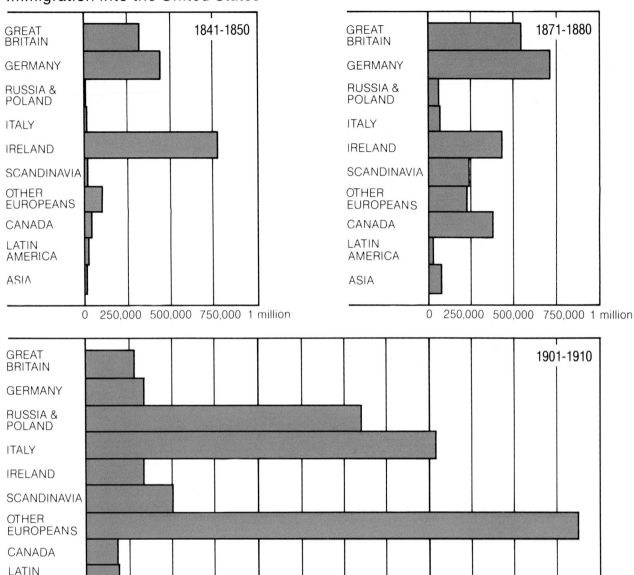

States. Then events turned the trickle into a flood.

Reasons for Immigration

The most important crop in Ireland was the potato. It was the main food of every family. In 1845 a disease struck the potato crop. For three years there was almost no harvest. A million people died of starvation or disease. Many others left Ireland. Most of them came to the United States. After the potato famine was over, Irish people continued to come to this country. By 1870, more than 2 million had come to the United States.

At about the same time, Germany, France, Finland, and the **Scandinavian** countries were also having troubles.

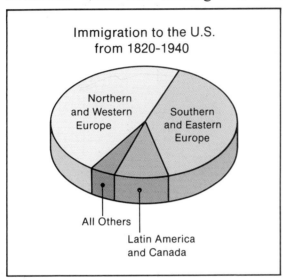

Immigration to the U.S. from 1820-1940

Northern and Western Europe

Southern and Eastern Europe

All Others

Latin America and Canada

Harvests there were also poor, and people went hungry. Besides, many citizens of these countries were not happy with their governments. Some countries did not allow religious freedom. Large numbers of families left their homelands to escape these hardships. Like the Irish, most of these people came to the United States.

During the years that followed the Civil War, families from northern and western Europe continued to come to the United States. Some Chinese and Japanese families came to California.

Then things began to change in Europe. The governments in northern and western Europe gave their people more freedoms. But trouble continued in southern and eastern Europe. People by the millions came to America from Austria-Hungary, Poland, Russia, Italy, and other countries.

New York City in 1942 and an immigrant family at Ellis Island

The Immigrants

Most of these people who came to the United States were very poor. They could not speak English. Many did not have relatives or friends here. If they worked hard, they could usually earn enough money to buy food and have a place to live. Many worked twelve hours a day, six days a week. Young children often worked as many hours as the adults. Often a family of six or eight persons lived in one room.

Immigrant families from the same country often settled near one another. They spoke their native language to each other. They started their own newspapers. They kept the holidays of their old countries. The grocery stores had their special foods. A settlement of this kind was nicknamed something like Little Italy, Little Warsaw, or Chinatown. Often these were parts of larger cities such as New York, Boston, and Philadelphia.

Even though life in America was hard for the immigrant families, few returned to their native lands. They believed that the freedoms in the United States were worth the difficulties they faced. They were especially thrilled that

Immigrant children saluting the flag

their children could get a free education here. Many of these parents had not been to school themselves and wanted their children to learn all they could.

Jewish Immigrants

Among the immigrants from eastern Europe were great numbers of Jews. Many people hated the Jews because of their religion. Russia was the home of more Jews than any other European country. Often the Russian government encouraged people to attack the Jews. The police stood by while mobs attacked Jewish neighborhoods, killing people and burning homes and businesses. Stories of freedom and riches in America caused many Jews to want to come here. Sometimes a whole village would come to America. These people called the United States the "Golden Land."

God had chosen the Jewish people for a special purpose. He wanted them to be a witness of His power and love to the rest of the world. He planned that Jesus, the Messiah or Saviour, would be born of a Jewish mother.

In Genesis 12:2-3, we find a wonderful promise that God made to Abraham, who was the "father of the Jews": "And I will make of thee a great nation, and I will bless thee, and make thy name great; and thou shalt be a blessing: And I will bless them that bless thee, and curse them that curseth thee: and in thee shall all families of the earth be blessed."

God also warned the Jews that He would punish them if they would not keep His commandments. They did not listen to His warning, and they disobeyed Him many times. The Bible tells us that they even worshiped idols. They would not accept Jesus as their Messiah. The punishment God had promised came upon them.

The Jews have been persecuted for hundreds of years. They have been treated more kindly in the United States than they have been in other countries. Perhaps this is part of the reason that God has blessed this nation so greatly.

Roman Catholic Immigrants

Many immigrants from Europe believed in the Roman Catholic religion. This religion is different from biblical Christianity in several ways (see the chart below). There is little stress on reading the Bible in Roman Catholic churches. So most Catholics do not know what the Bible really says about how to be saved. Only those who trust in the Lord Jesus alone as their Saviour will have their sins forgiven and go to heaven when they die.

The Statue of Liberty

One of the first things the immigrants saw when they entered New York Harbor was the Statue of Liberty.

The Statue of Liberty on Liberty Island

The Bible vs. Roman Catholicism

Biblical Christianity	Roman Catholicism
1. Salvation is by repentance and faith in Christ alone.	1. Salvation is by faith *and* works. To a Catholic, good works would include such things as baptism, church membership, and confession of sins to a priest.
2. The Bible is the final authority in matters of right and wrong.	2. Scripture *and* tradition (man's interpretation of Scripture) are the authority for Roman Catholics. Since 1870 the words of the pope have also been considered equal to the Bible.
3. Because they are saints of God, all Christians can come directly to Him in prayer.	3. Church members do not come to God directly. They confess their sins to a priest and often pray to Mary or other saints (men and women declared to be saints by the church). Church members believe that saints are in a better position to get prayer answered for them.

Her first title was "Liberty Enlightening the World." Now she is usually called the Statue of Liberty.

France gave the Statue of Liberty to the United States on July 4, 1886. It was a symbol of friendship between the two countries. It represents the liberty that citizens in free countries enjoy.

The Statue of Liberty

The Statue being repaired

The Journey Across the Atlantic

Most immigrants traveled to America the cheapest way possible. Many came in "steerage," which means that they were crowded into small rooms in the lowest parts of the ship. Steerage was kept for passengers who paid the lowest fares. (As late as 1910, a steerage ticket cost only ten to fifteen dollars.) Those traveling this way found no privacy and little comfort. Bunks were stacked so close together that often a person could not even sit up in bed. The ceilings of some steerage cabins were so low that only short people could stand up straight. Air did not flow well through the steerage area, and the smell was terrible—especially if someone had been seasick. Lice and sickness spread quickly in the close quarters. But immigrants endured the poor conditions. They knew that in three weeks or less they would arrive in the land of their hopes and dreams.

Ellis Island

An official entrance to America was opened in 1892 on Ellis Island in New York Harbor. For many years a stream of immigrants flowed steadily through this great center. All day long the newcomers with their bags and bundles passed through the pipe-lined pens in the "Gate to America." Over 16 million immigrants went through Ellis Island during the years it was open—between five and ten thousand people each day.

When a person arrived at Ellis Island, a large colored tag was tied on his clothes. The color identified what country's ship the person had traveled on. The immigrants were put into groups of thirty and taken to Registry Hall.

First, officials watched the immigrants walk up the long stairway. If they could not make the climb or puffed

Ellis Island

from the effort, officials labeled them for further health checks. Anyone over two years of age had to walk so that the health officers could see if he had a limp.

Doctors watched for special health problems. For example, if a doctor

thought that a person had a heart problem, he made a giant chalk *H* on his coat. They used other letters, too. The most dreaded letter label was *X*. This stood for mental problems and usually meant that the immigrant would be sent back. Those who had letters marked on them were given closer medical checks. If they could be helped, they were sent to the hospital there on the island.

After the health checks, the immigrants faced more questions from an officer: "What kind of work do you do? Can you read and write? Have you ever been in prison? How much money do you have? Where are you going? Do you have a job waiting for you there?"

Less than one-sixth of the immigrants were held back for closer checks or hearings. Immigrants who were held could stay on the island for four days to solve their problems. They could send telegrams to friends or relatives asking for help. Very few of the immigrants were rejected at Ellis Island.

By the late 1800s, some people in the United States became alarmed because of the millions of immigrants who were coming to this country. Northern cities were crowded with people who needed work. Employers sometimes took jobs away from workers born in this country and gave them to the immigrants, who were willing to take less pay. Of course, this caused trouble.

After a while, the government of the United States made laws to limit the number of foreign people coming into this country. By 1930 the great flood of immigrants was over. Most of the families that have come to the United States since then have been from Mexico or Puerto Rico. Others have also come from Vietnam and other parts of Asia.

Some Real Immigrant Families

The following pages contain true stories of some immigrant families. Many other American families—perhaps even your own—have stories similar to these.

The Maghans' Story

Kay Carswell was a tomboy. She like nothing better than to play with her brothers. Since she had eight brothers and sisters, there was always someone to play with.

Kay liked to play war because she had a real sword to use. The sword had grown dull and rusty over the years, but in her mind Kay could see her grandfather, Sir Robert Carswell, fighting for his king, George III. Carefully hung on the wall of Kay's home was the bayonet that had also belonged to Sir Robert. A bayonet is a knife that fits over the end of a rifle.

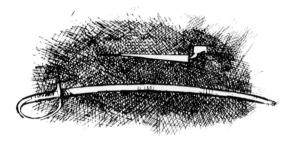

This bayonet was very sharp and not safe for the children to touch. The sword and bayonet were very special to the Carswell family because they were the only belongings of Sir Robert that his family in America still had.

Sir Robert had been born in Ireland. Ireland was a poor country back then, and it was hard to get a job there. The land was held by rich men who charged high fees to their renters. The land plots were very small, and the soil was not good for growing crops. The land had been farmed for centuries and was wearing out.

When Robert was old enough, he joined the British army. Since Ireland was a part of the British empire, Robert was a British soldier even though he was Irish. He fought in the wars against Napoleon of France in the early 1800s. He fought so well that the king of England honored him by making him a knight, giving him the title of Sir Robert Carswell. When Robert returned from the war, he became a farmer.

But things did not go well. In the 1820s the crops did poorly and a famine came. Potatoes were the main crop of the Irish. They were easy to grow and good to eat. Even though this famine was not as bad as the one in the 1840s, which you read about earlier, it scared Sir Robert. How would he ever earn enough money to afford a wife and family if the famines continued?

Also, there were religious problems in Ireland. Roman Catholics and Protestants did not get along well. In the north of Ireland, the Protestants had power. They made laws against the Catholics. They feared that if the Catholics gained control, Protestants would have to become Catholics. In the south of Ireland there were many more Catholics. The few Protestants in the area feared the "Papists," as the Catholics in Ireland were often called.

Sir Robert was a Protestant. He left Ireland and went to nearby Scotland. Because of his military record, he was able to get a job in Glasgow. He saved money and made a plan. People were going to North America. Things would be better there. He married a Scottish

girl and saved more money. Soon they would join others going to North America.

The cheapest fare to North America was also the shortest distance across the Atlantic. This was the route from Liverpool, England, to Montreal, Canada. There were already many Scottish and Irish people in Canada and the United States. Robert and his wife bought tickets and made the trip to America. Since no steamships were used on the oceans yet, it took them more than six weeks to make the trip by sailing ship to Montreal.

When Robert, his wife, and two children arrived in Canada, they found it crowded. So Robert went further west to Glasgow Station, Ontario, near Ottawa. There he and his family settled. When they got to their homestead claim, the family had each other, a basin of flour and fifty cents to their name. Their first home was really more a shack than a house. Their son John grew up, married, and had nine children of his own. One was a little girl named Kay.

Kay went to school in Winnipeg, Canada, became a schoolteacher, and taught in a country one-room school in Saskatchewan. During a vacation she went to a Methodist church picnic. Some young soldiers from a visiting World War I unit were at the picnic wearing their snappy tan uniforms. One of the soldiers was a tall, good-looking, soft-spoken young man from central Minnesota. His name was Albert

Maghan. He met Kay and soon wrote her father to ask permission to "court," or date her. Later Kay and Albert were married.

Kay went back to the United States with Albert. They lived on a farm in central Minnesota. They lived for a time at Sawbill Landing in northern Minnesota. Kay became an American citizen while Franklin Roosevelt was president. She and Albert raised a daughter and a son. Although it took many years for her family to reach the United States, Kay Carswell Maghan is happy that she is an American and that her children, Kathryn and Earl, are American citizens.

The Kvsvick's Story

There she was! The Lady with the Lamp! John Kvsvick had been searching the horizon for hours for a glimpse of the Statue of Liberty. Now he could see her gleaming in the sunshine. He had reached America at last. What an adventure for the nineteen-year-old Norwegian!

John's traveling papers were in order, so it did not take long to be checked at Ellis Island. He found his way to the railroad station and boarded a train for Minnesota. His brother Henry already lived there, so he helped John find work.

In Minnesota John lived and worked on a large farm. He earned fifteen dollars a month and was able to save almost all his money. After four years he decided to return to Norway to find a wife. He married Jennie Thomsen, and they had three children.

Jennie Thomsen in Norway

By 1900 John was becoming unhappy with his life in Norway. He could not earn enough money to take care of his family in the way he wished. Besides, his church did not preach God's Word as he thought it should be preached. John remembered the opportunities in America and decided to go back.

Sadly John Kvsvick told his little family good-by. "I will send money for you to come as soon as I can," he promised.

Back to Minnesota John went. This time he worked in a lumber camp. Eleven hours of hard work each day kept him from being too lonely. He earned thirteen cents an hour. In a few years he saved enough money to pay for his family to join him.

Jennie and the children went by ship to England and then to Quebec, Canada. They rode a train and a canal boat to New York. Another train took them to Minnesota, but the trip took a day longer than they had expected. That caused a problem.

John did not know what to do. His boss had given him only one day off from work to meet his family and get them settled, but no family came.

Jennie did not know what to do. She and the children got off the train, but no one met them. Jennie prayed for God's help. They were all tired and hungry. They could not understand what the people were saying. Clouds of huge mosquitoes swarmed about them. How they missed their home and friends in beautiful Norway!

At last the family decided to go to a hotel for the night. Early the next morning, Jennie found a man in a barbershop who could speak Swedish. They understood each other well enough for her to tell him her problem. He took Jennie to the lumber company office, where she was told in what part of the camp John was working.

Mrs. Kvsvick started looking for her husband. She searched among trees and piles of logs. She grew tired and frightened, but she kept on. About noon she found him on top of a pile of lumber. Tears came to her eyes as she called out to him. Soon the family was all together.

The Kvsvicks borrowed money to build a one-room house. After a while

they bought a cow. When other children were born, they added more rooms to their home.

John and his brother Henry decided to change their last name so that it would sound American. Their father's name was Jacob, so they chose to be called Jacobsen (Jacob's son). John was still not satisfied. "Jack is a nickname for Jacob," he thought. "I will change Jacobsen to Jackson. That is a real American name."

The Jacksons always worked hard. Jennie taught her girls how to sew, knit, and do beautiful embroidery. The family enjoyed good music and good books. They loved beauty in nature and in their home. The parents encouraged their children to go to college.

John and Jennie Jackson visited Norway two times, but they never wanted to stay there. They did not forget their old ways, but they had become real Americans.

Above: The Kvsvick family and the house that John built in America **Right:** The Kvsvick family in 1918

The Sabbadinis' Story

Signor Guiseppi Sabbadini was a sausage maker in Cortino, Italy. In the winter many families butchered a cow or pig, and Guiseppi was able to earn enough money to support his wife and six children. But in the summer things were different. People did not butcher in hot weather because the meat would spoil, so Signor Sabbadini could not make sausage. Often he could not find work of any kind. Then his family went without proper food and other things they needed.

The Sabbadinis were Roman Catholics. One daughter, Maria, decided to serve the church by becoming a nun. She left her family and entered a convent. The leaders of this convent said that she could never see her family again. After a few months, however, Maria became sick. Signor and Signora Sabbadini begged to see her, but the mother superior refused. Maria's sickness grew worse, and soon she died. The Sabbadinis were displeased because they had not been able to see her.

The Sabbadinis heard many stories about America. They heard that life was easy there. They heard that everyone could become rich if he wanted to. Even the poor people had plenty of food. The stories sounded too good to be true.

Young David Sabbadini had a problem. He was the oldest son, and he thought he should help the family. His father had taught him to make sausage, but it was hard to find a job as a sausage maker. He often thought about going to America, but he hated to leave his family. What should he do?

In 1910 David made his decision, and in a few weeks he was in New York. (The officials there spelled his name David Sabbadino, and David did not correct them.) The seventeen-year-old found out that the stories he had heard *were* too good to be true. Life was not easy in America, especially for immigrants who could not speak English. But David was willing to work. He cooked in a boarding house, worked in a mine, and helped build houses. He worked his way to California and back. He learned to speak German and Spanish as well as English.

David did not forget his family in Italy. He sent them money whenever he could. After several years, David Sabbadino started a small grocery store in Flint, Michigan. The Italian families in his neighborhood were pleased that he sold special spices and sauces that were used in Italian food. His

David Sabbadino's parents in Italy

homemade Italian sausage was popular in Detroit, Bay City, and other Michigan cities.

David married Madeline Buckarna, a young lady from Lebanon. David and Madeline had two children, Delores and Joseph. Mr. Sabbadino took his children to the Roman Catholic church a few times, but he did not really trust that religion.

Later Joseph accepted Christ as Saviour and became a Christian. Joseph asked his father to read the Bible. Mr. Sabbadino realized that he was a sinner. He learned that he did not need a priest to pray for him. He learned that he could pray in Jesus' name and that God would hear him and forgive his sins. Both David and Madeline asked the Lord Jesus to be their Saviour.

David Sabbadino and his family never became rich. They never became famous. But they did become a fine American family who loved their country and their Lord.

The Maszkos' Story

"You must go to America, Janos. If you don't, you will have to go back into the army. You know there is going to be a war soon. Oh, Janos, I could not bear it if you were killed. Our little Johann needs his father. And I need you too, my husband." Janos Maszko tried to comfort his weeping wife, but his own heart was heavy, for he knew her words were true.

The year was 1912. Janos and Mary Maszko lived in Liebnitz, Austria-Hungary. (That city is now Lubica, Czechoslovakia.) Janos had already spent three years in the army, but he had not liked army life. The officers were very stern, and the pay was only three cents a day. Janos had to learn how to use a machine gun. This gun had just been invented, and the young soldier shuddered when he thought of the killing that it would cause.

There was little freedom in Austria-Hungary, and the citizens did not have a chance to improve their lives. The poor people especially faced many hardships and troubles. Janos did not think that his homeland was worth fighting for.

The young couple made careful plans. Mary knew that she could support herself and Johann. She was a hunchback, but she was well educated and did beautiful sewing. Janos would go to America and get a good job. He would send for his family as soon as he earned enough money.

Two years passed before Mary and Johann came to America. How happy the little family was to be together again. They lived near Philadelphia, Pennsylvania, in a neighborhood that was mostly Polish and Hungarian. Little Johann never forgot the drooping mustaches and the long pipes of the Hungarian men.

All the families in the neighborhood were poor and ate simple meals. No one ate dessert except at Christmas and

Easter. Once a week Mary made bread. She blessed it by cutting a cross on the bottom of each loaf. Young Johann liked this bread toasted over the coals in the stove and spread with garlic-flavored lard. He liked to help make sauerkraut. His job was to tramp in the barrel of shredded cabbage as the spices were added.

Every immigrant family in the area had a story. Otillige Konshak often told what happened to her at Ellis Island when she came with her family to join her father.

When Otillige was a small child in Poland, she had many painful boils on her neck. The doctor did not treat them properly, and they left deep, ugly scars. Later the family came to America. The first doctor at Ellis Island who examined the girl told her mother, "I think your daughter is healthy, but I'm sure that the next doctor will say she must go back because of those scars."

Frau Konshak quickly thought of a plan. "Pull your shawl up around your neck, Tillie. Don't look up when the doctor speaks to you. Perhaps he won't look at you very closely."

Tillie lagged behind the other eight children of the family. Her heart thumped within her as she approached

The Konshak family (Tillie is in the second row.)

the impatient doctor. She looked at the floor as her mother had told her. The plan worked just as they had hoped. The doctor just glanced at her and let her pass. Happily, the whole family went together to meet their father.

The Konshaks and the Maszkos lived in different neighborhoods, but eventually these two immigrant families joined when Johann married Tillie's daughter, Evelyn. Together these two made a new family, an American family. They taught their children about their European heritage, but encouraged them to become good American citizens.

Johann Maszko with his parents and younger brother

Communists in Russia

The Isaaks' Story

Lichtfelde was a small village in western Siberia. Most of the people in the village belonged to a church group called the Mennonites. Their families had come from Germany many years before, and they spoke both Russian and German. The Mennonites had their own church and school. They set up the government for their village.

Most of the families in Lichtfelde were good workers, and they had prosperous farms and businesses. Then trouble came. In 1918 a civil war broke out in Russia, and the Communist army conquered all of Siberia. In 1920 the crops failed because of a lack of rain. Then disease spread throughout the land. Millions of Russian people were killed by the Communists or died of starvation or disease.

By 1928 life in Lichtfelde and other Mennonite villages was very hard. The Communists had closed the Mennonite school. The pastors, Sunday school superintendents, and choir directors had their citizenship taken away from them. They had to pay fines each month, and no store was allowed to sell them anything. The Communists required that the Mennonite farmers sell their crops for very low prices, and then they demanded such high taxes that no one could pay them. Some people were sent to prison and never returned.

The Isaaks were one of the best Christian families in Lichtfelde. Grandfather Isaak had been the mayor of the village. His sons, John, Peter, and Henry, were prospering in their work. The daughters had their homes and families. But the Isaaks knew that they could not be happy living in a Communist country. They also knew that people caught trying to leave the Soviet Union were killed or sent to prison.

John Isaak moved 4,500 miles to eastern Siberia. He hoped to find a way to escape into China and then to America. In January, 1929, Henry believed that the Lord wanted him to take his family to join his brother John.

Preparations for the trip began. Henry sold the farm and all of the family goods. The family prepared food and clothing for the long trip. They sewed their money into their clothes so that it would not be lost or stolen.

When other families heard what Henry and his family were planning, they decided to go with them. Soon a group of fifty-nine persons was ready to leave. Among them were Grandfather and Grandmother Isaak, Peter, three sisters, and all of their families.

The families traveled nine days by train to reach eastern Siberia. They did not take baths or change their clothes during the trip. Once there, they joined John and his family who were planning to escape to China.

The most dangerous part of the escape from the Communists was crossing the mile-wide Amur River, the border between the Soviet Union and China. The water was frozen, but the ice was rough. Guards patrolled the Soviet side.

Each of the ten families bought a horse and sleigh from families in John's village. Most of the snow had melted, but they were able to reach the river. The men wrapped the women and children in blankets. They packed them into the sleighs with straw and tied them in so that they would not be thrown out as they dashed across the ice.

By eleven o'clock at night everything was ready. Quietly the sleighs moved toward the river. Two gunshots rang out, but no one appeared. The frightened people prayed as they continued. Soon their guide called out, "My dear

people, all is clear. Turn right, toward the other side." Henry's horse turned, reared up on its hind feet, and then started running. The others followed!

By midnight, every family had reached the other side. God had helped them to escape!

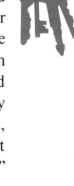

The families endured many hardships before they finally reached California, but they trusted God for protection. Psalm 5:2-3 encouraged the Isaaks when troubles came: "Hearken unto the voice of my cry, my King, and my God: for unto thee will I pray. My voice shalt thou hear in the morning, O Lord; in the morning will I direct my prayer unto thee, and will look up."

The Isaak family in China after escaping from the Soviet Union

The Isaak family settled in America

Things to know

1. A person who is born in a country is a _____ of that country.

2. A person who leaves one country and makes his home in another country is called an _____.

3. A count of the people living in a country is called a _____.

4. The government of the United States takes a census every _____ years.

5. The failure of the _____ crop in Ireland caused many people to leave that country between 1845 and 1850.

6. The Scandinavian countries are _____, _____, and _____.

7. God's special people are the _____.

8. Many immigrants from southern and eastern Europe believed in the _____ religion.

9. The Statue of Liberty was given to our country by _____.

10. The Statue of Liberty is on Liberty Island in _____ Harbor.

Things to talk about

1. People came to the United States from many countries and spoke many languages. Why do you think English is the main language of our country?

2. Why is it wrong to dislike a person because he looks different or speaks differently from you?

3. Do you think it was good for immigrants from one country to settle near each other when they came to America? How did it help them? Could it have hurt some of them? How?

4. Often people from different countries or different parts of the country make fun of each other and call each other names. Why do they do this? Is it right to do this?

5. Many immigrants love America more than people who were born here. Why do you think this is true?

Things to do

1. Ask your parents where your family's ancestors lived before they came to America. Try to find out when and why they came to this country.

2. Look in a recipe book to find foods from different countries. Help your mother make a special food to bring to share with your class.

3. Make an "Around the World" recipe book.

4. Label and color a map of Europe.

5. Color a map of Asia. Label Japan, China, and India.

6. Take a census in your school to find out how many students are in each class. Make a bar graph to show your information.

7. Write a story about an immigrant family coming to the United States.

8. Draw a picture of the Statue of Liberty.

9. Look through a phone book to find common names and unusual names. Make a list of each.

10. You can sometimes tell where a family is from by their name. Try to find out from which countries people with these names came:

    names ending in *sen,* such as Jensen or Andersen

    names beginning with *Mc* or *Mac,* such as McKee or MacDonald

    names beginning with *O,* such as O'Connor or O'Malley

    names beginning with *Van,* such as Van Gelderen or Vanderjagt

A Prosperous Nation

FIVE

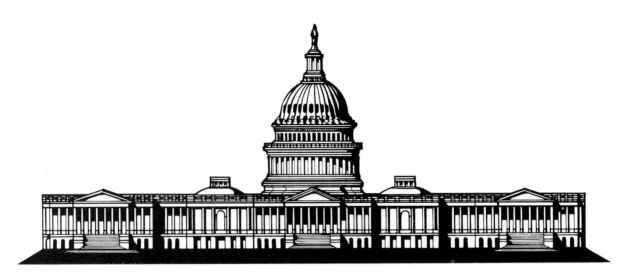

The Fifty-Star Flag When Alaska and Hawaii were added to the Union, a new flag had to be designed. On July 4, 1960, the fifty-star flag was first raised. This flag has five rows of six stars and four rows of five stars, making a total of fifty stars.

Although the American flag has changed many times over more than two hundred years, it has always been a much-loved symbol of a great nation.

UNIT GOALS

■ I will be able to name the major wars America fought in during our century and locate Germany, France, Japan, Korea, and Vietnam on maps.

■ I will be able to tell how Douglas MacArthur helped my nation and what made him a good leader.

■ I will be able to tell someone why communism is a threat to the American way of life.

■ I will be able to explain what the phrase "civil rights" means and will be able to list at least three of the many civil rights Americans have.

■ I will be able to give examples of two people who worked hard to help make America great.

TIME LINE

CHAPTER 15

THE BEGINNING OF OUR CENTURY

By 1900 the United States had become a large and prosperous nation. People from all over the world had come to fill the land that stretched from sea to sea. They built their homes and businesses here. Many Americans worked to make their nation great.

The year 1900 was a special year. Across America people celebrated the start of a new century. This new century was the twentieth century, the same one in which you live today. People in 1900 hoped that this would be America's greatest hundred years yet.

The World Goes to War

Before 1900 the United States had little to do with Europe. Americans were too busy. They had a large land to explore and settle. They traded with Europe, but they tried to stay out of Europe's problems.

In 1914 the countries of Europe went to war. This war was called the "Great War," but now it is usually called World War I. In this war the countries of Europe chose sides. Germany, Austria-Hungary, the Ottoman Empire, and Bulgaria were on one side. They were called the Central Powers. Fighting against them were the Allies—Great Britain, France, and Russia. Look on the map below to find the countries on each side.

Germany had the strongest army in Europe, while Great Britain had the strongest navy. Neither side, however, could quickly defeat the other. The war began in August, 1914, and by fall the enemies faced each other across a battle line. This line changed little during the rest of the war. The soldiers dug trenches along the battle line. Night and

Allied soldiers in one of their many trenches

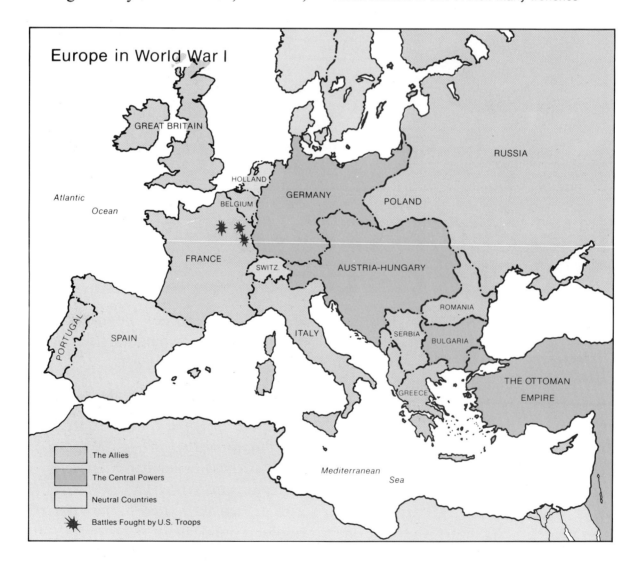

Europe in World War I

GREAT BRITAIN

RUSSIA

HOLLAND

Atlantic
Ocean

BELGIUM

GERMANY

POLAND

FRANCE

SWITZ.

AUSTRIA-HUNGARY

PORTUGAL

SPAIN

ITALY

ROMANIA

SERBIA

BULGARIA

GREECE

THE OTTOMAN
EMPIRE

Mediterranean   Sea

The Allies

The Central Powers

Neutral Countries

Battles Fought by U.S. Troops

The sinking of ships like the *Lusitania* (shown below) by the Germans angered many Americans.

day they lived in the trenches. When the officers gave the order to go "over the top," the soldiers attacked. Often the armies gained only a few yards in their attacks, while many soldiers were killed or injured.

In this slow, costly fighting it seemed that neither side would win. Both sides wanted help from America. They thought that America's money, goods, and men would help them win. But most Americans did not want to be drawn into the war. The United States declared herself **neutral;** that is, she did not want to take sides in the war. Even so, most of America's trade went to help the Allies.

The Germans became angry. To stop trade with the Allies, their submarines began sinking both Allied and American ships sailing to England and France. Many Americans lost their lives in these attacks. By 1917 the Americans were ready to fight to bring back peace. President Woodrow Wilson asked Congress to declare war on Germany. Congress voted to go to war.

The United States Enters the War

The United States was unprepared to fight when it entered the war. It had only a small army and few military weapons, but the American people quickly rallied to the war effort. Men between the ages of twenty-one and thirty registered for the **draft.** From this

President Woodrow Wilson prepares to draw for the draft lottery.

group the army selected its soldiers and began training them. Sometimes the new soldiers had to train with pieces of wood and broomsticks instead of real guns because there were not enough guns to go around.

American soldiers left on ships to go "Over There," meaning to Europe. Once there, they gave new life to the weary Allied troops, who had been fighting the Central Powers for three years. The fresh American soldiers helped turn the tide against the enemy.

An American Hero

Although the Americans were not trained for war, some became heroes. One hero was Sergeant Alvin York. Alvin had grown up in Tennessee, where as a young man he had accepted Christ as Saviour. As he grew up, he spent much time shooting guns and became an excellent marksman. When the United States went to war, he had a big decision to make. He did not think it was right to kill people, but he knew that he should serve his country. After

Sergeant Alvin C. York

spending two days and a night in prayer, he decided that God wanted him to go.

God had a special mission in Europe for York. One day he found himself alone, facing a German battalion.

York and the captured Germans

Bravely, he fought the Germans until they surrendered. For his skill and bravery, York received many medals and was made sergeant. Even though men praised him, Sergeant Alvin York said: "I am a witness to the fact that God did help me out of that hard battle for the bushes were shot off all around me and I never got a scrach. So you can see that God will be with you if you will only trust Him, and I say He did save me."

Everybody Works for Victory

As soldiers left for Europe, Americans at home stood behind them. Factories began making weapons and supplies. Factory workers worked

Many women helped the war effort by working in factories.

many hours to keep the "boys" in the army supplied. Many young factory workers had left their jobs to join the army. To replace them, more and more women took jobs in factories.

Women who did not work in factories also helped. Ladies' groups knitted warm clothing and made bandages for the soldiers. Some women joined the army as nurses and traveled to Europe to nurse wounded soldiers back to health.

All over the nation families supported the war effort. They had "meatless meals" to save food for the soldiers. They grew "victory gardens" to provide their own vegetables so that more food could go to Europe. Children and wives wrote letters to the lonely soldiers across the sea. They also collected scrap metal and other materials that could be used by factories to make weapons and supplies for the war.

American help, both in Europe and at home, brought victory for the Allies. They began to drive back the Central Powers. As one defeat followed another, the Germans agreed to lay down their weapons. On November 11, 1918, both sides signed the **armistice.** This agreement brought an end to World War I. Today we celebrate November 11 as Veterans Day. On this day we honor all American soldiers who have fought for their country.

Crowds in Paris celebrate the Armistice.

The Dazzling Decade

The ten years following World War I was a time of excitement and progress in America. Americans were glad that the war was over and the "boys" were home from Europe. They wanted to enjoy life. Business boomed, and many people became wealthy. The years from 1920 to 1929 are often called the "Roaring Twenties."

Many new inventions made life in America easier and more enjoyable. As more people put electricity in their homes, they added new home appliances. Women used washing

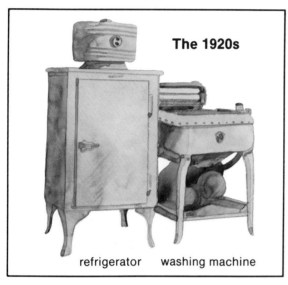

The 1920s

refrigerator   washing machine

machines and refrigerators for the first time.

A radio sat in nearly every living room. This invention brought news, information, sports, and comedy programs to families across America. These programs helped Americans feel closer to each other. People from the east coast to the west coast tuned in the same programs and heard what was happening in the whole country.

Americans also grew closer through travel. The Model T Ford and other cars became more and more common in the 1920s. Families used their cars to visit places in the nation that they might not have been able to reach before. With more people traveling, businessmen began new businesses. They put up gas stations to service

automobiles. They built tourist cabins for travelers to stay in overnight. Later motor hotels, or motels, were a familiar sight on American roadsides. To give travelers quick meal stops, some wise businessmen opened up the first drive-in restaurants.

The Twenties was also the decade of the first motion picture films. These early films were silent films. Instead of hearing the actors speak, moviegoers read their words on the screen. Many Americans looked on movie stars as heroes. They believed that fame made a person happy.

Other famous Americans of this decade were sports heroes. Attending ball games was a popular pastime for many people. Baseball was a special favorite, and baseball greats like Babe Ruth brought cheering fans out to

Babe Ruth

games. Basketball and football also grew more popular, and people flocked to college games. Another sport that drew much attention was boxing. The whole country waited to hear the results of the fights of champions like Jack Dempsey.

This was also a decade of fads and crazes. College men held goldfish-swallowing contests. Some crazes involved endurance contests, such as flagpole sitting. Alvin "Shipwreck" Kelly sat on a flagpole for a record twenty-three days and seven hours.

Up in the Air

Aviation was one craze of the Twenties that is today a major industry. The army had trained many pilots during World War I. After the war these men returned home, taking with them their love of flying. As stunt flyers, they showed Americans what airplanes could do.

A biplane in 1910

The first attempt to go from a plane to a moving car

The stunt flyers traveled across America, putting on air shows for crowds of people. The onlookers gazed in wonder as the pilots performed their daring stunts. The planes might fly straight up, roll over quickly, and fly upside down for a while. They could roll over and over and make loops and dips. Some planes carried acrobats. These daring men and women walked on the airplane's wings, did handstands, and even hung by their boots while in the air. One couple stood on the plane's wings and played tennis. Other acrobats sipped soda and read newspapers while hanging upside down.

A very famous early stunt flyer was Lincoln Beachey. Whenever he went up to do his stunts, he wore a suit, a high white collar, and a diamond stickpin in his tie. He always wore a golf cap—backwards. Once, while over a crowd, Beachey flung his arms open wide to greet the cheering people as he worked the plane's steering lever with his knees. He then began a display of stunts that kept the crowd on the edge of their seats. Beachey had one especially thrilling trick. His plane had only a ten-gallon gas tank, strapped to one wing.

Beachey would fly as high as he could until he ran out of gas. Then he turned his plane into a glider. He relied on gravity, wind currents, and his skill to bring him back down to the airstrip.

Beachey always looked for new ways to show off flying to Americans. He chose Niagara Falls on the U.S.-Canada border for one stunt. A crowd of 150,000 people came to watch him. He flew over the edge of the falls and dove abruptly into its mists. He flew downstream for a while, and then up, high over the cliffs on the Canadian side. There he landed, wet but safe, to the cheers of admiring fans.

Lincoln Beachey and his fellow stunt flyers did more than just thrill crowds. They introduced many Americans to flying. For a fee onlookers could join the pilot for a short ride. At first the price was high,

Women's Suffrage

"The right of the citizens of the United States to vote shall not be denied or abridged by the United States or by any state on account of sex."
Amendment 19 (1920)

Suffrage *is the right or privilege of voting. It is a right that most Americans today think they have always had, yet there was a time when many adults were not allowed to vote.*

In the early days of some colonies, voting was limited to free white adult males who owned land. These men also had to be church members and be able to read. More men gained the right to vote during the Civil War. People believed that if a man risked his life fighting for his country, he surely should be able to vote for its leaders. In 1868 black men gained suffrage rights.

But what about women's suffrage? Many women in the early 1800s did not believe that the right to vote was necessary for women. Later in the century, however, many people began to support women's suffrage. Women received more schooling than they had earlier. During the Civil War more women took jobs outside their homes as men went to war. Also, women worked together to fight the evils of slavery and drinking. Their success in these areas encouraged them to apply their efforts to other areas, especially voting.

Women who worked for the right to vote were often called suffragettes. *One of the early suffragettes was Elizabeth Cady Stanton. Elizabeth had studied law, but she could not become a lawyer because women were not allowed to practice law. In 1848 she began to work for women's rights as well as working against slavery and drinking. Elizabeth encouraged other women to support women's suffrage. One of these women was Susan B. Anthony.*

Susan B. Anthony

but as more pilots looked for riders, the price dropped to as low as $1.50. From these first rides in early, open airplanes, Americans built the best system of air travel in the world.

Troubles in the Twenties

The dazzling decade also had its dark side. With so many amusements and so much money, people often began to live only for their own pleasure. They cheated and disobeyed laws to get the things they wanted. They wanted the goods of the world and did not care about other people or God. The desire for wealth and fame made many of them miserable. Yet at this time, as always, God gave people an opportunity to repent. Many pastors and evangelists preached against the sin

*Miss Anthony led the suffragettes for the next fifty years. She often organized her followers to gather thousands of signatures on **petitions**. These petitions asked for laws to help women, including a law giving them the right to vote. The petitions were then sent to elected offficials to let them know how people felt. Many people did not like Miss Anthony's work. Sometimes they even threw garbage at her when she gave speeches about women's suffrage. But some people admired her courage. Ladies who favored the vote were often called "Suzy-B's."*

Susan B. Anthony believed that Congress should pass an amendment to the Constitution giving women the right to vote. When she died in 1906, her hope had not been fulfilled. But fourteen years after her death, the "Anthony Amendment" was passed. The twenty-nine words she had spent fifty years working for became the Nineteenth Amendment.

In more recent years, women who demand more rights are called feminists. The feminists have tried to add women's rights amendments to our Constitution. (One amendment has been called the Equal Rights Amendment, or ERA.) Although such amendments may sound quite harmless, they could greatly change women's lives, This is because the wording in these amendments might not limit the government's power in women's lives. Feminists often tell people that a women's rights amendment will guarantee equal pay for men and women in the same job. However, there are already laws in our land that make this guarantee. Unlike the earlier women's rights movement, today's women's rights movement is slowly trying to erase the God-given differences between men and women.

Today women have not only the right but also the responsibility to vote. All voters, men and women, should learn about the problems facing our country. They should also learn about the men and women running for office so that they will know who can best solve the problems. The right to vote has been a hard-won privilege in our nation. Every voter should guard his or her privilege carefully.

in America. They urged people to confess their sins and ask Christ to save them. They prayed that America would turn to God, who alone brings true joy and happiness.

Decade of Despair

The Twenties was a dazzling decade, but the brightness ended abruptly in 1929. That year began a period of hard times in America that lasted for the next ten years. This period is called the **Great Depression.**

The prosperity of the 1920s was not as strong as it seemed. Many people had spent more than they had earned. They had bought new cars and household appliances on **credit.** That means that they paid for only a part of the item and then made monthly payments called **installments.** As more and more people bought on credit, businesses received less money in payment. Banks lent money to people who were not able to pay it back. Sometimes banks lent out so much money that they had little left. Customers who wanted to withdraw their money were not always able to.

As the 1920s came to an end, Americans began to buy fewer new goods. Factories had produced more than the people could buy. Soon the factory owners started producing less. They laid off workers because the demand for new products was so low. These laid-off workers were unable to pay their installment bills for things they had bought. Across the country, businesses who needed these payments began to suffer. The banks ran out of money as people began to withdraw their savings to pay bills. Finally, in October of 1929, the stock market in New York City crashed. So many people had sold their stocks that there were no buyers. Prices dropped very low. The crash was the final blow to a weak **economy.**

Living in the Depression

American life changed greatly in the 1930s. Many people lost their jobs, while wealthy and poor alike lost their money and possessions. Nearly everyone was poor. Families lived on small amounts of food and wore old clothing.

Farmers suffered greatly. Many lost the farms that they had borrowed money to purchase and improve. Because of **droughts,** some farmers could not produce anything to sell. The droughts turned many areas of the United States into "dustbowls."

Farmers suffered many hardships during the Depression.

Unemployed men wait at a soup kitchen for a meal.

Without good crops the farmers were unable to repay their loans.

In the cities people worked for pennies a week. Men who had once been wealthy sold apples on street corners. Many people who had no work stood in long lines at soup kitchens to get a small portion of soup or bread. Some people who could not accept the loss of their riches killed themselves. They had trusted in their material goods to bring them happiness and peace.

In 1932 Americans elected Franklin Delano Roosevelt (often known as FDR) as their president. He promised the people relief from the depression. He called his plan the **New Deal**.

The New Deal included many programs to make new jobs. The government paid people to do these jobs. Under the New Deal, millions of Americans went back to work. They built roads, bridges, and dams throughout the country. Besides giving people jobs, these projects improved transportation and flood control. One program was called the Civilian Conservation Corps, also known as the CCC. Workers for the CCC planned and built many of our national parks. They took care of the land and opened wilderness areas to the public.

Recovery finally came to America. Although the New Deal helped America, it also caused problems. With the New Deal the government became more involved in people's private lives and businesses. Over the years this has meant more government control and interference. Another problem with the New Deal was that the government had to go into debt to pay for all the programs. This debt has kept growing, and today it is one of America's biggest problems.

"Wanted by the FBI"

When most of us hear the letters "FBI," we think of secret agents, wanted men, and fingerprints. These are some of the things for which the FBI, or Federal Bureau of Investigation, has become famous over the years.

"Wanted men" are the lawbreakers that the FBI is seeking to find. You may have seen posters of wanted men or women on a bulletin board in the post office. On the posters are "mug shots" (small pictures of the faces) and descriptions of the persons and their crimes. Most of the wanted men are considered dangerous. Almost all of them are eventually arrested. One-third of the suspects are found through tips given by helpful citizens.

FBI agents have a reputation for always getting their man. The more than 7,500 special agents who work for the FBI are well-trained men. They support the local police by investigating cases in which any federal laws have been broken or in which anything (a criminal, a victim, or stolen items) may have crossed state lines.

The Identification Division of the FBI has fingerprints for more than 94 million people. Not all of the people for whom the FBI has fingerprints are criminals. The Bureau also has fingerprints for certain government workers, as well as those of **aliens,** prisoners of war, and missing persons. Since each person has unique fingerprints, they are a positive means of identifying people. The FBI also has a file of footprints, although it is much smaller than the fingerprint file.

The FBI was formed in 1908 at the request of President Theodore Roosevelt. He said that it was needed to investigate cases of "land thieves" in the West and illegal practices of big businesses in the East. The Bureau grew in importance during World War I and World War II when it dealt with cases of spying and **sabotage.**

The FBI probably gained its greatest fame in the 1930s, when J. Edgar Hoover became its leader. The level of crime and violence had risen during the 1920s and 1930s. The public even seemed to accept violence and lawbreakers, especially those who broke the laws about

An FBI agent takes a suspect's fingerprints.

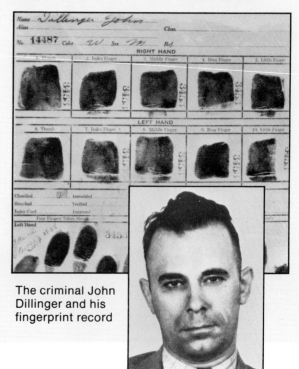

The criminal John Dillinger and his fingerprint record

J. Edgar Hoover

making and selling alcoholic beverages. (The manufacture and sale of alcoholic beverages was illegal in America from 1918 to 1933.)

In more recent years the FBI has also investigated cases involving civil rights. In these cases they have tried to be sure that citizens of all races are not deprived of any of the rights given them by the Constitution or by other laws. The Bureau has also worked to stop organized crime (crimes committed by large, well-organized groups). The FBI also investigates computer crimes.

Although the FBI has sometimes been criticized for its methods or its work, the Bureau continues to collect facts fairly and report them honestly. It upholds and protects the rights of Americans. Of course the FBI and local or state police do not catch all the criminals in the land. Even if people do wrong and are not caught, it does not make their wrongdoing right. Citizens should not tolerate wrongdoing and should help the police by reporting crime. Christian citizens especially should not break laws or cheat the government or others. Remember that "righteousness exalteth [builds up] a nation: but sin is a reproach [a shame] to any people" (Proverbs 14:34).

Problems in Europe

America was not the only country to suffer from the Depression. The whole world was affected. In Europe, power-hungry men used the troubled times to gain rule in their countries. Once in power they became **dictators,** leaders who had total control. Adolf Hitler became the dictator of Germany, and Benito Mussolini became Italy's dictator. Both men wanted to increase their power. They also wanted to do something to bring glory to their countries.

In 1936 Hitler and Mussolini made an agreement. They agreed to support each other in case of war. Together their countries were called the Axis Powers. The map below shows the Axis Powers. This agreement was the start of choosing sides for the Second World War. Hitler seemed eager to go to war.

The German-Italian Axis
1936

He wanted to prove to the world that Germans were better than any other people. He used the German army to take land from smaller, weaker nations around Germany. The people of Britain and France did not like Hitler's actions. However, they did not actively try to stop him. They remembered the horrors of World War I and wanted to avoid another war. They thought that if they let Hitler take a little territory, perhaps he would be satisfied and they would not have to go to war.

They were wrong about Hitler. His new lands did not satisfy him. He

The German army in Poland

wanted more. When Hitler invaded Poland on September 1, 1939, Britain and France declared war on Germany. This began the second great war of the century, World War II.

Things to know

1. The beginning of our century was the year _____.

2. A nation that does not take sides in a war is said to be a _____ country.

3. The agreement that brought an end to the shooting in World War I was called an _____ and was signed on _____, 19____.

4. The day that we honor all American soldiers who fought for their country in our nation's wars is called _____.

5. Another name for the "Dazzling Decade" from 1920 to 1929 is the "_____."

6. The period of the 1930s when people had to do without many things is called the _____.

7. The president during most of the 1930s was _____, and his program to give people relief was called the _____.

8. The two European leaders who became dictators were _____ of Italy and _____ of Germany.

Things to talk about

1. How many years are there in a decade? In what decade were you born? What decade are we living in now?

2. What are some ways in which ordinary American people helped to win World War I?

3. Why do we celebrate Veterans Day? What are some things people do to celebrate that day?

4. Why do you think people in the 1920s got involved in fads and crazes? What are some fads and crazes in this decade?

5. What are some evidences that some people in the 1920s lived only for their own pleasures and forgot God? What are some evidences that some people today are doing the same thing?

6. What is credit? What are some of the dangers of overusing it?

Things to do

1. Make a map of the European countries that fought in World War I. Color the Central Powers and the Allied Powers different colors. Label these countries.

2. Imagine that you are a nurse in a World War I hospital "Over There." Write a letter home to your family about the boys in the war and what you are doing to help them.

3. Make a list of things that American children today could do to help our government in a war. Make a list of ways American children could help save money.

4. Find out if there are any veterans attending your church. Write one of them a letter for Veterans Day and thank him for serving our country and for being willing to fight to protect our freedoms.

5. Make a list of things you could really do without to save your family money in a depression.

6. Make a list of questions about life during the Great Depression. Find someone who was working during the Depression, ask them the questions, and write down the answers.

CHAPTER 16

THE UNITED STATES IN WORLD WAR II

The Germans started World War II in 1939 by invading Poland. Their forces moved so quickly that people said they fought "lightning war." The Germans used this method successfully throughout the war. To weaken a country that they planned to invade, the German air force first dropped bombs on the larger cities. The bombing killed many people and filled the others with terror. Then tanks rolled in, followed by huge numbers of German troops marching in formation.

In the spring of 1940 the Germans attacked several European countries. They defeated Denmark in a day. Norway lasted about three weeks. Then in May the Germans invaded Belgium, the Netherlands, and France. Britain sent soldiers to help, but they could not hold back the strong German army.

British soldiers leaving Dunkirk

Deliverance from Dunkirk

The Germans moved quickly through northern Europe. They surprised a force of about 400,000 British and French soldiers in northern France. These soldiers were trapped near the city of Dunkirk on the English Channel (see map on page 220). With the Germans in front of them and the sea behind them, the armies had no place to go. The British sent ships across the English Channel to Dunkirk to rescue the soldiers. Before long they saw that these ships could not carry all of them. The British leaders asked the people of Britain for help. Soon hundreds of boats—barges, yachts, and even fishing boats—started across the Channel.

Earlier King George VI, the ruler of England, had called for a day of prayer for his nation. God answered. Winds and waves usually made crossing the Channel very rough. Small boats would have been sunk. But for nine days the Channel was almost smooth. Clouds and mists covered the harbor so that the German planes could not see where to drop their bombs. The British boats safely made trip after trip until most of the soldiers were rescued. Winston Churchill, the **prime minister** of Great Britain, called the rescue at Dunkirk a "miracle of deliverance."

Battle of Britain

Italy, led by Benito Mussolini, helped the Germans in the war against

France. In June of 1940 France surrendered. With this victory, Hitler and his allies controlled most of western Europe. Look at the map below to find the countries that they controlled. Britain stood alone against the German forces.

The Germans knew that the English were their strongest enemy. They began

London under attack by German bombers

to fly their planes across the English Channel to bomb cities in Britain. They destroyed many homes. British people in the cities sent their children to live with families in the countryside so that they would be safer. In the cities and countryside alike the British built bomb shelters underground. When sirens sounded, the people knew to go into the shelters for safety.

The Germans also tried to keep ships from bringing goods to British ports. They set up a blockade and sank many ships. In spite of these attacks, the British stayed strong. Many British were killed or wounded, but they did not give up. The Germans did not conquer Britain.

In June of 1941 Germany and its allies surprised almost everyone. They began a lightning attack on the Soviet Union and headed for Moscow, the capital city. But winter came early to the Soviet Union, and the Axis armies were trapped in that vast land. The Soviets began to fight back. Hitler's lightning attack failed, and the Germans spent many months and lost many soldiers in this country.

The United States Joins the Allies

Ever since the end of World War I, Americans had wanted to stay out of other countries' problems. They did not want to fight again, even if Europe was at war. Some Americans thought that there was no reason for their men to die in a European war. Others feared that America was unprepared and would be easily defeated. Even so, Americans did help the Allies in some ways. They sent food, weapons, and other manufactured goods to Europe.

American young men had to register for the draft.

At this time fighting was also going on in Asia. Japan had invaded China and controlled many islands in the Pacific. The Japanese were allied with the Germans and Italians. Together these countries were known as the Axis Powers.

On Sunday, December 7, 1941, the Japanese made a surprise attack on Pearl Harbor, a large American military base in Hawaii. America was stunned. The next day President Franklin D. Roosevelt asked Congress to declare war on Japan. Congress voted to go to war against all the Axis countries. Because so many countries were in the war, it came to be called World War II.

The Japanese attack on
Pearl Harbor

The Americans fought mostly in the Pacific, but they helped the Allies in other places, too. They fought in North Africa and Europe. The Americans played a big part in the great Allied invasion of France.

From D-Day to the End

By 1944 the Allies were strong enough to retake France. They hoped to defeat the Germans in France and push them back to Germany to end the war. The Allied commander, General Dwight D. Eisenhower, and his staff had planned for months. Almost 3 million men gathered in England. Everything they needed to invade France was collected there. They had thousands of trucks and tons of ammunition, food, and medical supplies.

The Allies decided to invade France at Normandy Beach. Find Normandy on the map on page 220. Finally, on June 6, 1944, everything was ready. The day of the planned invasion was called D-Day. Over 4,600 ships carried men and supplies to France. Many soldiers landed by parachute in France. Hundreds of planes flew over the French coast. The planes kept German troops away from the beaches and also bombed German supply factories. The fighting was very hard, but the Allies won that day and began their march across France. Their final goal was to reach Germany.

As the Allies marched and fought, they freed prisoners of war. They also came upon huge prison camps filled with starving people. These were

Allied forces landing on the beaches of Normandy

American soldiers using a flamethrower in Iwo Jima

concentration camps that the German leaders had built for anyone who disagreed with their ideas. Because Hitler especially hated the Jews, he ordered them arrested and put in the prison camps. Six million of them were murdered or starved to death.

By March of 1945, American troops reached the Rhine River, which separates France and Germany. By the next month the soldiers reached the Elbe River farther east. There they waited for the arrival of their Soviet allies, who had been fighting their way across Germany from the east. Once the war was over, the Soviets kept most of the lands they freed from German rule. Sadly, the people in these countries have since suffered under Communist rule.

Hitler killed himself at the end of April, 1945, and the weary Germans surrendered a few days later on May 7. That day was called V-E Day— Victory in Europe Day. Winning in Europe caused great rejoicing, but America and her allies knew that their fight was not over. They still had to defeat Japan.

The War in the Pacific

For many months after Pearl Harbor, the Japanese seemed to win everywhere they fought. Many islands and countries fell to the Japanese. They took many prisoners and forced them into large concentration camps. There the prisoners lived in terrible conditions, and many were tortured and killed.

World War II in the Pacific

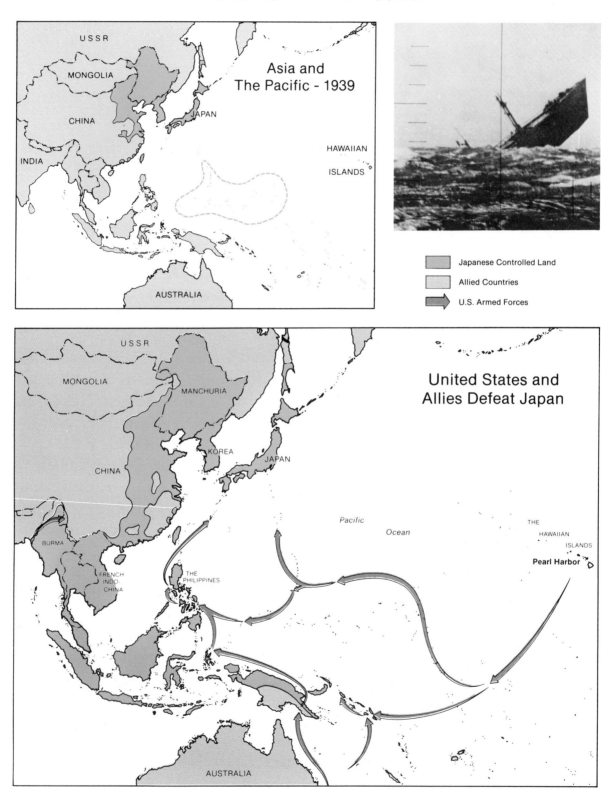

Asia and The Pacific - 1939

USSR
MONGOLIA
CHINA
JAPAN
INDIA
HAWAIIAN ISLANDS
AUSTRALIA

Japanese Controlled Land
Allied Countries
U.S. Armed Forces

United States and Allies Defeat Japan

USSR
MONGOLIA
MANCHURIA
KOREA
JAPAN
CHINA
BURMA
FRENCH INDO-CHINA
THE PHILIPPINES
Pacific Ocean
THE HAWAIIAN ISLANDS
Pearl Harbor
AUSTRALIA

Find Burma on the map on page 224. The United States had been using a little road across the mountains and jungles of this country to get supplies to the Chinese army, which was also fighting Japan. The Japanese conquered Burma and closed the road. With the road closed, brave American pilots flew supplies over the border to China. Their route took them "over the hump" of the Himalayas, the world's highest mountains.

In the Philippine Islands the Americans fought hard against the Japanese. In spite of a lack of supplies, they held them back for five months. The American troops had to eat mules and monkeys because they had no other food. At last they had no choice but to surrender. Their commander, General Douglas MacArthur, promised, "I shall return."

Look at the map on page 224 to find the islands that the Japanese controlled. The Americans knew that it would be hard to capture all of them. Instead, the United States followed a plan called "island hopping." They decided to retake only the most important islands, with the goal of reaching Tokyo, Japan's capital. The plan was successful. On each island they took, they built an air base. Each island brought U.S. forces closer to Japan. Each new air base allowed U.S. planes to fly closer to Japan and bring supplies to the forces that had to "hop" to the next island. They also provided fuel for the bombers. In World War II airplanes could not fly as far without refueling as they can today. The closer islands made it easier for Americans to bomb Japan's ports and factories.

By January of 1945, the Americans' island hopping landed them in the Philippines again. General MacArthur returned, just as he had promised. He came with 600 ships and 250,000 men.

General Douglas MacArthur returning to the Philippines

As he waded ashore, he said, "People of the Philippines, I have returned. . . . Rally to me." He had returned to free the islands and to rescue those in the prison camps. But while the Americans were gone, the Japanese had tortured and killed many soldiers and Christian missionaries in the islands.

As the Americans got closer and closer to Japan, the fighting became more fierce. It took twenty-five days to take the tiny island of Iwo Jima and three months to capture the island of

U.S. Marines raising the flag at Iwo Jima

Okinawa. During this fighting the Japanese made air raids on American

Aircraft Carriers: Eyes and Wings for the Navy

World War II brought changes and progress in air transportation. The aircraft carrier was very important in the Pacific during the war. It changed the way of fighting not only in this war, but also in future wars.

An aircraft carrier is a floating airport. It has hangars with spare parts for making repairs aboard ship. It carries fuel and ammunition for the planes. It also has living quarters for the crew.

Aircraft carriers are very useful because they can move easily from place to place. Our military air bases can be built only on lands owned by the United States or on lands rented or borrowed from other countries. These are not always good locations. Aircraft carriers can sail almost anywhere large ships can go. They can be moved quickly to a place of battle. They can be moved just as quickly out of danger.

Airplanes taking off from the aircraft carriers during World War II were the "eyes" of the fleet. They scouted the enemy and brought back information. The planes could also drop bombs on enemy lands, ships, or submarines. Bad weather conditions such as ice, rough seas, and fog were almost the only things that kept these planes down.

In 1910 Eugene Ely, an American aviator, flew the first plane off a ship. He used a wooden platform built over the ship's deck for a runway. The Navy did not want him to try his takeoff. They feared that the plane would land in the water—and Eugene Ely did not even know how to swim! But he did take off.

Landing on a ship was even harder. When Eugene Ely succeeded in taking off from a ship, he still had to land at a regular airstrip. The next year he landed a plane on a ship. He stopped the plane in only thirty feet by using an "arresting gear." This gear was made of large ropes stretched between sandbags. Modern aircraft carriers use the same idea to catch plane wheels, but they have better ways of doing it.

Today aircraft carriers are longer than three football fields and carry five thousand or more men. Each ship ships. *Kamikaze* pilots committed suicide by crashing planes loaded with explosives into American ships, hoping to sink them. They believed that dying for their emperor was the highest sacrifice they could make.

Victory in Japan

Harry Truman, who became president after Roosevelt died in 1945, had a big decision to make. American scientists had invented a new weapon—the atomic bomb. President Truman had to decide whether to use its terrible power against the Japanese. He knew that thousands of soldiers would be killed if American forces invaded Japan. The United States tried to get Japan to surrender. American planes dropped leaflets on Japan, telling the Japanese people that something terrible would happen if they did not surrender right away. The Japanese would not surrender, so President Truman decided that the atomic bomb must be used.

carries ninety to one hundred jet fighter planes. The wings on the planes fold upward so that they will take up less space when not in use. Huge elevators lower the planes from the deck to hangars below. Catapults, like huge slingshots, speed a plane from standing still to 161 miles per hour in less than 250 feet.

Nuclear aircraft carriers can go for thirteen years without refueling. Much of our military sea power rests on these aircraft carriers, the eyes and wings of the Navy.

On August 6, 1945, American airmen dropped the first atomic bomb on Hiroshima, Japan. The bomb killed or burned 180,000 people. Still the Japanese did not give up. On August 9 a second bomb was dropped on a giant Japanese naval base located at Nagasaki. The next day Japan asked for peace. On September 2, 1945, General Douglas MacArthur accepted the formal surrender on board the battleship *Missouri* in Tokyo Bay.

Happy Americans cheered in the streets as V-J (Victory in Japan) Day was celebrated across the nation. World War II was finally over, six years after it began.

How Americans Fought for Their Country

More than 15 million men and women joined the Armed Forces during World War II. The men got the nickname "G.I.'s" because their clothes were all "government issue."

Some women had served in the military in World War I, but many more served in World War II. Their duties included secretarial and medical work. They joined the WACS (Army), WAVES (Navy), SPARS (Coast Guard), and Marines. Other women helped the war effort by working outside their homes. Some of them took jobs left by the men who went to fight.

Americans were able to succeed because God gave them strength. They worked unusually hard and invented new methods to make things. The leader of the German air force had jeered, "The Americans can't build planes—only electric ice boxes and razor blades." But Americans built over 300,000 airplanes in five years. They also produced tanks, guns, ships, and many other war supplies. The American people showed that they were willing to do without household goods to help their country. They gave time and money. They gave their lives. They were proud to help free the world of evil men like Adolf Hitler.

The United Nations

After the war, the countries of the world joined together to try to keep the peace. Almost fifty nations met in San Francisco, California, to form a new organization, called the United Nations (U.N.). The U.N. has two main parts: the Security Council and the General Assembly. The Security Council has five member countries— the U.S., the USSR, Britain, France, and China. The Assembly has every country of the world as a member. The U.N. listens to problems between

The United Nations Building in New York

countries. The members try to solve the world's problems in this way.

The U.N. moved its headquarters to New York City, in buildings next to the East River. Although an organization to keep peace sounded like a good idea, in real life it has not worked very well. Some of the members are selfish; they do not do what is good for all the nations. People cannot depend on each other for peace in the world.

Christians who study the Bible know that there will never be peace in the world until Christ, the Prince of Peace, returns. However, a person can have peace in his heart if he lets the Lord rule his life.

Douglas MacArthur
(1880-1964)

Douglas heard the bugle sound. He ran to the parade ground on the Texas military post where his father was serving. He skidded to a stop and snapped to attention. His favorite event of the day—flag lowering—was about to begin. He loved to see Old Glory against the beautiful Texas sunset. His heart always beat faster when he saw the flag go up and down.

Douglas MacArthur's parents were his first teachers. Along with regular subjects, they taught him the importance of duty. He was told to do what was right, no matter what it might cost. "Always our country was to come first," he wrote of those days. There were "two things we must never do: never lie and never tattle." The only time he was to tattle was when another person had done something that was wrong before God.

Douglas was born in 1880 in Arkansas. He always considered himself a Virginian, though. His parents were away from that state only because his father was in military service. His grandfather was a judge whom Abraham Lincoln admired. Douglas's father, who became a general himself, fought in the Civil and Spanish-American wars and also in some Indian skirmishes. When his father went to capture Geronimo, the Apache Indian chief, young Douglas was with him.

His mother, Mary Hardy MacArthur, was a southern girl whose ancestors had lived at the early Jamestown settlement. His uncles from her side of the family had fought under Robert E. Lee and Stonewall Jackson. So it is not too surprising that young Douglas wanted to be a soldier when he grew up.

When Douglas was three, he and his two brothers, Arthur and Malcolm, all got the measles. His brother Malcolm died from the disease. Their mother was saddened and her sons became very devoted to her, seeking to please and honor her in any way they could. They wanted only to make her happy again. Years later, after his father and his brother Arthur died, Douglas wrote her letters and called and visited as often as he could. He tried to think of ways to follow the command of Scripture: "Honour thy father and mother . . . That it may be well with thee, and thou mayest live long on the earth" (Ephesians 6:2-3). Perhaps that is one of the reasons Douglas MacArthur lived to be eighty-four years of age.

Douglas was an average student in elementary school. Later he went to a military school near Fort Sam Houston in Texas. It was there that he began to change. "There came a desire to know, a seeking for the reason why, a zest to learn the truth, a search for fact."

Douglas wanted to go to West Point, the United States Military Academy. He studied hard for the entrance tests. The night before, he could not sleep. His mother said, "Doug, you'll win if you don't lose your nerve. . . . Be self-confident, self-reliant, and even if you don't make it, you will know that you have done your best. Now go to it." Douglas did and he got the highest marks. His careful preparation had led to success. "It was a lesson I never forgot. Preparedness is the key to success and victory."

MacArthur entered West Point in June, 1899. There he worked hard and played hard on the baseball and football teams. He became First Captain of the Corps, the highest position given to a student. He had the highest grade average any West Point cadet had made in twenty-five years. There were those in his class who were smarter, but Douglas knew what duties had to come first, and he did them. His determination to do what he believed to be right guided his actions throughout his life.

During World War I, MacArthur served his country in Europe. He was wounded

twice and received five stars for his bravery.

In 1919 MacArthur became the head of West Point Military Academy. He changed the course of study for the school and made all the **cadets** take part in sports. He wrote the motto that is still on the wall of the West Point gym: "Upon the fields of friendly strife are sown the seeds that upon other fields, on other days, will bear the fruits of victory."

MacArthur gained the rank of general in 1930, and was appointed chief of staff for the whole army. He was the youngest man ever to have that job.

During World War II, MacArthur served in the Pacific. At the end of the war, he became commander of the American troops sent to Japan as an **occupation force**. He helped Japan write a new constitution, made the nobles in Japan less important, and gave Japanese women the right to vote. He invited American missionaries to Japan to bring the gospel. The Japanese people grew to love Douglas MacArthur and thought he was a fair man.

On June 25, 1950, a Communist force from North Korea attacked South Korea. General MacArthur was named commander of the United Nations force that had the responsibility to defend South Korea.

MacArthur believed the Communists were a deadly enemy. He believed that if they were not defeated in Asia, they would continue to take over lands there. But he was not allowed to win the war in Korea. President Truman would not permit General MacArthur to bomb important bridges, supply centers, or electrical plants needed by the Communists. These bases were located in China, and the president feared that such attacks would lead to an even greater war. MacArthur did not approve of the way the war was being fought. The general complained to several men in Congress. Soon President Truman took his position of commander from him and called him home. The Korean War ended in 1953, but the Communists were not defeated.

In his retirement years, MacArthur was called to West Point to receive an award. There he gave one of the most famous speeches in American military history. He began the speech with these words: "Duty, honor, country: Those three hallowed words reverently dictate what you ought to be, what you can be, what you will be."

Things to talk about

1. How did God answer the prayers of the British people?

2. Do you think English parents did right when they sent their children away from home during World War II? Why?

3. Why did the Allies choose Normandy Beach as the attack spot?

4. Why was much of the fighting against Japan in World War II done from aircraft carriers?

5. What are some of the ways in which the planes in World War II differ from the planes of today?

6. Do you think President Truman was right to use the atomic bomb in the war?

7. Why did V-J Day mean so much to the average American family?

8. What are some things women did to help win the war?

9. Why does the United Nations not work very well?

Things to know

1. Four important Allied nations of World War II were _____, _____, _____, and _____.

2. Three important Axis nations of World War II were _____, _____, and _____.

3. The United States was attacked by Japan on _____, 19____, at _____, Hawaii.

4. The general who headed the war effort in Europe was General _____.

5. The big Allied invasion at Normandy was called _____ and took place on _____, 19____.

6. The general who was important in the war in the Pacific was _____. He promised the people of the Philippines, "_____," and later kept his promise.

7. The country on which the atomic bombs were dropped was _____.

8. The organization founded to try to keep future wars from breaking out was the _____.

Things to do

1. Color a set of maps of Europe. Show (1) the countries captured by Germany, (2) the Allied nations and the Axis nations, and (3) Europe as it is today.

2. Imagine that you were a boy or girl in London during the war. Write a letter to your grandparents who live in Edinburgh, Scotland, a city that was not bombed, and tell them about your daily life in London and your move to the country.

3. Imagine that you are on an aircraft carrier. Write a letter telling about a day on this floating town in World War II.

4. Make a list of what you would name things today and write a sentence telling why you chose the name for each. What would you name—
a new ship?
a new aircraft carrier?
a new kind of airplane?
a new space vehicle?
a new automobile?

5. Draw a line down the center of a piece of paper. Write "Camping trip" on one side and "Invasion trip" on the other. What would you carry on a camping trip? What things would a soldier have to carry for an invasion? Remember that you have to carry everything on your back!

Douglas MacArthur Review

1. Why did Douglas MacArthur become interested in the military at a young age?

2. How did MacArthur apply Ephesians 6:2-3 in his life? How old was he when he died?

3. What was MacArthur's attitude toward winning awards and prizes?

4. What did MacArthur learn was to be the key to success in getting into West Point and then in other areas of his life?

5. What three wars did MacArthur fight in during our century?

6. List some ways in which MacArthur helped the country of Japan after World War II.

7. Why was the war in Korea confusing to Americans?

8. What three words did MacArthur believe determined what you ought to be and what you can be?

CHAPTER 17

YEARS OF CHANGE AND CHALLENGE

World War II was over. American military forces came home, and life in the United States returned to normal. The years after the war were years of change. The United States added two new states to the Union. Scientists developed new products, such as television sets, calculators, and computers, for American homes and offices. They also improved many older inventions. Americans were busy making better cars, better airplanes, and better homes.

Americans also faced challenges in these years. Communism opposed the American way of life. The space race took Americans to the moon. Black Americans worked for equal treatment under the law. All these challenges have caused many changes in American life. In this chapter, you will read about both changes and challenges.

Lituya Bay in Alaska

Alaska

In 1741 a Danish sea captain sailing for the Russian navy sailed north along the coast of Asia. His ship, the St. Peter, reached an island near the southern coast of Alaska. Men in another ship, the St. Paul, explored along the coast of Alaska itself. They claimed all of that land for Russia.

A few Russian fur traders and missionaries moved into "Russian America." They built trading posts and churches. They traded with the Indians and the Eskimos. But Russia did not send families to start colonies on the American continent.

In 1867 Russia offered to sell Alaska to the United States. William Seward, the American secretary of state, gladly accepted the offer. He agreed to pay $7,200,000 for the great country. This price came to about two cents an acre.

Many Americans thought that the purchase was a great mistake. They called Alaska "Seward's Icebox" and "Seward's Folly." Since Andrew Johnson was president at the time, some called it "Johnson's Polar Bear Den." They did not know that the land was more than twice as big as Texas. They did not know that it was a land of great riches.

Gold was discovered in Alaska in 1896 near the border between Canada and Alaska. When news reached the United States, another gold rush began. Mining towns of tents and shacks sprang up almost overnight. A few men quickly made fortunes. Many more found no gold at all.

The men who returned to the United States told of the wild and beautiful land they had seen. They told of the treasures of timber, fish, and furs in Alaska.

As the years passed, businessmen went to Alaska. They started fish canning factories and logging camps. They discovered coal and oil, which are now Alaska's most important resources. Farmers settled on the rich coastal soil in southern Alaska. Alaska became a state in 1959, but much of the land in the state has not yet been settled. It is still called our country's last frontier.

Hawaii

The Hawaiian islands lie about two thousand miles southwest of California in the blue Pacific Ocean. These

Honolulu, Hawaii

small islands were discovered in 1778 by an English sea captain, Captain James Cook. He named the islands the Sandwich Islands. The people called their land "Owyhee," which means "Big Island." The word Hawaii comes from that name.

Missionaries first went to Hawaii in 1820. They built schools and churches. They learned the language that the native people spoke and made a system of writing it down. The eager islanders learned to read and

A Hawaiian plumeria

write. Soon the missionaries had translated the Bible and printed textbooks for the islanders. The people also began to publish newspapers in their language.

In the years that followed, many ships stopped at the Hawaiian islands for water and supplies. Stories of Hawaii's rich soil and comfortable weather made people want to go there. The rulers of the islands gave land to American settlers. Families from China, Japan, Britain, and other countries went there, too, but the Americans controlled most of the businesses. One king agreed that only Americans could use Pearl Harbor, the best harbor of the islands. The Americans built large pineapple and sugar plantations.

In 1891 trouble arose between the American settlers and Queen Lilioukalani. The queen was forced off her throne, and the islands became an independent nation. Soon, however, they became part of the United States. Hawaii became the fiftieth state in 1959. It is our only state that is made up of islands.

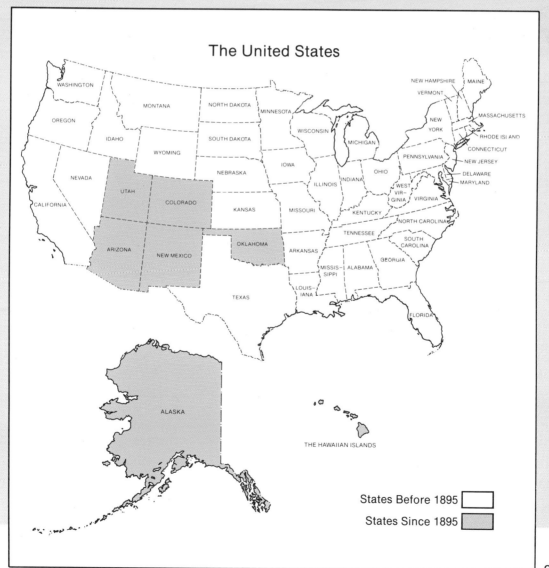

The United States

States Before 1895 ☐
States Since 1895 ▨

237

The Communist Challenge

After World War II ended, President Truman and later presidents faced great problems. Although the Axis powers had been defeated, another, greater enemy arose to threaten freedom. This enemy was communism.

The Communist way of life differs from America's way of life. Communism is based on the idea that the government should own and control property and businesses. Our system teaches that property and businesses should be owned and controlled by individuals. Communism promises that all citizens in Communist countries will have the same amount of money and goods no matter what talents they have or how hard they work. The American system rewards those who work hard and use their talents wisely. Communism appeals to many people by promising that the government will give them a better life. In America people are urged to improve their lives by their own effort.

Most important, communism differs from the Christian way of life. Christians believe that God directs people's lives. Their decisions and actions should be based on the teaching of God's Holy Word. Communism teaches that there is no God to influence the lives and decisions of people. They do not believe there is a heaven. They think that this is the only world anyone will ever know. Communists hate Christianity. They want others to follow the Communist way and spread their ideas throughout the world.

Unfortunately, some Americans do not believe that communism is a threat to the American way of life. They are not willing to fight against it. Many people have seen or read of the horrors of war. They know that if we go to war against the Communists, both sides might use new weapons that could kill millions of people. Other Americans are selfish. They are so concerned about making money that they do not pay much attention to what is happening to others. As long as they do not think they are in danger from communism themselves, they are not concerned about others who are.

Both the **free world** (those countries against communism) and the Communists try to influence other countries to follow their way of life. They do this by **foreign aid,** or giving money or goods to needy countries. Communists also use other ways to get countries to become Communist. Sometimes they encourage civil war among the people of a country. They come in and train men to use **guerrilla warfare**, give them weapons, and pay them. Guerrilla warfare uses small groups of soldiers that make quick, scattered attacks. This warfare makes the government unable to rule the country. The Communists then promise the people peace. In this way they win many people over to their side.

In this chapter you will learn that these two ways of life have often come into conflict during the last few decades. The two largest, strongest nations in the conflict are the United

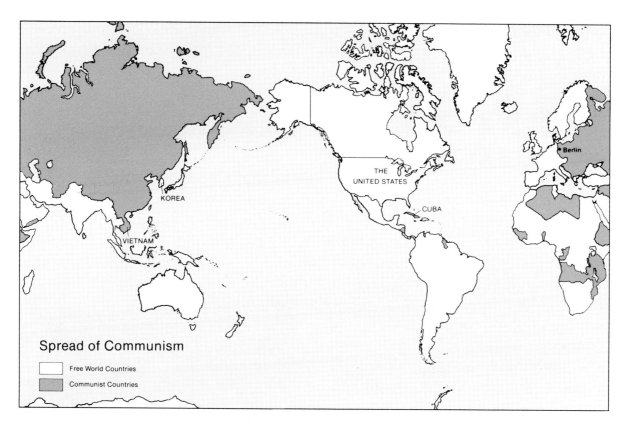

Spread of Communism

☐ Free World Countries

■ Communist Countries

States, leader of the free world, and the Soviet Union, leader of the Communist world. In two wars during these years, American soldiers have fought and died. More often there has been no fighting in the struggle. Conflicts have arisen over the space race, the Olympic games, and foreign aid. Because the struggle has not always been a hot, shooting war, it is often called the "Cold War."

The Berlin Airlift

One of the first conflicts of the Cold War came about when the Allies had to decide what to do with Germany after World War II. The Allied leaders decided that it was best to divide Germany into four zones. Each zone would be controlled by an Allied country. That country would help to rebuild it and see that it had a good, strong government. The French, British, and American zones were in the western part of Germany. The Soviet zone was in the eastern part.

Berlin, one of Germany's most important cities, was in the Soviet section. Like the rest of Germany, the city of Berlin was divided into four parts. Each country was given a way

American soldiers checking cars entering West Berlin

to get to its part of the city by a narrow strip of land called a **corridor.** Roads and railways were built along these corridors. Planes from the west were able to fly over them.

Then in one day everything changed! The Soviets in control of East Germany announced that they were going to keep the other Allies out of Berlin. They were going to keep any supplies from getting in by closing off the corridors. They began to operate a blockade of West Berlin on June 22, 1948. In this way they planned to quickly take over all of the city.

Much to the Soviets' surprise, the American air force came up with a daring plan to save the people of Berlin. They would keep the Berliners from starving by flying in *all* the supplies they needed.

Before long, the Air Force project, called "Operation Vittles," was under-

way. All available cargo planes received orders to fly to air bases in West Germany. From these bases they could fly to West Berlin. Over three hundred Air Force cargo planes were used in "Operation Vittles." American pilots worked in shifts, and the planes flew twenty-four hours a day. A planeload of goods landed in West Berlin every three minutes.

Tons and tons of goods were flown in. All the food the Berliners needed

A crowd of Germans watching a supply plane land

A C-54 supply plane landing in Berlin

Crews preparing sacks of flour to be flown to Berlin

came in on the planes—canned goods, meats, fresh vegetables, and milk. Materials needed for rebuilding arrived, too. Even coal was flown in to run the plants that made electricity for the German people. As the days grew shorter and fall turned to winter, the Air Force flew in more and more coal to heat homes.

Men in the Air Force started their own program that they called "Little Vittles." The men collected candy, clothing, and small gifts to bring the children of Berlin. Cargo planes would drop large packages of these gifts near the airfields. Inside were notes that said, "For You. With love from the people of America." Some of the children in West Berlin began to write

Coal being unloaded in Berlin

soldiers and their families who had put their addresses and messages inside the packages.

Eleven months after the Communists had announced their blockade, they gave up their idea. It had not worked. West Berlin was still a free city!

The Korean War

The failure of the Berlin blockade did not stop the Communists. They had already made gains in other places. After World War II they had taken the northern half of the nation of Korea, while the southern half remained free. Mainland China also fell to the Communists. (Find China and Korea on the map on page 239.) When North Korean forces invaded South Korea, the United Nations sent troops into Korea to stop the Communists.

Marines landing in Korea

President Truman sent thousands of American soldiers to help the South Koreans. Under General Douglas MacArthur, the U.N. forces drove the North Koreans back. When it looked as if the war was almost over, thousands of Chinese Communists poured in to help North Korea. These new forces pushed the U.N. army back. Fighting dragged on for over two more years before both sides agreed to stop fighting. Korea remained as it had been before the war, a divided nation.

During the fighting American soldiers were taken prisoner. In the prison camps they were **brainwashed** by the Communist enemy. They were told that Americans had left them without any help and no longer cared what happened to them. They were given very little food and forced to sit for hours and hours with light bulbs shining in their faces. They were beaten and then told to admit that they were spies.

Some Americans gave in to this strain; others heroically suffered through it. Those with strong religious faith were the prisoners best able to stand up to their tormentors. Some prisoners quoted Scripture verses to themselves. The verses that they had memorized kept these men from losing their faith under the enemy's pressure. Psalm 91:4b says, "His truth shall be thy shield and buckler."

Vietnam

Several years after the Korean War, the United States again faced trouble in Asia. Indochina had been a French colony, but the people there did not want to be part of France. Both the Communists and non-Communists fought to be free. In 1954, they defeated the French, and their country was divided into four parts—North Vietnam, South Vietnam, Laos, and Cambodia. North Vietnam was Communist, and South Vietnam was not. Of course the Communists wanted all of the country. They helped Communist rebels in South Vietnam and later sent troops there to take it over.

The United States government sent money and then weapons and

South Vietnamese soldiers trained by American military advisers

ammunition to aid South Vietnam. Next, military men flew there to teach the Vietnamese officers the best ways to fight their enemy. Finally, American troops went over to help fight.

Fighting in Vietnam was difficult because it was not the kind of war that Americans were used to fighting. Much of the fighting was guerrilla warfare. Also, the people on both sides looked alike. They were the same race and did not wear uniforms. No one could trust anyone else. Even children helped set traps for the soldiers.

Many American newspaper and television reporters opposed the war and spoke out loudly against it. Some American college men who were supposed to enter the military refused to do so. They burned their draft cards in front of television cameras. Others

went to Canada to escape being drafted. Some marched in the streets and started riots against the government. All of these men were breaking the law. They did not respect and honor their country as they should have. They also tried to keep other people from serving their country.

The war dragged on for years. America spent millions of dollars and sent thousands of soldiers to help South Vietnam and end the war. The government also tried to hold peace talks between North and South Vietnam. Nothing seemed to work. Finally, the United States pulled its men out and left the fighting to the South Vietnamese soldiers.

Although South Vietnam still received money and supplies from the United States, it could not hold out against North Vietnam. The southern half of the country fell to the Communists. Many of the people escaped from the Communists and fled to other nations. Some of these Vietnamese came to the United States.

A Vietnamese fishing boat

The Challenge to Keep the Peace

Even though the Cold War has at times become a hot war, Americans have always wanted peace. Of course, Americans do not really want to have to use their weapons. They know how dangerous these weapons, especially nuclear weapons and chemical weapons, can be. To help keep the peace, many American leaders have met with other world leaders to discuss the build-up of weapons, or the **arms race.** These world leaders all *say* that they would stop building the weapons—and even throw some away—if the other countries would also promise to stop building weapons.

Controlling the arms race would mean that all countries must do what they promise. Each country must trust the others. Yet the Communists have shown again and again that they cannot be trusted. They do not keep their word. Even if the United States threw away some of its weapons, we could not be sure that the Communists would do the same.

The United States needs strong armed forces to help protect our freedom. This does not mean that the United States wants war or is going to fight. It means that other nations, including the Communists, will respect us because of our strength. We as Christians need to remember, too, that our trust is not in guns, missiles, or even men. Our trust is in God. In Psalm 20:7 David reminded his people: "Some trust in chariots, and some in horses, but we will remember the name of the Lord our God."

The Challenge in Space

During the 1950s, still another front was added to the Cold War. This time the struggle was in outer space. On October 4, 1957, Soviet scientists surprised the whole world. Using a rocket, they launched the first space satellite, *Sputnik,* into orbit around the earth. Millions of Americans heard the signals from this beeping, basketball-sized object on radio broadcasts. Soon after *Sputnik,* the Soviets launched a much larger satellite called *Sputnik 2.* It carried a black-and-white dog named "Laika."

Americans panicked. They feared that if the Soviets could send rockets into space, they could easily fire missiles at cities in the United States. While American scientists had been inventing color televisions, transistors, and microwave products, the Soviets had been building rockets and missiles. The United States began to work hard on its own space program. Within a few months the United States launched a grapefruit-sized satellite called *Explorer I.*

In May of 1961 the first American astronaut, Alan Shepard, went into space. Less than a year later, John Glenn became the first American to orbit (go completely around) the earth. President John F. Kennedy announced that the United States planned to put an astronaut on the moon by the end

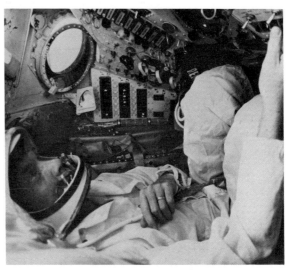

John Glenn in the *Mercury* space capsule

of the decade. The National Aeronautics and Space Administration (NASA) was started to help reach this goal. On July 20, 1969, Neil Armstrong

An *Apollo 15* astronaut on the moon

and Edwin Aldrin, Jr., actually walked on the moon. Michael Collins piloted their space capsule, *Apollo 11*. Millions of Americans proudly watched the "moon walk" on television. After setting foot on the surface of the moon, Armstrong said, "That's one small step for a man, one giant leap for mankind."

In the 1970s the Apollo project was replaced by Project Skylab, the launching of the first orbiting space station. Plans were also made for a series of space shuttles. These would save millions of dollars for NASA because they could fly missions into space and then return to earth to be used again. The earlier space capsules could not be reused. The first space shuttle was named *Columbia* after Christopher Columbus.

The Challenge of Civil Rights

The years following World War II were also years of challenge and change for black Americans. Until this time in many parts of our country, blacks lived under laws different from those for whites. Laws kept blacks **segregated,** or separate, from whites. Many people did not think that segregation was fair.

They felt that all Americans, black or white, had certain rights called **civil rights.** Civil rights are the rights guaranteed every United States citizen by the Constitution. In the decades after World War II, blacks tried hard to gain their civil rights.

The government did not act quickly on civil rights. Some laws were passed to help blacks. The courts decided some cases in favor of ending segregation. But as blacks grew impatient, they decided to try other ways to get their rights.

One woman who tried another way was Rosa Parks, a black seamstress. Just before Christmas in 1955, she got onto a city bus in Alabama. The bus had two sections of seats, one for whites and one for blacks. The law said that black people had to sit in the back section of the bus. Sometimes the black section filled up, while there were empty seats in the front part. Even then the blacks were not allowed to sit in the front, but had to stand in the back. Because she was tired of having to sit in the crowded back, Mrs. Parks sat in the white section up front. When Mrs. Parks sat up front, she broke the law. Because she broke the law, she was arrested. She went to jail to pay for her crime. Other blacks started a bus **boycott** and refused to ride the bus at all for a whole year.

The leader of the bus boycott and other civil rights activities over the next few years was a black minister named Martin Luther King, Jr. By the early 1960s blacks had tried to eat at lunch

Dr. Martin Luther King, Jr.

counters, ride on buses, swim at beaches, and worship at churches that kept blacks out. Congress did pass several civil rights acts between 1957 and 1965. These were efforts to see that no race would be treated unfairly in voting, in education, in public places, or in work. However, these laws were not always enforced.

In the eyes of many blacks, however, the changes had come too slowly. Only five days after President Lyndon B. Johnson signed a civil rights act, riots broke out. Over the next few years blacks rioted across the country, and whites grew fearful. Millions of dollars' worth of both white and black property was destroyed in major cities like Detroit, Los Angeles, and New York. Martin Luther King, Jr., was murdered. This caused even more rioting. As fires smoldered in burned buildings, blacks began to see that rioting only destroyed what they had. It also made whites less likely to cooperate with them, and slowly the riots ended.

Over the years blacks saw some change. More black children attended public schools with white children. Some cities with large white populations even elected black mayors. Black people were able to earn more money than they had before. Today many opportunities are open to people of all races. Of course, to achieve success, anyone of any race must be willing to work hard. For blacks, success has often meant working even harder than others.

The Challenge of Science

Since World War II, the world has seen an explosion in the growth of scientific knowledge. The moon landing you read about earlier is a good example of how far science has come since 1945. New inventions and important discoveries in medicine have changed how we live.

Electricity has made possible many of these changes. Early radios, televisions, and even computers used large amounts of electricity. These devices had vacuum tubes to control the electrical flow in them. Vacuum tubes were big, costly, and easily broken. These problems set many people to work looking for a replacement for vacuum tubes. The answer was invented in 1948 by a team of men. Their invention was the transistor. This small piece of wires and silicon directs the flow of electricity. (Silicon is a material found in sand.) Transistors are much smaller than vacuum tubes. They also put out less heat and do not break easily. Transistors even cost less than vacuum tubes.

Because the invention of the transistor was first announced in December, the inventors called it "a Christmas gift to the world." Companies began to use transistors in many products. Radios, calculators, and television sets cost less when made with transistors. More and more people could afford these products.

The tiny transistor brought big changes to American life by making radios and television sets household items. In the 1970s a tinier invention brought more changes to American life. This invention was a single chip of

Changes in the Telephone

The telephone has had many designs since Alexander Graham Bell invented it in 1876. Early telephones had separate ear- and mouthpieces. Because these phones had no dials, all calls had to be placed through an operator. Today many phones have push buttons instead of dials, and a person can call almost anywhere in the world without an operator's help.

1876   1896   1907   1964

Changes in the Automobile

Automobiles were first made in the United States in the 1890s. These early models, often called "horseless buggies," were open, two-seaters. Later, automakers built bigger, closed-in cars designed to travel long distances. Today people ride in comfortable, gas-saving models. Some modern cars even have built-in computers.

Changes in the Home

Inventors of this century have brought many changes to the home. Before 1900 women used wood-burning stoves for cooking. Electric and gas stoves and electric iceboxes were common by the 1930s. Today housewives use microwave ovens and frost-free refrigerators.

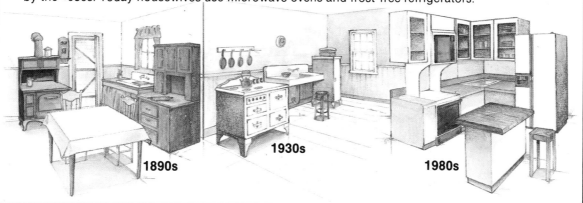

Changes in Clothing

Clothing styles have changed greatly in the last century. Ankle-length skirts and high-topped, buttoned shoes for women have given way to knee-length dresses and low shoes. Men's clothing has changed less, but men's shirts no longer have the detatchable collars and cuffs of the early 1900s.

silicon that holds many transistors. A chip the size of your fingernail could do the work of many transistors. Because they were smaller, silicon chips used less electricity and cost less than transistors.

Chips began to replace transistors in radios, television sets, and calculators, which became smaller and cheaper. However, the most important use of the chip has been in computers.

Today small desk-top computers can do the work that in the 1950s took a room-sized computer to do, and they can do it in less time. The invention of the silicon chip allowed more people to buy their own computers. This began the Computer Age for the American people.

One of the most important medical discoveries since World War II was the finding of a vaccine for polio. The following story about that discovery was written by a high school teacher. At that time, she was about the same age as you are now. She lived through what you are now reading about in a history book.

The silicon chip at the right is smaller than a dime, yet it helped make all these inventions possible.

"Thank You, Dr. Salk!"

It was a hot summer day and we had nothing to do. Perhaps Mother would let us go swimming or go to the city playground. "Mom," we said, "it's so hot out. May we go swimming?"

Mom dried her hands and looked at us. "Girls," she said, "I'm afraid not. I heard on the radio that both the beach and the playgrounds are closed."

"Why?" we moaned before Mom could explain.

"They're closed because of polio. Some people say we're having an epidemic." I had learned that an epidemic occurs when a disease spreads rapidly and widely through an area. Polio was a contagious disease—one that could spread easily from person to person.

It was 1952. That was the year that the number of polio cases reached its peak. There were fifty thousand reported cases of polio across America. There were many more unreported cases, because in its milder forms, polio was not even recognized. Mild cases seemed like the flu, and the patients were usually well in two weeks or so. But many children in the early 1950s suffered some sort of lifelong effect from polio.

During that year we often read about polio in the newspaper. We heard about polio every day on the noon news. I didn't really want to hear about more children getting polio. Polio was awful. Some children who had had polio were paralyzed so that they would never walk again. I'd seen pictures of children whose arms and legs were drawn up in strange positions because their muscles did not work anymore.

The children that were the saddest to see were those who had bulbar polio. This type of polio paralyzed the breathing system so that the victim could not breathe without a machine called an iron lung. Many of these victims died before they could be helped.

Every night when I went to bed, I thanked the Lord that my sister and I had not caught polio. I prayed that no one in my family would get it. Every time I had any ache or pain, I was afraid it was polio and that I was going to end up crippled.

The Lord was already working to bring an answer to my prayers and the prayers of many others. In 1949 a scientist from Harvard, Dr. John Enders, found a way to grow polio viruses in a dish. Using Enders's

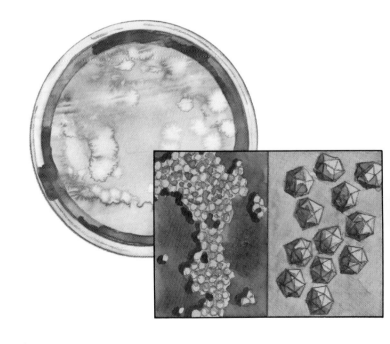

Dr. Jonas Salk

who had been crippled by it and could never again run in gym class or go bike riding with me. My mom signed the permission for me to have the "Salk shot," as we called it then. My dad gave me a dollar to pay for it. I walked to the junior high school and got in line. When my turn came, the nurse daubed rubbing alcohol on my arm. It felt cool. I bit my lip and tried not to wince as the doctor stuck the needle in. I felt a little sting, and my arm was a bit sore. Within the next several months,

research, Dr. Jonas Edward Salk of Pittsburgh tried to develop a vaccine that would give protection from polio. He and his helpers worked almost day and night for three years. They grew the vaccine in the laboratory and tested it on chickens and monkeys. In 1952 they had a vaccine that worked well on monkeys. But would it help humans?

Dr. Salk and his helpers gave each other shots to try out the vaccine. In 1954 it was considered safe enough to be tested on large numbers of people. Then it was given out to doctors across the nation.

Soon there was an article in our newspaper about the vaccine. It said that all children aged fourteen or under should go to the junior high school for immunizations on a certain day. I hated shots, and my parents knew it. But I did not want to get polio. I had friends

I had two more Salk shots. A year later I had a booster shot to continue the protection.

I remember reading about Dr. Jonas Salk at that time in a new book in the library. I thanked the Lord then for a doctor whom God had used to stop a dreaded disease. Once I was riding in the car with my Mom and was playing a thinking contest she had made up. We would each think of five

famous people that we would like to meet and then each tell why we wanted to meet them. I remember that one of the five people I wanted to meet was Dr. Salk. I told Mom that I wanted to say, "Thank you, Dr. Salk, from all the kids in my town. Because of your work, we never had polio."

Things to know

1. The conflict between communism and the free world is often called the _____ War.

2. Warfare that uses small groups of soldiers that make quick, scattered attacks is called _____.

3. American troops fought in wars against the Communists in the two Asian countries of _____ and _____.

4. The build-up of weapons by countries is called the _____.

5. The nation that launched the first successful space satellite called "_____" was _____.

6. The letters in NASA stand for _____.

7. The two Americans who walked on the moon were _____ and _____, and their spacecraft was called _____.

8. Rights that are guaranteed every United States citizen by the Constitution are called _____.

9. The invention of the _____ made the Computer Age possible.

Things to talk about

1. Why do you think some people became Communists?

2. How does communism differ from our American way of life? How does communism differ from our Christian way of life?

3. Why should Christians be against communism?

4. What is the difference between a "cold war" and a "hot war"?

5. Why was *Columbia* a good name for a space shuttle?

6. What are civil rights?

7. What are some ways the computer affects your life?

8. What events of today do you think people will be reading about in history books twenty years from now?

Things to do

1. Ask a grownup to tell you some things he remembers about the United States during the Vietnam War.

2. Make a list of all the verses you know completely by heart right now that you think would help you if you were being brainwashed. Make another list of verses that you think would help you if you were being brainwashed by someone. Learn the four best verses by memory. List the names of some hymns that you think you could recall to help you.

3. Suppose you go with your mother to a shopping center. Someone at a table is passing out entry blanks for a children's contest. You are asked to make a poster or write a story to encourage disarmament (throwing away weapons). What would you do? Make a list of the reasons you could give the people for not entering their contest.

4. Make a special time line starting in 1957 and going to the present and put important events of the space race on it.

5. Imagine that you have been asked to be the first young person to ride with some astronauts on a space shuttle. Make a list of some questions you would like to ask or things you would like to find out.

6. Make a list of five rights that you have as an American citizen.

7. Play the thinking game described in the last paragraph of the chapter.

EPILOGUE

A LEADER AMONG NATIONS

The United States of America is the greatest nation in the world. Its citizens have more freedom and more opportunities to be successful in life than people anywhere else in the world. Perhaps you wonder why this is true. Christians know that God deserves the credit for the blessings that we enjoy in this country.

Many of the settlers of the first English colonies came to this country for the freedom to worship God. They were willing to suffer great hardships for the privilege of reading the Bible, going to church, and establishing laws based on God's Word. These people also were willing to obey the command in the Bible to work. They read in Colossians 3:23, "And whatsoever ye do, do it heartily, as to the Lord, and not unto men." They believed the teaching of II Thessalonians 3:10— "that if any would not work, neither should he eat." God blessed these people, and the colonies grew and prospered.

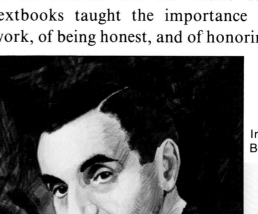

In 1776 the thirteen colonies declared that they were a separate and independent nation. The leaders of this new nation believed in God. They were not all born-again Christians, but they honored God and His Word. During the War for Independence and the writing of the Constitution, the people and their leaders prayed to God for protection and for wisdom so that the nation would be preserved. Again God kept His promise to bless those who honor Him and His Word.

The nation grew westward for the next hundred years. Many of the families that settled the vast western land took a Bible with them to their new homes. The most important book in the schools was the Bible. The textbooks taught the importance of work, of being honest, and of honoring

Irving Berlin

God Bless America

Israel Baline was born to a poor family in Russia in 1888. His father tried to support the nine children by singing in the synagogue. One day in 1892, a band of Russian soldiers rode into their Jewish village. They destroyed houses and the synagogue and killed and injured many people. The Baline family watched in terror as their home burned to the ground. They determined to leave Russia and go to America.

The Balines lived in terrible poverty in New York. After four years the father died, and the children all worked to help provide for the family. Little Israel earned money by selling newspapers and also by singing on the streets of Chinatown. Later he became a singing waiter and started to write his own songs. He began to sell his music, and by 1920 he had become rich. In the meantime he had changed his name to Irving Berlin.

In 1938 a singer named Kate Smith wanted a new patriotic song to sing for an Armistice Day radio program. She asked Irving Berlin to write something that would raise the spirits of Americans who were discouraged

by the Depression at home and by the rise of dictators overseas. Mr. Berlin had just visited Europe and had seen the conditions there. He thought about his own early life in Russia and the great opportunities he had in the United States. His heart filled with love for America, and he was glad to grant Miss Smith's request.

As Mr. Berlin was trying to think of a new song, he remembered something he had written years before. He got out "the yellow and frayed manuscript" of "God Bless America," made a few changes, and gave it to the singer. Miss Smith, along with her listeners, was overjoyed with the song, and it became popular immediately. Today it is sometimes called the "second national anthem."

God. Almost every new town built a church. Many people did not accept the Lord Jesus as their Saviour, but nearly everyone respected God and those who tried to live for Him. God continued to bless the United States.

It was and still is easy to see how God has blessed us. The United States has some of the best farmland in the world. Early settlers found great forests spreading over hundreds of miles. They were filled with deer, beaver, and wild fowl. The rivers and oceans were filled with fish. There were mountains of coal and iron and lands rich with gold, silver, and oil. God had provided all of these riches for the people of the United States to use.

Favorite American Foods

Graham crackers

Sylvester Graham was a preacher in the 1830s. He believed that people were not eating a healthful diet. He urged women to stop buying bread from bakeries and to make it at home using whole grain flour. Some of his followers started health-food stores that sold graham flour, bread, and crackers.

Potato chips

George Crumb, an American Indian, was the chef at a hotel in Saratoga Springs, New York, in the middle 1800s. A dinner guest kept sending the French-fried potatoes back because he thought they were too thick. Mr. Crumb became irritated. He shaved a potato into the thinnest possible slices and fried them in hot oil. The customer was delighted with the "Saratoga chips," and a new snack was born.

Hot dogs

Just before the Civil War, Charles Feltman opened a stand at Coney Island, New York, to sell sausages in rolls. He was from Frankfurt, Germany, and he called the sausages frankfurters. In 1906, a sports cartoonist was eating a frankfurter at a ball game. He thought that it looked like the body of a dachshund. He drew a cartoon to show his idea and labeled it "Hot dog!" The name stuck.

Hamburgers

Hamburgers without a bun were introduced in the Midwest in the early 1800s by German immigrants. Hamburg is the name of a city in Germany. Hamburgers in a bun were first sold at a fair in St. Louis in 1904. They became popular in the 1920s when the White Castle snack bar started selling a small, square patty of meat for a very low price.

Ice-cream cones

A Syrian food peddler sold thin, sweet waffles at the St. Louis fair in 1904. When a nearby ice cream stand ran out of plates, he twisted hot waffles into cone-shaped containers. They cooled into crisp cups that were the beginning of the ice-cream cones we eat today.

Coca-cola

John Pemberton was a druggist in Atlanta, Georgia. In 1886 he made a syrup from coca leaves and cola nuts. He mixed the syrup with water and sold it for a nickel a glass. He called it Coca-cola. The drink did not become popular. The next year another druggist bought the formula for the syrup. He mixed it with carbonated water. People liked this much better. Soon bottling companies were started so that Coca-cola could be sold more widely. The familiar flared bottle was designed in 1916.

God is in control of all things. He allowed millions of immigrants to come to the United States. They brought money and ability and joined Americans born in the United States to build great factories, mines, and other businesses. Many brought only their muscles to make the businesses productive. Some immigrants who had brilliant minds made valuable scientific discoveries, composed great music, or wrote outstanding books. Most, however, were ordinary people who never became rich or famous.

All of the immigrants brought their customs, their beliefs, and their hopes with them. They worked, played, and learned together with the Americans. God used this mixture of people to produce a nation that leads the world.

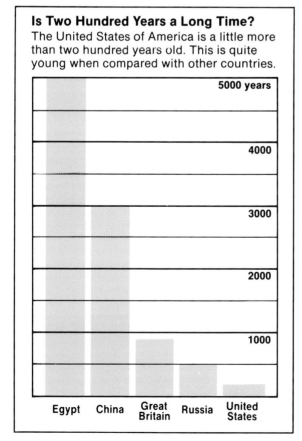

Is Two Hundred Years a Long Time?
The United States of America is a little more than two hundred years old. This is quite young when compared with other countries.

God's people should be willing to obey the Bible at all times. Today, in some countries, a person is in danger of losing his job, his home, and even his life when he becomes a Christian and tries to live for God. Being a Christian is the most important thing in a person's life. God's people in America should remember to thank Him for the freedom He has given them. They should do whatever they can to protect that freedom for themselves and for their children.

In Psalm 33:12 we read, "Blessed is the nation whose God is the Lord." God is not the Lord of most of the people of the United States today. Many people never go to church, never read the Bible, and never try to please Him. Their main interest is getting money so that they can buy a big home or nice cars, and have an easy, comfortable life. Many of the leaders of the United States do not care about what the Bible says. Some even make laws to make it difficult for Christians to live for God in the way they believe is right. God does not promise to bless a nation that does not honor Him.

The Bible tells us in I Thessalonians 4:13-17 that one day Christ is coming to take His people to be with Him:

But I would not have you to be ignorant, brethren, concerning them which are asleep, that ye sorrow not, even as others which have no hope. For if we believe that Jesus died and rose again, even so them also which sleep in Jesus will God bring with him. For this we say unto you by the word of the Lord, that we which are alive and remain unto the coming of the Lord shall not prevent them which are asleep. For the Lord himself shall descend from heaven with a shout, with the voice of the archangel, and with the trump of God: and the dead in Christ shall rise first: Then we which are alive and remain shall be caught up together with them in the clouds, to meet the Lord in the air: and so shall we ever be with the Lord.

We do not know when this will happen. We do not know what will happen in this country before He comes. We do know that God's promises are true. He has promised that He will never leave us or forsake us. "So that we may boldly say, The Lord is my helper, and I will not fear what man shall do unto me" (Hebrews 13:6).

A PICTURE HISTORY OF THE
U.S. CAPITOL
BUILDING

1840

1859

Today

1861

The States of the Union

State	Capital	Entered Union	Order Entered	Post Office Abbreviation
Alabama	Montgomery	1819	22	AL
Alaska	Juneau	1959	49	AK
Arizona	Phoenix	1912	48	AZ
Arkansas	Little Rock	1836	25	AR
California	Sacramento	1850	31	CA
Colorado	Denver	1876	38	CO
Connecticut	Hartford	1788	5	CT
Delaware	Dover	1787	1	DE
District of Columbia	Washington	1791		DC
Florida	Tallahassee	1845	27	FL
Georgia	Atlanta	1788	4	GA
Hawaii	Honolulu	1959	50	HI
Idaho	Boise	1890	43	ID
Illinois	Springfield	1818	21	IL
Indiana	Indianapolis	1816	19	IN
Iowa	Des Moines	1846	29	IA
Kansas	Topeka	1861	34	KS
Kentucky	Frankfort	1792	15	KY
Louisiana	Baton Rouge	1812	18	LA
Maine	Augusta	1820	23	ME
Maryland	Annapolis	1788	7	MD
Massachusetts	Boston	1788	6	MA
Michigan	Lansing	1837	26	MI
Minnesota	St. Paul	1858	32	MN
Mississippi	Jackson	1817	20	MS
Missouri	Jefferson City	1821	24	MO
Montana	Helena	1889	41	MT
Nebraska	Lincoln	1867	37	NB
Nevada	Carson City	1864	36	NV
New Hampshire	Concord	1788	9	NH
New Jersey	Trenton	1787	3	NJ
New Mexico	Santa Fe	1912	47	NM
New York	Albany	1788	11	NY
North Carolina	Raleigh	1789	12	NC
North Dakota	Bismarck	1889	39	ND
Ohio	Columbus	1803	17	OH
Oklahoma	Oklahoma City	1907	46	OK
Oregon	Salem	1859	33	OR
Pennsylvania	Harrisburg	1787	2	PA
Rhode Island	Providence	1790	13	RI
South Carolina	Columbia	1788	8	SC
South Dakota	Pierre	1889	40	SD
Tennessee	Nashville	1796	16	TN
Texas	Austin	1845	28	TX
Utah	Salt Lake City	1896	45	UT
Vermont	Montpelier	1791	14	VT
Virginia	Richmond	1788	10	VA
Washington	Olympia	1889	42	WA
West Virginia	Charleston	1863	35	WV
Wisconsin	Madison	1848	30	WI
Wyoming	Cheyenne	1890	44	WY

The Presidents of the United States

	President	Years in Office	State	Birth and Death
1	George Washington	1789-1797	Virginia	1732-1799
2	John Adams	1797-1801	Massachusetts	1735-1826
3	Thomas Jefferson	1801-1809	Virginia	1743-1826
4	James Madison	1809-1817	Virginia	1751-1836
5	James Monroe	1817-1825	Virginia	1758-1831
6	John Quincy Adams	1825-1829	Massachusetts	1767-1848
7	Andrew Jackson	1829-1837	Tennessee	1767-1845
8	Martin Van Buren	1837-1841	New York	1782-1862
9	William Henry Harrison	1841	Ohio	1774-1841
10	John Tyler	1841-1845	Virginia	1790-1862
11	James K. Polk	1845-1849	Tennessee	1795-1849
12	Zachary Taylor	1849-1850	Louisiana	1784-1850
13	Millard Fillmore	1850-1853	New York	1800-1874
14	Franklin Pierce	1853-1857	New Hampshire	1804-1869
15	James Buchanan	1857-1861	Pennsylvania	1791-1868
16	Abraham Lincoln	1861-1865	Illinois	1809-1865
17	Andrew Johnson	1865-1869	Tennessee	1808-1875
18	Ulysses S. Grant	1869-1877	Illinois	1822-1885
19	Rutherford B. Hayes	1877-1881	Ohio	1822-1893
20	James A. Garfield	1881	Ohio	1831-1881
21	Chester A. Arthur	1881-1885	New York	1830-1886
22	Grover Cleveland	1885-1889	New York	1837-1908
23	Benjamin Harrison	1889-1893	Indiana	1833-1901
24	Grover Cleveland	1893-1897	New York	1837-1908
25	William McKinley	1897-1901	Ohio	1843-1901
26	Theodore Roosevelt	1901-1909	New York	1858-1919
27	William Howard Taft	1909-1913	Ohio	1857-1930
28	Woodrow Wilson	1913-1921	New Jersey	1856-1924
29	Warren G. Harding	1921-1923	Ohio	1865-1923
30	Calvin Coolidge	1923-1929	Massachusetts	1872-1933
31	Herbert C. Hoover	1929-1933	California	1874-1964
32	Franklin D. Roosevelt	1933-1945	New York	1882-1945
33	Harry S. Truman	1945-1953	Missouri	1884-1972
34	Dwight D. Eisenhower	1953-1961	New York	1890-1969
35	John F. Kennedy	1961-1963	Massachusetts	1917-1963
36	Lyndon B. Johnson	1963-1969	Texas	1908-1973
37	Richard M. Nixon	1969-1974	California	1913-
38	Gerald R. Ford	1974-1977	Michigan	1913-
39	James E. Carter	1977-1981	Georgia	1924-
40	Ronald W. Reagan	1981-	California	1911-

WASHINGTON

River

Columbia

OREGON

IDAHO

MONTANA

NORTH DAKOTA

SOUTH DAKOTA

Missouri

Great

Platt e

Plains

River

NEBRASKA

Rocky

WYOMING

Sierra Nevada

NEVADA

UTAH

Mountains

COLORADO

KANSAS

Arkansas

River

CALIFORNIA

Colorado

River

ARIZONA

NEW MEXICO

OKLAHOMA

Red

TEXAS

Rio

Grande

ALASKA

River

Yukon

Alaska Range

HAWAII

0   100   200   300

scale in miles

same scale as large map

MINNESOTA

Lake Superior

WISCONSIN

MICHIGAN

Lake Michigan

Lake Huron

MAINE

NEW HAMPSHIRE

VERMONT

MASSACHUSETTS

RHODE ISLAND

CONNECTICUT

Lake Ontario

NEW YORK

IOWA

River

Lake Erie

PENNSYL-
VANIA

Mountains

NEW JERSEY

OHIO

ILLINOIS

INDIANA

DELAWARE

River

Washington, D.C. ✪

MARYLAND

Ohio

WEST
VIRGINIA

VIRGINIA

MISSOURI

River

KENTUCKY

Mississippi River

TENNESSEE

Appalachian

NORTH CAROLINA

River

ARKANSAS

SOUTH CAROLINA

River

GEORGIA

ALABAMA

MISSISSIPPI

LOUISIANA

FLORIDA

United States
of America

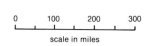

0   100   200   300

scale in miles

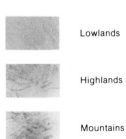

Lowlands

Highlands

Mountains

Nations of the World

ASIA

Pacific

Indian Ocean

AUSTRALIA

ANTARCTICA

Ocean

NORTH

AMERICA

CENTRAL

AMERICA

Atlantic

Ocean

Ocean

SOUTH

AMERICA

EUROPE

AFRICA

267

GLOSSARY

A

alien A person from another country.

anthem A song of loyalty or praise.

armistice An agreement by both sides in a war to stop fighting.

arms race The attempt by the Communists and the free world to build more nuclear weapons than each other.

artillery Large guns or cannons that are too heavy to be carried.

assembly line A line of workers and equipment along which products are passed as they are being put together.

Axis Powers The countries which the United States fought against in World War II—Germany, Italy, and Japan.

B

boll The round seed pod of the cotton plant.

boll weevil A beetle with a long snout. Boll weevils cause great damage to cotton plants.

boycott The effort of a group of people working together to refuse to buy from or deal with a store, company, person, or nation. A boycott is used as a way of protesting or forcing a change.

brainwash To attempt to force someone to accept beliefs and attitudes he does not hold.

brand A mark burned into the skin. Brands are put on cattle to show who owns them.

C

cadet A student in a military school.

canal A body of water, usually man-made, that connects two or more points. Canals are used for travel, shipping, irrigation, or drainage.

census An official count, usually by a government, of the people living in a given area. A census may also include the age, sex, job, and other information about the people being counted.

centennial A one-hundredth anniversary or a celebration of it.

chaplain A clergyman who holds religious services for a school, prison, military unit, or other group.

chuck wagon A wagon equipped with cooking equipment and food supplies.

citizen Someone who is a member of a country, either by being born there or by choosing to become a member.

civil war A war between groups that belong to the same country or community.

civilized Changed from a simple or rough condition of life to a more highly developed one.

communicate To pass along or exchange thoughts, ideas, or information.

concentration camp A camp where prisoners of war or political prisoners are kept.

conflict A fight or struggle.

contagious Easily spread by direct or indirect contact.

continental divide A long, high ridge in a continent. The water on one side of the ridge runs in the opposite direction from the water on the other side.

conveyor belt A moving belt used to carry objects from place to place.

corridor A narrow strip of land through territory held by another country.

cotton gin A machine that separates cotton fibers from the seeds.

craft 1. An occupation requiring skill with the hands. 2. A boat.

crane A machine for raising and carrying heavy weights by means of a swinging arm or an overhead track.

credit A system of allowing customers to pay for something a little at a time instead of paying for it all at once when they buy it.

D

decade A period of ten years.

depression A time when business is bad and many people are out of work.

dictator A ruler who has complete power over the government of a country.

draft The selection of persons for a special service or job.

drought A long period of dry weather.

E

economy The way a country develops, divides, and uses its money, goods, and services.

epidemic A disease that spreads widely and rapidly.

expedition A long trip, usually for exploring or studying something unknown or far away.

F

filament A very fine wire or thread. The filament in a light bulb is heated by an electric current until it gives off light.

firebreak Land cleared of all materials that could burn. It is used to stop a fire from spreading.

flagship The ship that carries the leader of the fleet and flies his flag.

fleet A group of ships working together under one commander.

ford A place in a river shallow enough to walk or ride across.

foreign aid Money or goods sent to help other countries.

fortify To make stronger or more secure.

free world The countries of the world that oppose communism.

freight Goods carried in a train, plane, truck, or other vehicle.

G

gap A narrow place through which one can pass between mountains.

guerrilla warfare Fighting by small bands of soldiers who move and attack quickly.

H

heritage Everything that has a part in making a person who he is, what he is like, and what he does.

hull The body of a ship.

I

immigrant A person who comes to a country in order to live there permanently.

immunization   A means of preventing people from getting a disease.

indigo   A dark blue dye. It can be made from the indigo plant or man-made.

installment   One of a series of payments that must be made by someone who is buying something on credit.

integrity   Honesty; sincerity.

interchangeable parts   Parts of products made so that the parts of one product will fit every other product of the same kind.

invade   To enter with force.

isle   An island, especially a small one.

L

launch   To set in motion with force.

livestock   Animals raised on a farm.

longhorn   A breed of cattle with long, spreading horns.

M

malice   A desire to hurt others or to see them suffer.

mass production   The process of making a large number of products that are all alike in a short period of time.

maul   A heavy, long-handled hammer used to drive stakes or wedges.

missile   An object that is thrown, fired, or dropped at a target.

mouth   The part of a river that empties into a larger body of water.

mustang   A small, wild horse of western North America.

N

native   A person born in a particular country or place.

neutral   Not supporting any side in a war, argument, or fight.

New Deal   A plan made by President Franklin Roosevelt in the 1930s to help the economy of the United States.

nominate   To name as a candidate for an office.

nuclear weapons   Weapons using atomic power.

O

oath   A calling upon God to witness to the truth of a statement or to witness that one intends to do what is promised.

occupation force   An army staying in an area after it has been conquered.

open range   Pastureland owned by the government that anyone can use.

P

pan   To rinse soil in a pan to find bits of metal.

paralyzed   Unable to move.

patent   A document given by the government to an inventor or a company. A patent gives a person or company the right to be the only one to make or sell an invention for a certain number of years.

pelt   An animal skin with the hair or fur still on it.

platinum   A valuable, silver-white metal that does not tarnish.

population   The number of people who live in a certain place.

port   A city with a harbor for ships to take on and unload goods.

prime minister   The chief governmental officer of a country.

proclamation   An official public announcement.

prospector   Someone who searches or explores an area for gold or other valuable minerals.

R

remuda A herd of horses provided for cowboys' use.

rendezvous A planned meeting.

reservation An area set aside by the government for a certain purpose.

S

sabotage The attempt to hinder a nation's war effort by destroying property or interfering with industry.

scythe A tool with a long, curved blade attached to a long, bent handle. It is used for mowing and reaping grains and grass.

secede To remove oneself from a group or an organization.

segregate To separate or keep apart from others.

self-sufficient Able to supply one's own needs.

silicon A common material in the earth; sand is composed mostly of silicon.

sod 1. Grass and soil forming the surface of the ground. 2. A piece of such soil held together by matted roots and removed from the ground.

source The beginning of a stream or river.

spacious Having a great deal of space.

spar A pole used to support sails on a ship.

spike A very large nail.

stanza One of the divisions of a poem or song. It is made up of two or more lines.

sublime Of great value.

suffrage The right to vote.

suicide The act of killing oneself on purpose.

swing station A place where pony express riders stopped to get fresh horses.

T

territory A part of the United States not included within any state. It makes its own laws.

toll road A road that could not be used without a payment of a fee.

train 1. A connected line of railroad cars. 2. A moving line of persons, vehicles, or animals.

transcontinental Reaching across a continent.

transistor A small device that controls the flow of electricity.

trench A long ditch with earth piled up in front to protect soldiers.

turnpike A road, especially a wide highway. People have to pay a toll on certain turnpikes.

U

united Brought together or joined so as to form a whole; made one.

V

vaccine A material that is injected into a person to protect against a disease.

valiant Acting with or showing courage; brave.

vigilante One who volunteers to help punish criminals and to keep peace.

W

wrangler A person who cares for saddle horses.

Y

yarn A long tale of adventure, often one that is made up or exaggerated.

Pronunciation Guide

Pierre Charles L'Enfant	/pē âr' shärl lôn fôn'/	Sioux	/sōō/
Benjamin Banneker	/băn' ĭ kər/	Nez Perce	/nĕz pûrs/
George Drouillard	/zhôrzh drōō' yär/	Kiowa	/kī' ə wô/
Toussaint Charbonneau	/tōō săn' shär bōn nō'/	Kvsvick	/kŏŏs' vĭk/
Sacajawea	/săk ə jə wē' ə/	Sabbadini	/săb ə tē' nē/
Shoshone	/shō shō' nē/	Maszko	/măts' kō/
Sequoya	/sĭ kwoi' ə/	Isaak	/ī' zək/
John McLoughlin	/mək lôf' lĭn/	Maghan	/mā' hăn/
		kamikaze	/kä mĭ kä' zē/

INDEX

Photo Credits